THE COMMUNIST PARTY OF INDIA

THE COMMUNIST
PARTY OF INDIA

A Short History

by

M. R. MASANI

WITH AN INTRODUCTION
BY GUY WINT

In association with the
Institute of Pacific Relations

DEREK VERSCHOYLE
LONDON
1954

First published in 1954 by
Derek Verschoyle Ltd
Thirteen Park Place, St James's
London SW1

Printed in Great Britain by
Adlard & Son Ltd
The Bartholomew Press, Dorking

Contents

5

Introduction

The contemporary history of Asia is strongly dramatic. In the two great land masses, India and China, new orders of government and society came into existence within two years of one another. In India, the Congress State succeeded the British Raj in 1947. In China two years later the Communist party became masters of the whole country, and dedicated it to the principles of Marxism, Leninism and Stalinism as interpreted by Mao Tse-Tung.

The systems in India and China are opposite poles. The rule of law genuinely prevails in India. The subject enjoys the right not to be ordered about arbitrarily by the government; and the courts zealously uphold his right when he has recourse to them. There are no armies of forced labour. The press is free as the wind (notwithstanding certain reserve powers taken by the government two or three years ago for use in case of emergency because of communal feeling, and as yet not employed). The government, in the provinces and at the centre, is responsible to parliaments elected freely and honestly by the huge populations on the basis of universal suffrage.

China on the contrary is a totalitarian dictatorship under which the people are considered as so much raw material to be moulded according to the doctrine, passing ideas and needs of the Communist government.

Though India and China are thus in contrast – India the great example of liberalism in Asia, China the first full-fledged example of Asian communism – they have one characteristic in common. In neither can it be the aim of government simply to keep an existing social machine in smooth function. In each country the urgent need is for a radical transformation; and the governments are under immense pressure to make themselves responsible for bringing this about. The bane of both countries is poverty and technical and industrial backwardness. The demand of all the educated classes is that this state of affairs should be brought to an end. They want their countries modernised, made strong in relation to other countries, and equipped with industry. They want to end for ever the familiar sights of Asian penury–the beggar, the under-nourished masses, the hovels and slums, the dirt, disease and squalor.

Inevitably and without intention, India and China have become symbols of the different methods by which economic and social change may be brought about. India stands for releasing the energies of the individual–though it will systematise them within the framework of a general plan. It puts its trust in the galvanising effects of supplies of capital raised by voluntary saving at home and by loans from abroad. China stands for a military type of organisation, with a chain of command reaching from the Politburo at Peking down to the meanest peasant and factory worker. Everything is to be determined by government and by compulsion. Capital is to be raised by forced savings. Labour is to be mobilised by conscription. Recent eyewitness reports from China speak of the huge gangs of forced labour, miserably paid, fed and equipped, which are being used upon the hydraulic projects on the Chinese rivers, and contrasts them with the freely recruited labour on such works as the Damodar project in India.

Whichever country shows the more impressive economic progress, India or China, is likely to be accepted as the social, and perhaps the political, leader of Asia. All the countries of South Asia are watching the competition. At present, though there is plenty of sympathy for Communism, the intelligentsia of most of these countries may have a bias in favour of free systems. But they are not indissolubly attached to them. The prime interest is in material advance. If it appears, from the result of the test in India and China, that by sacrificing freedom there can be a quicker advance materially, much of the intelligentsia will not hesitate to turn Communist. Even in India itself this may happen. If on the other hand the progress under the liberal system is striking–if the Colombo Plan achieves its results–there will be an immense strengthening of the confidence in liberal and democratic ideas.

Because of the 'neutralist' foreign policy which India is trying to pursue, Indian leaders such as Mr Nehru would deny that India is competing with China for prestige and primacy in Asia. But regardless of the wishes of the leaders, facts and circumstances press the two powers into contest.

While the Indian Government pushes on with its plans of social and economic reform, while its Planning Commission supervises the monumental Five Year Plan, the efforts to make the present free system a success are under constant attack from the Indian Communist Party. They are boring from within, trying to frustrate all that is done by government in India. The more they succeed, the more they might tip the scales in China's favour in the international competition. The true strength of the Indian Communist Party was first shown when it was able for a time in a period of confusion to establish a virtual shadow government in two districts in Hyderabad state. Two years ago in the Indian general elections it won some notable successes in the South, especially in Madras, Hyderabad and Travancore-Cochin. Though the total votes which it received are still a small fraction of those of Congress, and though even the Socialists won in the whole country twice as many votes as the Communists, the Communist party, by its energy and discipline, has since then been able to win general acceptance as the principal opposition to Congress—and a formidable opposition.

Mr Masani's book is the first comprehensive study of the Indian Communist Party which has appeared in this or any other country. It is a very useful contribution to our knowledge of what is happening in Asia. It is really indispensable to anybody concerned with the prospects in India. The study of the Communist Party in China was neglected almost until it became the master of the country. Today it is hard to discover many facts of its early history, so many of the documents having perished in its vicissitudes. Had it not been for the diligence of Mr Masani, the facts about the early days of the Indian party might also have been allowed to pass into oblivion.

Most of the current books on India describe what the Indian Government is doing to forestall the threat of Communism. It may be hoped that its acts will yield the success which is hoped for, and that Communists will never come to power at Delhi. But it is valuable to have a book describing, not what the government is doing to counteract the Communists, but what the Communists are doing to thwart the government. Intelligence about the high command of an adversary is one of the first needs for tactics and strategy.

GUY WINT

CHAPTER ONE

India at the end of
World War I

In October 1917, Russia went through a revolution which brought the communist dictatorship into power. Six months later, on 22nd April 1918, when Mr Edwin Samuel Montagu, British Secretary of State for India, and Lord Chelmsford, the Viceroy, signed their momentous *Report on Indian Constitutional Reforms*, they already found it necessary to refer thus to the influence which the Russian Revolution was having on the political consciousness of large sections of the Indian people: 'The revolution in Russia in its beginning was regarded in India as a triumph over despotism; and notwithstanding the fact that it has since involved that unhappy country in anarchy and dismemberment, it has given impetus to Indian political aspirations.'[1] What was the state of India as it emerged from World War I and faced the impact of the October Revolution, and in what directions was its political, economic and social life bent?

Five trends could be noticed by observers who surveyed the scene. First, there was persistent and challenging opposition to the administrative measures of the British Government in India which were regarded by Indian public opinion as being repressive of the agitation for self-government. Secondly, there was ever widening discontent with policies and measures regarded as evidencing racial discrimination. Thirdly, an increasing amount of energy was to be found directed towards social reforms, educational progress and industrial advance. Fourthly, there was a demand which found increasing support in favour of the liberalisation of existing political institutions having as its goal full self-government on the part of the Indian people. Finally, there was a growing desire to raise the status of India in the British Empire and the world. 'Dominion

Status' was the goal which the largest number of educated Indians then aspired to and it was believed that this would allow the Indian people to play an equal and honourable part in the comity of the nations of the world.

These were India's chief preoccupations when World War I broke out in 1914. By the time that war ended, it was obvious that it had affected the political and economic situation in India in several ways. Indian troops had fought gallantly alongside of British armies in various parts of the world, and much material support had been contributed. The war, of course, had caused much disturbance to Indian trade in its earlier phases but, in due course, this was followed by a considerable expansion of industrial activities. While the bulk of the educated classes were in tune with the ideas which inspired loyalty towards the Allied Powers, small groups of revoluntionaries, particularly in Bengal and Punjab, had sought to utilise the opportunity to advance their cause. The Ghadr (rebel) Party, which drew its funds from America and Germany, made plans for running arms and ammunition into India and launching an armed rising. In pursuance of the call of the Ghadr Party, no less than 8,000 Sikhs returned to the Punjab from the USA, Canada and the Far East, and among these were active agents of the Ghadr Party. While no large scale rising resulted, this factor had its part to play in influencing opinion.

The war gave the Indian people a new sense of self-confidence and pride and the emphasis shifted from the more limited demand for self-government to an assertion of the right of self-determination popularised in the West by President Wilson of the USA. A demand went up that these war aims should be applied to India.

It was at this stage that Mahatma Gandhi emerged on the Indian scene and succeeded in welding into a powerful mass agitation the widespread aspiration for home rule and the Muslim slogan for the restoration of the Khilafat which had just been abolished. Freed from the preoccupations of the war, the British Government was able to turn its attention to the situation in India and, on August 20, 1917, Mr Montagu, the Secretary of State for

India, made the following announcement in the House of Commons:

'The policy of His Majesty's Government, with which the Government of India are in complete accord, is that of the increasing association of Indians in every branch of the administration and the gradual development of self-governing institutions with a view to the progressive realisation of responsible government in India as an integral part of the British Empire. They have decided that substantial steps in this direction should be taken as soon as possible, and that it is of the highest importance as a preliminary to considering what these steps should be that there should be a free and informal exchange of opinion between those in authority at Home and in India. His Majesty's Government have accordingly decided, with His Majesty's approval, that I should accept the Viceroy's invitation to proceed to India to discuss these matters with the Viceroy and the Government of India, to consider with the Viceroy the views of local Governments, and to receive with him the suggestions of representative bodies and others.

'I would add that progress in this policy can only be achieved by successive stages. The British Government and the Government of India, on whom the responsibility lies for the welfare and advancement of the Indian peoples, must be judges of the time and measure of each advance, and they must be guided by the co-operation received from those upon whom new opportunities of service will thus be conferred and by the extent to which it is found that confidence can be reposed in their sense of responsibility.

'Ample opportunity will be afforded for public discussion of the proposals which will be submitted in due course to Parliament.'[2]

Economic and Social Conditions

The condition of the Indian people, as it was thus launching on increasingly rapid strides towards free nationhood, was marked unfortunately by two dominating conditions. One was the poverty, ignorance and degradation of immense masses of the Indian people. The other was that Indian society was characterised by a series of divisions and cleavages of race, religion, caste and language which constantly threatened its solidarity and came in the way of a realisation of full nationhood. There was inequality too between town and countryside. By rural standards, all town dwellers, including industrial workers, were a privileged class. While the bulk of taxation was borne by the agrarian classes, the State spent most of the money in the cities and towns. As Gandhi used to put it, the people in the towns and the cities had been riding, like the Old Man of the Sea, on the back of the rural Sinbad. They would do everything but get off his back.

The Indian peasant was as yet inarticulate. Indebtedness was his greatest curse. It was universal throughout the countryside, though its extent could not be precisely estimated. A Royal Agricultural Commission, which was to be appointed shortly, found that 'money-lenders were steadily adding to their landed possessions in most provinces'. Rural indebtedness was both a cause and a consequence of the poverty of the large part of the Indian peasantry. The principal factors which tended to make indebtedness chronic and onerous were: the excessive pressure of the population on the land, the excessive sub-division and fragmentation of farm plots, the decay of village industries subsidiary to agriculture, the insecurity of harvests and periodical famines. There was no demand for agrarian legislation or land reform nor for a parity in prices between rural and industrial products. It was Gandhi who took public affairs down to the level of the village and gave the first stirrings to agrarian consciousness. The urban industrial proletariat, though insignificant numerically – numbering barely a million – was steadily growing and becoming an important force and a Royal Commission had to be appointed in 1929 to inquire into problems of industrial labour. An essential point which distinguished industrial labour in India from its counterpart in the West was the migratory character of the workpeople. Most workers in towns and cities retained their link with the village from which they came and to which they returned for a few months every year. The labouring classes were, therefore, slow to organise themselves into a force capable of having their grievances redressed. State legislation for the regulation of working conditions was in its infancy. The strange environment in the cities, poor diet, hard conditions of work and living – all these factors made it difficult for a new recruit to take to his new avocation with zest and with a

will to make good. Absenteeism and loitering were naturally the result. No wonder the efficiency of the worker, or the effort put in by him, was much poorer than that of the Western worker with whom he was often compared.

At the other end of the political scale stood the intelligentsia, many of whom were associated with the British in ruling the country and ordering its affairs. While statistics in regard to the national income and the distribution of wealth were practically non-existent, such evidence as was available showed that not only was the average income miserably low (it was estimated ten years later to be Rs 65 per annum or $14), but that the distribution of the national income was marked by even more gross inequalities than in most parts of the world. The Indian Maharaja, the big feudal landlord and the rising industrialist and bureaucrat stood like lofty mountain peaks above the plains of poverty.

The state of education of the Indian people was just as alarming, only six per cent of the population being able to comply with the test of literacy which consisted in reading and writing a letter in one's own script. It was higher in large cities where it rose to about thirty per cent. The knowledge of the English language was confined to some two million people, less than one per cent of the population.

The frail structure was riddled by the caste system of which the essential elements were endogamy, a hierarchy headed by the Brahmins, restrictions on social intercourse in the matter of food and drink, occupational discrimination and inequality before the law. Moreover, the 'untouchables' were often banned from using public places like schools, wells, bathing places, temples and cremation grounds and, in certain provinces, even their contact or proximity was regarded as a pollution.

Another feature of the social organisation was the joint family system, a remnant of the primitive tribal community, which was found in all classes of society, with both patri-leneal and matri-leneal traditions. The system had its advantages but it often led to family discord and encouraged idleness and dependence even among the able-bodied. It was, however, disintegrating under social and economic forces like the rising spirit of independence and self-respect among the younger generation, the increasing struggle for existence and a migration of able-bodied members of the family to industrial centres. Probably traceable to the joint family system was the custom of child-marriage common at that time. Marriage often took place at the instance of the family even when the bride and bridegroom were still in their childhood.

A bird's eye view of the vast sub-continent had provoked a comment that India was still a country 'marching in uneven stages through all the centuries from the fifth to the twentieth'.

The civil servant, the police official, the judge, the lawyer, the doctor, the college professor, the landlord and the industrialist were intellectually the products of British rule. They had imbibed the principles of British liberalism as they were preached in the nineteenth century and were steeped in the traditions of British constitutional history. The Indian intellectual began to claim that the care of his backward brethren in the villages should be entrusted into his hands.

The response that Gandhi was able to evoke with the slogan of *swaraj* (self-government) and *swadeshi* (home-made) showed that the country was ripe for radical change and that the first stirrings of a new consciousness were manifesting themselves. The question was one of the emancipation of the *ryot* (peasant).

This situation might have been easier to face were it not for the size of the country and the immensity of its problems. British India had then two and a half times the population of the USA. One in five of the world's inhabitants was an Indian. Two provinces, Bengal and United Provinces, contained between them as many people as inhabited the British Isles. While, however, in England and Wales four-fifths of the population lived in towns, in India a similar proportion of the Indian people lived in villages. It was estimated then that 226 out of 244 million people in British India lived in villages. Agriculture was the basic industry of the people. Of every 100 Indians, 71 were devoted to agriculture, 12 to industry, 5 to trade, 2 to domestic services, $1\frac{1}{2}$ to the professions and $1\frac{1}{2}$ to Goverment services.[3]

It was obvious that in terms of the immensity of the problem any radical improvement would take time. If ever there was a case to prove the 'inevitability of gradualness' as propounded by Sydney and Beatrice Webb, it was India.

This was appreciated by the first generation of India's national leaders like Dadabhoy Naoroji and Gopala Krishna Gokhale. It was Mr Gokhale who said:

'There is work enough for the most enthusiastic lover of his country. On every side, whichever way we turn, only one sight meets the eye, that of work to be done; and only one cry is heard: that there are but few faithful workers. The elevation of the depressed classes, who have to be brought up to the level of the rest of our people, universal elementary education, co-operation, improvement of the economic condition of the peasantry, higher education of women, spread of industrial and technical education, building up the industrial strength, promotion of closer relations between the different communities – these are some of of the tasks which lie in front of us, and each of them needs a whole army of devoted missionaries.'

Constitutional Development

In 1919 the British Parliament, as a result of the Montagu-Chelmsford proposals of 1918, enacted the Government of India Act which gave India a new constitution and took a step forward in the direction of 'the progressive realisation of responsible Government in India'. This act called for decreased intervention by the British Secretary of State for India and Parliament in the day to day administration of the country and provided that normally power should rest in the hands of the British Governor-General and his Executive Councillors in New Delhi, a larger proportion of whom were from then on to be Indians. The central Government was not yet made responsible to any popularly elected legislature, but a bicameral legislature consisting of a Council of State and a Legislative Assembly was set up at the Centre which would function as a consultative and deliberative body in relation to the Governor-General and his Council in roughly the same manner as the German Reichstag of the Imperial days functioned in relation to the Kaiser and his Chancellor. This Assembly was to be elected in the main on a restricted franchise.

17

B

In the Provinces or States, one step further was taken in that the State Governments or Cabinets were to be divided into two sectors, one consisting of the British Governor and his Councillors who, like the Governor-General and his Councillors, would be above responsibility to a popular legislature and, on the other hand, of the Governor and his Ministers, who would be responsible to the provincial Legislative Council, which in turn was to be popularly elected on a franchise which gave the urban and the tural middle class a vote for the first time in the country's history. This split responsibility of the provincial government was known as 'diarchy'. In both the Centre and the Provinces, the Governor-General and the Governor had power to veto legislation.

In the sphere of municipal and local Government, complete popular control was instituted. In regard to public services, any racial barriers that still existed in the regulation of appointments were to be abolished altogether and the progressive Indianisation of both the civil and military services was contemplated.

It was provided that, at the end of ten years of the working of the new Constitution, a Commission was to be appointed to review the constitutional position both at the Centre and in the Provinces. This Commission was to be appointed with the approval of the British Parliament and similar Commissions were to be appointed at intervals of not more than twelve years thereafter.

This then was the state of India when the international communist movement first cast its eyes in the direction of the Indian ocean and surveyed the scene and its possibilities.

CHAPTER TWO

Early Years
up to 1929

The First World War came as a shock in India, as elsewhere, to many people who had come to regard the kind of world they inhabited as something permanent. They began to seek some solution of the social and economic ills that appeared to have contributed towards bringing about the ghastliness of a global war. Just when this heart-searching and stock-taking were going on throughout the world, the Russian Revolution led by Lenin and Trotsky broke out. Its denunciation of the existing system and sweep of promises of a better future based on peace, equality and social justice took many people by storm. In the heat, passion and idealism thus generated, much was not seen and a good deal excused.

It was on this wave of idealism that communism came to India. Here it mingled with another stream – nationalism – sometimes supporting it, sometimes opposing it. India was then waking from a long slumber into a new consciousness of its pride and dignity and was, under the leadership of Mahatma Gandhi, preparing to launch her first mass struggle against British rule. By minds caught up in this emotional surge, triumphant Bolshevik Russia was received favourably and looked up to as a new liberating force. The professed repudiation – probably largely sincere at that stage – by Lenin and Trotsky of the legacy of Tzarist imperialism was perhaps the biggest single factor in creating this favourable response.

Though communism, ideologically, is a creed professedly based on the strength and interests of the proletariat, and though during the War years the increased tempo of the country's industrialisation had created a sizeable labour force, the strength of communism

19

in India was in the beginning, as it is even at the present day, mainly intellectual.

The intellectual and emotional climate in India in the early twenties was receptive to the ideas of communism. In such a climate, the Communist International sought to forge the necessary organisational links. This monograph is primarily the story of the structure so reared. Communist ideas and ideals are discussed not in the abstract but only in so far as they are embodied in the communist programme, actions and organisation in India.

The Bolshevik leaders turned their eyes very early to India. As far back as 1918, the wireless stations of the Soviet Government broadcast a report of a memorandum handed to the Central Executive Committee of the Soviets by some unnamed and almost certainly fictitious Indian delegation. The delegation requested the Soviets for assistance and called upon free Russia to stretch a fraternal hand to oppressed India.[1] Messages sent out a year later spoke of the fact that the Russian Communist Party had decided 'to take concrete measures to spread revolution in the East' and that the Third International was about to establish sections in Oriental countries.[2]

In 1919, the Third International decided to support nationalist movements in the East 'as they tend to upset the existing authority while not opposing revolutionary aspirations.'[3] In September 1920 was convened at Baku, through the efforts of Zinoviev and Radek, a Congress of the Peoples of the East, reportedly attended by delegates from thirty-seven countries, including India. In 1920, at the Third Congress of the Comintern, Lenin said:

'British India is at the head of these countries, and there revolution is maturing in proportion to the growth of the industrial and railway proletariat on the one hand and to the increase in the brutal terrorism of the British – who are more frequently resorting to massacres (Amritsar), public floggings, etc. – on the other.'[4]

In his work *On the Foundations of Leninism*, Stalin wrote in 1924 that in India 'the imperialist chain may break earlier than in other countries'.

Chapter 6 of the *Programme of the Communist International*

adopted by the First World Congress on September 1920 in Moscow deals with the strategy and tactics of the Communist International in the struggle for the dictatorship of the proletariat. The first part deals with ideologies inimical to communism. Amongst these is Gandhism and on this subject the programme says clearly:

'Tendencies like Gandhism in India, thoroughly imbued with religious conceptions, idealize the most backward and economically most reactionary forms of social life, see the solution of the social problem not in proletarian socialism, but in a reversion to these backward forms, preach passivity and repudiate the class struggle, and in the process of the development of the revolution become transformed into an openly reactionary force. Gandhism is more and more becoming an ideology directed against mass revolution. It must be strongly combated by Communism.'

On 9th February 1924 Soviet Foreign Minister Chicherin speaking for Moscow proclaimed that 'Future India must stand at the head of the Free Eastern Republic'.[5]

Channels of Communication

To achieve this purpose, Moscow developed and perfected channels of contact with India. Communist activity became evident in all the border countries – Tibet, Sinkiang, Afghanistan, Persia. The Comintern had considered three main lines of penetration – the central line through Afghanistan, the Eastern line through Sinkiang and the Western line through Persia. These communications were effected by Comintern agents, some of them recruited later from the members of the Ghadr Party[6], who joined the Comintern for nationalist reasons but in the process became good communists.

The earliest recruits, apart from a few political exiles and wandering intellectuals, were made by the communists among the Muhajirin, fanatical Muslims who left India as an unholy land in protest against the Afghan War of 1919. It is understood that something like 100 of them got to Tashkent, where Mr M. N. Roy and others indoctrinated them. They were then sent back to India in ones and twos, some overland and some by sea, from 1921–22 onwards. Much money and effort were spent on them, but the results were meagre. Majid and Shaukat Usmani of the Meerut Conspiracy Case belonged to this group. Round about 1924, certain others among them were put up as accused in Conspiracy Cases in Peshawar. Fazl-I-Ilahi Qurban was one of them. Though he returned to India by sea, he was tried at Peshawar and sentenced to three years imprisonment. He is probably the only one of the Muhajirin recruits who is still active, being one of the leading lights of the Pakistan Communist Party.

In August 1924, the Executive Committee of the Communist International issued instructions to Tashkent that a new propaganda base in Northern Afghanistan should be established at Maza-i-Shariff. Almost immediately, a steady increase in the number of Russians entering Afghanistan became evident. While Afghanistan was the base of operations, India, however, was the main objective. It was also thought that a Bolshevised Afghanistan would expedite the process of Bolshevisation in India. In an article by an Indian communist in Europe, it was said: 'The very existence of a pro-Bolshevik Afghanistan will be the greatest signpost of Bolshevism to the tribes of the North Western Frontier Province who will pass the message onward to India.'[7]

Similar activities were started in Persia, but it was always kept in mind that the line of communication between Persia and India ran through Afghanistan.

These channels were reinforced by channels opened up in Sinkiang, a large country to the north of India over which Russia had always cast covetous eyes. Soviet Russia was making feverish efforts to infiltrate Sinkiang and, as a preliminary, succeeded in negotiating a trade pact with that country. A Russian newspaper *Echo* in Shanghai wrote in May 1928: 'Now that they (the Bolsheviks) have taken possession of the region, they know that by doing so they are becoming directly connected with Northern India *via* Kuldja, Aksu, Kashgar, and on to the Pamirs. From Sinkiang there are several routes to India ... The Bolsheviks are not losing time and are forwarding in the direction of India large

quantities of communist literature, ammunition and other supplies.'[8]

The next country in the line of march was Tibet, then as now
an important gateway to India. Communist emissaries started
visiting Lhasa in 1922. In 1930 the Communist International
'decided to instruct the IKKI (International Executive Committee)
to take steps to combine the existing revolutionary groups in
Tibet into a national party and to nominate comrade Dordzhiyev
(Dorjieff) as President of the Central Committee of the proposed
new Party.' The equivalent of £20,000 was assigned for these
activities.[9]

All these contacts were further strengthened by communist
activities in China. The possibilities of a communist revolution in
China, not in relation to China, but as further opening up channels of penetration into India, were regarded as fruitful by Soviet
leaders. As early as 1925, Zinoviev proclaimed that instead of the
'well-trodden paths to India through Persia and Afghanistan', it
was China that had 'become for us the central starting point for
action in India'. The fighting slogan of the communists was *Via*
revolutionary China to the Federal Republic of the United States
of India'.[10]

Despite all this activity, the overland routes were not to play as
important a part as the sea routes. Realising the value of th's,
particular attention was paid by the Communist Parties, b. .n
India and abroad, to recruiting Indian and other seamen . European and American ports so that they might serve as couriers.
Shamsul Huda of the Meerut Conspiracy Case was one of those
so recruited in America. Nalini Gupta of the Cawnpore Conspiracy Case travelled to and fro as a seaman. So did Ayodhya Prasad
of the Meerut Conspiracy Case and Amir Haidar Khan and many
others. They carried with them letters, propaganda literature and
sometimes money.

M. N. Roy

Alongside of these activities on the borders, Moscow was also
trying to establish a section of the Communist International in
the heart of India itself. Organisationally, Mr M. N. Roy was

perhaps the first link between the Communist International and nascent Indian communism which was throughout the greater part of the twenties still at the level of ideas. It was in 1920 that M. N. Roy made his first appearance in Russia. Arriving that year in Europe, he placed himself at the head of a small but extremely virile group of Indian exiles in Berlin. Round about 1921-22, Roy began to publish from various places in Europe an English periodical, first entitled *Vanguard* and later *The Masses of India*. A large number of copies of this journal were sent to individual nationalists, trade unionists and intellectuals in India. These journals undoubtedly supplied the inspiration for an English weekly entitled *Socialist* published in Bombay by S. A. Dange in 1923 and a Bengali weekly *Janavani* published in Calcutta about the same time by Muzaffar Ahmad. The inevitable rivalries occurred even at that early stage. Virendranath Chattopadhyaya, who had appeared earlier on the scene, was the chief rival. M. N. Roy, however, overcame all opposition and succeeded in securing his own recognition by the Moscow leaders as the spokesman of India. In July 1924, the Comintern decided to adopt M. N. Roy's advice that the Communist Party of India should be established as a branch of the Communist International.[11]

It was when the first of Roy's followers began to arrive in India, the finished products of Moscow's infant Oriental Academy, that organised communism came to India. Roy recalls that among his pupils in Moscow was the Indo-Chinese communist Ho Chi-Minh.

In the vanguard were Nalini Gupta and Abani Mukherji, who returned to India, one on Roy's behalf in 1921 and the other in 1923 on behalf of Chattopadhyaya. Both had been members of terrorist organisations in Bengal prior to their departure abroad. Their activities fructified in the Cawnpore Conspiracy Case in 1924. The accused in that case were S. A. Dange, Muzaffar Ahmad, Shaukat Usmani and Nalini Gupta.

Round about 1924, the Communist International appears, however, to have developed some doubt about Roy's ability to deliver the goods and to place less reliance on his infallibility where Indian affairs were concerned. New tactics became clearly discernible in Moscow's handling of the Indian situation. Zinoviev demanded and obtained the adoption of a scheme of direct contact between the Comintern and the Communist organisation and groups in British India. Actually, the contact was not direct, since London soon became the organisational link. In course of time, the Communist Party of Great Britain tended to monopolise India as its own province, thus following ironically the imperialist relationship which it constantly denounced. R. Palme Dutt, one of the outstanding members of the Communist Party of Great Britain, became the Pundit to lay down the law to the Indian Communist Party, a rôle he still plays. Dutt has throughout been in closer touch with Moscow than most of his colleagues in the British Party. His wife, a Finn, was one of the Comintern's earliest recruits. High in the confidence of the Kremlin, it is understood that she was consulted by Dutt about all his pronouncements and directives.

Emissaries from Europe

The orientation of this new policy caused the despatch to India, in spite of Roy's vehement protest, of the first of a series of British communists in the person of Percy E. Glading, *alias* R. Cochrane, who was later, in 1938, to be imprisoned for espionage for the Soviets in Woolwich Arsenal, where he was then employed. Glading was followed by George Allison, *alias* Donald Campbell, a prominent member of the British Communist Party, who arrived in Bombay in April, 1926. Allison had visited Moscow in 1924 and had remained there till July 1925 and was sent to India to develop the left-wing inside the Trade Union Congress but to keep out of party politics except in an advisory capacity. This injunction he failed to carry out and the prominent part which he took in labour troubles in Bombay and Bengal eventually led to his apprehension in 1926 and his subsequent prosecution and conviction on a charge of using forged documents and of having counterfeited the seal and stamp of the British Foreign Office on his passport. He was sentenced to eighteen months' rigorous imprisonment and was deported on the expiry of his sentence.

Allison's place was taken by Philip Spratt, a Cambridge University graduate, who arrived in India in December 1926, ostensibly on behalf of a firm of booksellers but in reality to open in India a Labour Research organisation (on the model of the Labour Research Department in London, where he had worked for some time) through which Soviet money could be received and distributed. When Spratt arrived in India, though the Communist Party of India had been formally in existence for about a year and a half, it had barely a dozen nominal members and hardly any perceptible activity. In actual fact, Spratt took up the work which Allison had perforce to abandon, and his devotion, energy and advice became available to the Indian group along with a not inconsiderable amount of financial assistance.

Spratt was joined in September 1927 by Benjamin Francis Bradley, also a capable worker, who took a similarly active part in the organisation of the Workers' and Peasants' Party and of the employees of cotton mills and the railways. The last of this ring of foreign agents was Hugh Lester Hutchinson, who was not a member of the Communist Party. He came to Bombay in September 1928 after a short stay in Berlin. Hutchinson's mission did not, however, prove to be a success.

During these early days Spratt's hand was everywhere. He planted the seeds of revolt in the Punjab. It was Spratt's untiring energy that brought into being a Workers' and Peasants' Party in the United Provinces, which held its inaugural conference at Meerut in October 1928. Within a month, branches had been formed in Delhi, Meerut, Gorakhpur, Jhansi and Allahabad. Spratt worked in 1927 mainly with the Bombay group, in 1928 with the Bengal Party. He played a large part in uniting the Punjab groups into one party and in the formation of those in the United Provinces into another. And all the time he was carrying on correspondence with his counterparts on the Continent and in England, informing them of the progress achieved, discussing difficulties, receiving instructions.[12]

Literature

A steady and expensive stream of literature had been flowing into India ever since communist activity in the country started. Various subterfuges were resorted to in order to frustrate the censorship. Communist dailies were frequently wrapped in one or two pages of the London *Times* or the *New York Herald Tribune* or other papers of similar standing. Books were found wrapped in the dust covers of popular novels or religious works. Addresses of firms or shops were used as a cover to which such literature was sent. The Indian distributor of a communist weekly gave a publisher abroad the following instructions: 'Please send these twelve copies in three packets of four copies each in plain wrappers as usual so as not to attract attention.'[13]

Methods used by the British administration to stem this stream of literature included a recourse to Section 19 of the Sea Customs Act which provided that the Governor-General in Council could prohibit the bringing into India of any particular class of goods. In exercise of this power, a notification was framed in 1927 prohibiting the import into India of any publication issued by, or emanating from, the Communist International or any organisation affiliated to, or connected with, it.

Finance

The question arises as to how the communists were able to finance their operations in those early years. Apart from what little they could raise internally, it is clear that the larger part of their financial support was and is today derived from abroad. The Indian communists have always feigned righteous indignation at any mention of this fact. As it happens, however, a certain amount of document-ary proof exists of the foreign help made available during this period. Sometimes these funds were sent quite openly. Indeed, in these cases, Indian communists were enjoined to give news of the receipt of these remittances the widest possible publicity and to emphasise the source from which they came. Examples of this method of dispatch were two sums of Rs 20,917 and Rs 14,101 which were sent during the Bombay textile strikes to Mr S. H. Jhabawala, Vice-President of the (local) Textile Labour Union, and later President of the Bombay Mill Workers' Union, for the relief of the strikers. These grants were professedly made by the Textile Central Committee in Moscow. The first consignment was wrongly directed and, to the great consternation of the leaders of the Workers' and Peasants' Party, it fell into the hands of Mr N. M. Joshi, then a moderate trade union organiser.[14]

Other funds, meant for the communist apparatus, were sent through devious channels and with the greatest secrecy. Spratt constantly complained about money difficulties and once drew a budget estimating his needs at a modest sum of Rs 2,400 a month. He said that it would only mean an increase of 33⅓ per cent on the then allowance made to him, which was therefore, presumably in the neighbourhood of Rs 1,800 per mensem.[15]

Spratt received the equivalent of nearly £1,000 during the eighteen months which ended on 30th January 1928. Of this, three sums totalling £700 were despatched from London by Samuel Montagu and Co, Olive N. Parsons and Douglas Parsons. Douglas Parsons was a noted British communist and was at that time the general manager of the Communist organ, the *Sunday Worker*. His wife Olive was the daughter of a director in Samuel Montagu and Co. Spratt also received £200 (and Bradley £100) from H.P. Rathbone and £40 from Robin Page Arnot. Bradley also received six other remittances amounting to £300 in the course of a year, and acknowledged receipt to the Workers' Welfare League of India, a CP front in London.[16] As the communist movement in Britain was itself then in an impoverished state, it is obvious that the original source of supply of these funds was Moscow. A case in point was the suggestion that came from Moscow in August 1925 that Clemens Palme Dutt should be sent to India as the representative of the Colonial Bureau of the Communist Party of Great Britain. When London replied that the Communist Party of Great Britain had barely enough funds to pay C.P. Dutt's fare, M.N. Roy replied that Dutt was being sent on behalf of the Eastern Department of the Communist International and that his deputation need not involve the CPGB in any expenditure.[17]

Secret Communications

The question of financial aid raises the question of the means of communication and the methods of secrecy by which the Party's work was and is carried out. Communications were sent in figure ciphers, invisible ink and cryptic language. Sometimes, the cryptic language took the form of a grotesque sort of correspondence as if between clergymen, in which the Workers' and Peasants' Party were described as 'Methodists' and the CPI as 'YMCA'. All the leading participants had of course been given pseudonyms: Allison was 'David', Spratt was 'Desmond', Bradley 'Fred', Clemens Palme Dutt 'Douglas'. C. P. Dutt was a constant user of such forms of address as 'Dear brother in God'. The meanings of words were sometimes interchanged. For example, 'send' meant 'receive' and 'receive' meant 'send'. Thus, in a letter dated 14th June 1927, Spratt sent the message: 'You should receive some sort of MSS by the end of August. Ask Baker about it. It should not be sent directly by me or Ambrose.' The message transcribed, really meant: 'You should send some money by the end of August. Ask Saklatvala about it. It should not be received directly by me or Muzaffar Ahmed.' To disguise the name of a person, vowels in it were substituted by those which next precede them in the alphabet (U for A, A for E). Similar order was taken with the first and last consonants in the name. Thus, Cunfa equalled Dange, Fhusa meant Ghate and so on.[18]

During all this period, although international communism functioned through the Workers' and Peasants' Party and the communists continued to grow in strength, there was little sign of activity on the part of the parent body, the Communist Party of India, which had formally been formed by Satya Bhakta in 1925, while the real fathers of the cause convicted in the Cawnpore Conspiracy Case were still in prison. Documents which came to light later in the course of the Meerut Conspiracy Case showed that the Party's members had concentrated so much effort on building up the Workers' and Peasants' Party that the CPI had perforce been almost neglected. To such a pass had things come that S.V. Ghate in May 1928 seriously suggested that the Workers' and Peasants' Party should control the Communist Party – a complete reversal of the orthodox procedure prescribed by Moscow. The constitution and programme of the CPI had, it is true, been formulated in May 1927, and an executive committee was in existence and had met in Madras six months later, but it was obvious that drastic reorganisation was called for.

Sixth World Congress

Meanwhile, Moscow had not been inactive. It was watching the developments in the Communist Party in India and other similarly placed countries with great interest and had made its own decisions about it. The Sixth World Congress of the Communist International met and passed a resolution on 1st September 1928, entitled *The Revolutionary Movement for the Colonies and Semi-Colonies*, on which Mao Tse-tung, who became head of the Chinese Communist Party two years later, was to base his entire strategy. Under the heading 'Communist Strategy in China and similar Colonial Countries', the resolution stated:

'As in all colonies and semi-colonies, so also in China and India, the development of production forces and the socialisation of labour stands at a comparatively low level . . . In the revolutionary movement of these countries . . . the following kinds of tasks can be pointed out . . .

'Emancipation of the country from the yoke of imperialism and establishment of the dictatorship of the proletariat and peasantry; consolidation of the hegemony of the proletariat . . .

'Strengthening of the Communist Party and its conquest of a firm leading position among the toiling masses . . . How far the bourgeois-democratic revolution will be able in practice to realise all its basic tasks . . . will depend on the course of the revolutionary movement of the workers and peasants . . .

'The bourgeoisie of China, India and Egypt . . . attempts by means of empty nationalist phrases and gesture to keep the petty-bourgeois masses under its influence and to induce imperialism to grant certain concessions.

'Without the liberation of the toiling masses from the influence of the bourgeoisie and of national-reformism, the basic strategical aim of the Communist movement in the bourgeois-democratic revolution . . . cannot be achieved.

'In India, Egypt . . . etc . . . it is necessary to carry through much work in the building up and consolidation of the Communist Party and trade union organisations of the proletariat . . . in the winning over of the masses and their liberation from the influence of national-reformist bourgeoisie, before it is possible to advance in these countries with definite prospects of success to the realisation of such tasks as those which were fully carried out in China during the Wuhan period.

'. . . It is necessary by means of correct communist tactics, adapted to the conditions of the present stage, to help the toiling masses in India, Egypt, Indonesia and such colonies to emancipate themselves from the influence of the bourgeois parties . . . (Swarajists, Wafdists, etc). It is necessary to reject the formation of any kind of *bloc* between the Communist Party and the nationalist-reformist opposition; this does not exclude the formation of temporary agreements and the co-ordinating of separate activities in connection with definite anti-imperialist demonstrations, provided that these demonstrations of the bourgeois opposition can be utilised for the development of the mass movement, and provided that these agreements do not in any way limit the freedom of the Communist Parties in the matter of agitation among the masses and among the organisation of the latter . . . Even such movements as Gandhism in India, Sun Yat Senism in China, Sarekat Islam in Indonesia, were originally radical petty-bourgeois ideological movements which became converted into a bourgeois nationalist-reformist movement.'

Under the heading 'Communist Strategy and Tactics', the Resolution went on:

'The fundamental slogans, through which the Party must seek to win over the masses are: Overthrow of imperialist domination . . . Union with the USSR and the world proletarian movement.'

Dealing specifically with India, the Resolution stated:

'The basic tasks of the Indian communists consist in struggle against British Imperialism for the emancipation of the country . . . The Union of all communist groups and individual Communists scattered throughout the country into a single, independent, and centralised Party represents the first task of the Indian communists . . .

'In the Trade Unions, the Indian communists must mercilessly expose the national-reformist leaders and carry on a decisive struggle for the conversion of the trade unions into genuine class organisations of the proletariat and for the replacement of the present reformist leadership by consistent revolutionary representatives from the mass of the workers . . .

'The communist must unmask the national reformism of the Indian National Congress and oppose all the phrases of the Swarajists, Gandhists, etc, about passive resistance.

'It must be remembered that under no circumstances can the communists relinquish their right to open criticism of the opportunist and reformist tactics of the leadership of those mass organisations in which they work.'

The Assembly Letter

But the Comintern did not wait for the World Congress to meet and pass a resolution. A letter which is called the 'Assembly Letter', because it was later read out in the Indian Legislative Assembly on 10th September 1928, was sent out to India. It was dated 30th December 1927, and is believed to have been written by M. N. Roy as a member of the Executive Committee of the Communist International in Moscow, and despatched through Clemens Palme Dutt to Muzzafar Ahmed.[19] This letter was a comprehensive one and dealt with the organisation of the CPI and of the Workers' and Peasants' Party and the inter-relation, co-ordination and international affiliation of these parties as also questions concerning the emigrant section and financial support.

This letter said that: 'The communists will become the trusted leaders of the masses only by giving concrete form to the latter's unconscious demands.' It emphasised the need of participation by the communists in the daily struggles of the mass of the Indian people. There was no illusion, however, about the legality of such participation, for the letter went on to point out that legality could only be had at the expense of the *raison d'être* of the Party. The letter insisted, therefore, on the formation of an illegal Communist Party. But as legality was an essential pre-requisite to the conduct of effective propaganda among the masses, a Workers' and Peasants' Party must also be built up to take the place of the Communist Party when the latter became illegal and make open preparations for the great day when the Communist Party could openly assume the leadership of the revolution. This veiled Communist Party was to be a much broader organisation, a rallying ground of all exploited social elements. There followed a draft of the new Party's programme of which it was said that the social elements ready to fight for this programme were not all necessarily communists and never would be communists, but under the influence of the proletariat and led by the CP while subscribing to the programme of socialism. There was also a word of criticism of the WPP, as it was then. The Workers' and Peasants' Party was too openly identified with the Communist Party. 'It is publicly known that practically all the members of the Central Committee of the Communist Party are the leaders of the WPP. Of course, in fact, it should be so, but the cat had been unnecessarily let out of the bag by publishing the list of the CC of the CP'.

The letter continued: 'As far as the Workers' and Peasants' Party is concerned, the question is answered. It should affiliate itself with the League Against Imperialism.[20] That will serve our purpose. Through that you will have the relations and aid you need, but you will not be accused of having relations with Moscow. The WPP can eventually become the recognised organ of the League in India.'

Of the CPI, the letter said: 'The CP must unquestionably be a section of the Communist International. It is practically treated as such, but no formal request to this effect has yet come from our Party in India . . . A Communist Party must be an organic part of the world communist organisation. It cannot be otherwise and call itself "Communist". Those who smell foreign dictation in this organisational principle of a body that carries on a relentless struggle throughout the world are not Communists.'

The last section of the 'Assembly Letter' dealt with financial matters: 'Arrangements have been made to continue the aid for the three papers and also for the monthly in the North, if necessary. Besides provision has also been made for the other necessities specified in a report received two months ago . . . This is a temporary arrangement and things will be in better shape in the new year (1928) . . . The new arrangement will be according to a plan which will be communicated to you in due time.'

33

C

Party Reorganisation

Soon after the Comintern Resolution of September 1928 was passed, the Communist Party met in Calcutta, in December 1928. It was at this meeting that the swing to the Left in obedience to the decisions of the Sixth World Congress was applied to India, a trend that was to continue till 1934–35. A new Central Executive was first elected. The main decisions were to make the Party active and to do propaganda in the name of the CPI, to affiliate to the Communist International, to adopt the colonial thesis of the Comintern as the basis for work, and to send Muzaffar Ahmed to Moscow as a delegate to the Executive Committee of the Communist International. A revised constitution was subsequently issued which differed materially from the earlier one. It began by describing the Party as a section of the Communist International and then categorically stated that the Party's object was the attainment of socialism in accordance with the programme of the Communist International and the policy adopted from time to time by the Party with the agreement of the Communist International.[21] Roy's instructions had thus been obeyed to the letter.

The Party's next meetings were held in Bombay from 17th to 19th March 1929, when Dr G. M. Adhikari, as the expert in method, presented concrete proposals for further reorganisation which were accepted in theory. The Party was to be organised in *five* departments (for trade unions, peasants, propaganda, organisational and secretariat development and political control) and a sub-committee was appointed to work out details. On the following day, however, the majority of the members were arrested, thus putting an end to the first period in the story of communist activity in India. During this period, the non-Marxian Communist Party of India, set up in 1924, had thus been transformed, step by step, into a body owning full allegiance to the Communist International. This gradual development was guided and closely supervised throughout by the Comintern itself, and the formal act of affiliation was but the final step in the development of a plan which was hatched over a period of time.

Communists in Trade Unions

Perhaps from a short-term point of view, the greatest success of the communists during the first period was the influence they had managed to acquire in India's nascent Trade Unions and their success in distorting, disrupting and splitting them to their advantage.

The First World War had given a considerable push to the industrialisation of India. In the process, a sizeable labour force was created. The influence of Western ideas of labour organisation and social justice became noticeable. The inspiration came primarily from the British Labour Party. Rising prices and the consequent unrest encouraged the birth of trade-unions. The first Union to be formed was the Madras Union established by Mr B. P. Wadia in 1918. In 1920, the All India Trade Union Congress was established for purposes of co-ordination, and in 1925 was formed the All India Railwaymen's Federation. The early leaders like B. P. Wadia of the Theosophical Society and N. M. Joshi of the Servants of India Society were genuine trade unionists, interested in the welfare and wages of the labourers, trying to develop a tradition of collective bargaining. Thus, by 1925–26, labour organisations had under such auspices acquired a certain strength and stability and their spokesmen in the Legislatures had succeeded in giving legislative expression to some of the workers' needs.

The communists just then appeared on the scene. In conformity to the principles of communism, their sole objective was the capture of key trade unions with a view to utilising this organised force for the political ends of the Party. Already, as early as 1921, the Red International of Labour Unions (Profintern) which guided their operations, had unsuccessfully invited the AITUC to affiliate. From 1926 to 1928, the influence of the communists increased immensely. The communists started several weekly journals, like *Kranti* in the Marathi language.

By the end of 1928, the extremists as represented by the Workers' and Peasants' Party had obtained, particularly in the city of Bombay, a voice in the control of trade union activity. The influence of the moderate element decreased. Strikes were being fomented and the oft-repeated policy: 'First disturb the masses' placid contentment and then inculcate the principles of Communism' – was being pursued with vigour under the guidance of European emissaries and trained indigenous workers. When discontent reared its head amongst the cotton textile workers in Bombay at the beginning of 1928 and amongst the railway workers at Lillooah a few weeks later, the Workers' and Peasants' Parties were able to take full and speedy advantage of the opportunities so presented. The textile strike in Bombay lasted from 16th April to 6th October 1928, and was characterised by a great deal of violence and intimidation.[22]

The Sixth World Congress of the Comintern had in the course of its Resolution already laid down the rôle of communists in the Trade Unions. Equipped with these instructions, the communist leaders met in Calcutta at the end of the year 1928, and formally proclaimed what they had already been practising. Strikes became the order of the day. Four years later, a communist journal in London was to observe: 'During the strike struggles of 1928–29 the workers of India emerged as a political force, a development of immense significance, and took an active part in the nation-wide struggle for independence. A new milestone was thus reached: the workers had realised for the first time their revolutionary rôle among the various forces for national emancipation.'[23]

Meerut Conspiracy Case

Communist activity was abruptly cut short by the arrest under instructions of the British Government in India of thirty-one of its most important leaders from different parts of India on 20th March 1929, including Philip Spratt, Ben Bradley, Muzaffar Ahmed, Shaukat Usmani and S. A. Dange. Lester Hutchinson was arrested a few weeks later.[24] The arrests were accompanied by comprehensive search operations throughout the country and a good deal of the inner working, plans, secret codes, letters written in cryptic terms or in invisible ink and secret documents were disclosed, which were later on supported by a vast mass of direct and documentary evidence, including testimony of the accused themselves.

From these documents, which became available for open investigation, the duties and tasks of the Communist Party of India as enjoined from time to time by the Comintern were for the first time brought into daylight. These injunctions were concentrated on organisation: take part in the every-day struggle; do not disregard the smallest demand; be conspicuous in all strikes and demonstrations; every strike, large or small, is a lesson; train leaders from the rank and file; inculcate discipline; expose reformists; oppose all phrases about non-violence or passive resistance; deprecate tactfully the influence of religion; denounce capitalists; explain that the Government is an instrument of the capitalists; introduce political subjects and issues; create discontent and intensify it where it exists; demonstrate the international character of the class struggle; praise the Red International of Labour Unions (Profintern) and denounce the International Federation of Trade Unions, Amsterdam; and draw illustrations from Russia.

All this was in consonance with the programme laid down by the Communist International in 1928, and the stages in which it was to be realised and the tactics which were to be followed at different stages. The International had said: 'The principal task in such countries (China, India, etc) is, on the one hand, to fight against feudalism and the pre-capitalist forms of exploitation and systematically to develop the agrarian revolution; on the other hand, to fight against foreign imperialism for national independence. As a rule transition to the dictatorship of the proletariat in these countries will be only possible through a series of preparatory stages and as the outcome of the whole period of transformation of bourgeois democratic revolution into socialist revolution'.

Summarising the developments of communist activity in India in the twenties, we can do no better than give the findings of the lower Court which made a preliminary enquiry into the case and finalised its hearing of the case on 14th January 1930. The Court found:

'It has been definitely proved that (1) the Communist International was founded in 1919, with its headquarters at Moscow, as the supreme head of all Communist organisations throughout the world; (2) its chief aim

37

is to establish Workers' Republics in every country; (3) for this purpose it has as its fixed policy the exciting of violent revolution in all countries; (4) in particular it has turned its attention to India and determined to cause a revolution which has for its immediate object the overthrow of the sovereignty of the King Emperor in British India; (5) with this object it has formed a conspiracy with persons and bodies in Europe and India and elsewhere to excite the Indian workers and peasants to revolution; (6) these persons and bodies, who may be called conspirators, have laid down a general plan of campaign under the direction of the Communist International; (7) this plan includes the formation of such bodies as a Communist Party of India and Workers' and Peasants' Parties; (8) the immediate work of these parties is to gain control of the working classes by organising them in Unions, teaching them the principles of Communism, inciting them to strikes in order to educate them and teach them solidarity, and in every way to use every possible method of propaganda and instruction; (9) the workers are thus to be taught mass organisation with a view to the declaration of a general strike followed by revolution; (10) the peasants are to be organised in a similar manner so as to form an effective reserve force for the proletarian masses and to effect an agrarian revolution; (11) in pursuance of these aims a Communist Party of India and four Workers' and Peasants' Parties, in Bombay, Bengal, the Punjab and the United Provinces, were formed; (12) these bodies were given financial aid from Moscow and their policy was dictated from Moscow, directly and *via* England and the Continent, through communications conducted in a secret and conspiratorial manner; (13) in addition to this, several persons, such as Allison, Spratt and Bradley were sent out to India for the express purpose of organising the work and fomenting revolution; (14) in pursuance of these directions and with the financial help thus obtained, these bodies have organised unions, conducted demonstrations, edited papers, instituted youth movements, initiated and conducted strikes and used all possible methods of propaganda; (15) in these activities all the accused, with the exception of Dharamvir Singh, are shown to have taken part with full knowledge and approval of their aims and objects and directly or indirectly in league with the conspirators outside India.'[25]

The Additional Sessions Judge, who then took up the actual trial of the case, pronounced judgement on 16th January 1933, sentencing all but four of the thirty-one accused persons to varying terms of imprisonment. Muzaffar Ahmed was sentenced to a life term, S. A. Dange, S. V. Ghate, K. N. Joglekar, R. S. Nimbkar and Philip Spratt to twelve years, Bradley, Mirajkar and Usmani to ten years' transportation, and so on down to the lightest sentence of three years' imprisonment.

On appeal to the Allahabad High Court, while the Chief Justice confirmed all the findings, he scaled down considerably the sentences passed in the Sessions Court in view of the fact that all the accused had already undergone more than four years' confinement before their case came before him. As a result of this clemency, P. C. Joshi, Gopal Basak, Shakshul Huda and Dr Adhikari were released. By the end of 1933, all save Spratt, Muzaffar Ahmed, S. A .Dange and Shaukat Usmani had regained their liberty. Spratt was released in September 1934, and the rest in the autumn of 1935.

At this stage it may be appropriate to refer to one or two interesting features of the trial. One was the fact of widespread nationalist sympathy for the accused at Meerut. By playing upon the liberal principles and anti-British emotions of the nationalist leaders, the communists were able to enlist for their legal advice and defence the services of younger nationalist spokesmen. Among the team of lawyers, many of whom functioned without fee or at financial loss, were men like Pandit Jawaharlal Nehru, now India's Prime Minister, Mr. Farid-ul-huq Ansari, now a leader of the Socialist Party, and Mr. Kailash Nath Katju, at present Home Minister in the Indian Government.

The other feature was the long duration of the proceedings in the successive Courts. The Chief Justice went into this question in appeal and observed: 'The accused took an inordinately long time in reading out well prepared statements which the Court had to take down word for word. In most cases they had nothing more than an exposition, on an elaborate scale, of the doctrines of communism, its tenets and its programme. There has been an extravagant waste of time and energy in the dictation and recording of these statements'.[26] These tactics were, of course, similar to those employed elsewhere by the communists, who regard the 'courts' as bourgeois fads to be turned into platforms for communist propaganda.

What had been the effect of the arrest and the prosecution of the leading communist agents while these legal proceedings were dragging on through the years? The outstanding fact is that the removal of the thirty leading communists in March 1929 had dealt a heavy blow to the Communist Party of India. The industrial situation improved noticeably. There was a cessation of strikes in general. The removal of the leaders had created a vacuum which was filled by very inferior material. Rivalries and petty squabbles grew within the Party. A prominent Calcutta communist was forced to admit that 'from June 1929 to October 1929 the time was very bad with us'.[27] In actual fact, the only practical event of any importance during the last nine months of 1929 was a short-lived strike in Bombay.

CHAPTER THREE

The Wilderness
1930 - 1935

The period covered by the years 1930 to 1935 was one of great political awakening for large masses of the Indian people hitherto touched very lightly by developments in the realm of government. Major political campaigns which included in their scope calls for the encouragement of Swadeshi (home-made) goods and the boycott of British goods also gave a fillip to the industrial progress of the country.

It was precisely at this time when, as a result of the blow struck by the Meerut prosecutions, the communist leadership had been removed from the scene and the Party was disintegrating that the Indian National Congress under Gandhi's leadership launched in 1930 and again in 1932 on mighty mass struggles for national independence which took the form of civil disobedience and open violation of repressive laws, boycott of British goods and the refusal by peasants to pay the land tax. In the course of these campaigns hundreds of thousands of men and women of all walks of life courted imprisonment and served terms in prison ranging from a few weeks to as many years. For the first time peasants, clerks, students and housewives faced the policeman's baton and went cheerfully to prison out of love of their country and its freedom.

The part played by the CPI at such a stage of political advance is naturally of considerable significance. The claim has been made that, throughout the world, communists are in the forefront of the fight for the emancipation and national independence of peoples oppressed by imperialism. The record of the Indian communists during the period under review makes queer reading against the background of such a claim.

41

Far from taking a leading part in the rousing of the people's political consciousness and the resistance to British imperialism, the communists were nowhere to be found in this revolutionary framework. In point of fact, they not only held aloof from this anti-imperialist struggle but did everything they could to weaken and sabotage it. While love of Indian-made cloth and goods was sweeping the land, they sported suits made of foreign cloth as a gesture of solidarity with the British workers in Lancashire. When the people were being educated by Gandhi in methods of non-violent resistance, they asserted academically the right to use violence. Faithful to the letter of the Moscow directive of the Sixth World Congress, the Indian communists insulted on the sands of Chowpathy in Bombay the national flag of the independent India yet to be born, for had not the Comintern laid down that bourgeois nationalists and left nationalists were the deadliest foes of the world revolution?

To the communist in India as elsewhere the struggle for national independence was not so much a struggle for national liberation, as one for strengthening a sector of world capitalism and imperialism. The Comintern in 1928 had resolved:

'The bourgeoisie of China, India and Egypt . . . attempts by means of empty nationalist phrases and gestures to keep the party-bourgeois masses under its influence and to induce imperialism to grant certain concessions.

'It is necessary by means of correct communist tactics, adapted to the conditions of the present stage, to help the toiling masses in India, Egypt, Indonesia and such colonies to emancipate themselves from the influence of the bourgeois parties . . . (Swarajists, Wafdists, etc).

'The communists must unmask the national reformism of the Indian National Congress and oppose all the phrases of the Swarajists, Gandhists, etc, about passive resistance.'

A document entitled 'Platform of Action of the CP of India'[1] which appeared in *Pravda* in 1930 said: 'The greatest threat to the victory of the Indian revolution is the fact that great masses of our people still harbour illusions about the National Congress and have not realised that it represents a class organisation of the capitalists working against the fundamental interests of the toiling masses of our country'.

This thesis also appeared in the *International Press Correspondence*, the official organ of the Communist international, and later on in the London *Daily Worker*. It was later translated into Urdu and other languages of India, and it particularly denounced Mahatma Gandhi. It said: 'The policy of Gandhism, on which the programme of the Congress is founded, uses a cloak of vague talk about love, meekness, modest and hard-working existence, lightening the burden on the peasantry, national unity, the special historic mission of Hindustan, etc. But under this cloak it preaches and defends the interests of the Indian capitalists, the inevitability and the wisdom of the division of society into rich and poor, eternal social inequality and exploitation'.

The Platform of Action continued:

'The greatest threat to the victory of the Indian revolution is the fact that great masses of our people still harbour illusions about the National Congress and have not realised that it represents a class organisation of the capitalists working against the fundamental interests of the toiling masses of our country . . .

'The National Congress, and particularly its "left" wing, have done and are doing all in their power to restrain the struggle of the masses within the framework of the British imperialist constitution and legislation . . .

'The most harmful and dangerous obstacle to victory of the Indian revolution is the agitation carried on by the "left" elements of the National Congress led by Jawaharlal Nehru, Bose, Ginwala and others . . .

'The exposure of the "left" Congress leaders, who may once again undertake to set up a new Party or organisation like the former League of Independence, in order once again to bamboozle the mass of workers is the primary task of our Party. Ruthless war on the "left" national reformists is an essential condition if we are to isolate the latter from the workers and mass of the peasantry and mobilise the latter under the banner of the Communist Party and the anti-imperialist agrarian revolution in India.'

Feeling this way about the great Civil Disobedience campaigns

43

of 1930 and 1932, in the course of which hundreds of thousands of Indians courted arrest and baton charges, the Indian communists could not but keep away from the greatest mass campaign India had till then witnessed in her entire struggle for national freedom. This abstraction completely isolated the communists. They were later to regret and admit their mistake.

Factions Within Party

This tactical weakness was supplemented by organisational weakness. Indeed, there was no central organisation as such, but only factional groups. There was the Bombay group led by Dr G. M. Adhikari, who was sent to India at the end of 1928 after having lived for some years in Germany. Another group was the Calcutta group, manned by Muzaffar Ahmed. The third group was in Northern India, with P. C. Joshi very active in it. When some of these men were removed by arrest, these groups broke up into subgroups, each claiming direct relations with the Communist International. Which of them was entitled to this claim it is not easy to say. Perhaps the Cominterm welcomed them all, but bound itself to none.

At this period of general splintering, M. N. Roy added to the confusion by appearing in India in person and organising a rival party. After his removal from the Executive Committee of the Communist International as a result of a quarrel with Stalin and his subsequent expulsion from membership of the International in 1929, Roy evidently made up his mind to create a party of his own, but not independent of the Communist International. Roy evidently hoped that his party would in due course be accepted by the International as the officially recognised one.

Moscow's Concern

In brief, the condition of the CPI was so unsatisfactory that it made Moscow sit up. Molotov, in an unusually subdued note presented before the Communist Party of the Soviet Union, said: 'In India, a communist organisation is in the course of formation;

44

this will undergo the impending revolutionary struggle before it can take its place as the Bolshevik vanguard of the Indian proletariat'.[2]

The plenum of the Executive Committee of the Communist International met in Moscow in August 1932 and prepared a report setting forth the part which India was to play in the year 1933. It was as follows: to strengthen the Communist Party politically and organisationally; to train Bolshevik cadres; to wage a stubborn struggle in the reformist trade unions; to develop a wide anti-imperialist front; to liberate the masses from the influence of the Indian National Congress; to make agitational and organisational preparations for a general strike; to give the greatest support to the peasant movement for the non-payment of taxes, rents and debts; and to popularise the basic slogans and tasks of the agrarian revolution.

Moscow's concern for Indian communism was more than merely exhortative. As soon as old emissaries like Philip Spratt and Bradley had been arrested, a new supply was shipped. In 1927 came S. Saklatvala, a Member of the British Parliament but himself of Indian origin. In 1928 the country was visited by J. W. Johnstone of the American Communist Party and J. Ryan of the Australian CP. Canadian and Russian agents were also among those deputed to India.

In 1930 came one Prem Lal Singh, an Indian student who had just completed a course in Lenin University. But he achieved nothing and after six months returned empty-handed. At about the same time arrived in Bombay an American antiquarian, named William Nathan Kweit, accompanied by his wife Helen Howlen. They were joined in July 1930 by another American, Herry Somers, who posed as the representative of a cellulose company. These latter were apprehended and deported under the Foreigners' Act in September 1930.

M. N. Roy's arrival in India did not please Moscow and Muhammad Ali *alias* Seppasi, who had been along with Roy a member of the Foreign Bureau, was despatched to India to counteract his influence. But there was some hitch over his false passport and he could not reach India.

Then came another American, H. G. Lynd, who arrived in

Bombay in February 1931 and posed as a skin merchant. He brought money and instructions with him and was more successful than any of his predecessors. He was followed by Amir Haidar Khan, John Magnus Clark, William Bennett and Mrs Constance Marry Sargent. All these agents proved a failure, except Amir Haider Khan, who established himself in Madras as a factor of some importance and was in correspondence with communist groups elsewhere.[3]

These emissaries brought money for the Party. For example, when Henry G. Lynd came to India in 1931, the Bombay Party was immediately placed in funds to the extent of Rs 12,000. Similarly, Clark and Bennet brought with them considerable sums the spending of which they could not account for. Another agent, Mrs Constance Marry Sargent, was apprehended in Bombay with an ingeniously devised receipt in her personal baggage.

An important centre of recruitment to the CPI was that among Indian students studying in British Universities. Among the papers siezed by the London police when they raided the headquarters of the Communist Party of Great Britain in King's Street, Covent Garden, in 1926 were those which revealed that the CPGB had been making systematic attempts to infect Indian students at Oxford and elsewhere with their ideas. Two non-Indian students were the agents employed for this task. These men attended meetings of the Indian Majlis. Prior to the exposure of their plans, these agents had arranged for interviews between Shapurji Saklatvala, the well-known communist MP, and promising Indian students. As a result of these disclosures in the British press, the CPGB functioned more carefully. It confined its attention to such ready-made Indian organisations as the London Branch of the Indian National Congress, of which Saklatvala eventually got control in 1930 after a struggle lasting over two years. This, however, was a pyrrhic victory, for this Branch was disaffiliated by the Indian National Congress in August 1931. Study circles formed by Clemens Palme Dutt from 1926 onwards had a somewhat chequered existence.

In July 1930, the CPGB adopted a lengthy resolution on the subject of India, clause 7 of which read as follows:

'The party must work actively among the Indian residents in Britain (workers, sellers, students, etc) and establish the best possible connection with India through them.'[4]

Thereupon communist fronts such as the League Against Imperialism and the Workers' Welfare League of India concentrated on these tasks. Saklatvala's main student collaborator at this stage was a dynamic young student named Niharendu Dutta Mazumdar, who, ironically enough, was later to break with communism in India, became a Minister in Dr B. C. Roy's Congress Cabinet in Bengal, and be defeated by a communist candidate in the general elections in 1951. Mazumdar's student group, on the periphery of which the present writer himself was somewhat precariously perched, consisted of young men of the best families in various parts of India. In the early thirties, Saklatvala's special position *vis-á-vis* India was undermined and Rajni Palme Dutt emerged as the rising star in the firmament.

In the summer of 1935, when the present writer visited Britain as Secretary of the Congress Socialist Party, he met the current products of these activities who confessed their communist views and condemned the Congress Socialist Party as 'reformist'. By the time this writer returned to London a couple of months later the Seventh World Congress had met in Moscow and these same young men expressed to him a desire to join the Congress Socialist Party on their return to India. This they did a few months later, under instructions not to join the Communist Party in India, but to form the Progressive Writers' Association and to infiltrate into the Indian National Congress and the Congress Socialist Party. It is not an accident therefore that the aristocracy of the Communist Party, as of other parties in India, is to-day drafted to a certain extent from the class of people whose parents could afford an expensive foreign education.

Meanwhile, the flow of literature in India continued owing to loop-holes having been discovered in the law. It was found necessary by the Government on 10th September 1932 to issue a fresh Customs Notification which superseded the Notification of 28th May 1927 and prohibited the bringing into India of 'any docu-

47

ment issued by or emanating from (1) the Communist International or (2) any organisation affiliated to or controlled by or connected with the Communist International or (3) any person holding office in any such organisation or (4) of any document containing a substantial reproduction of the matter contained in any such document'.

Despite this tightening up of the administrative censorship, imports appear to have continued almost undiminished. During the year 1934, the total number of communist newspapers and periodicals held up in the mails was in the neighbourhood of 15,000 copies comprising some fifty different papers from no less than ten different countries in Europe, Asia and America.[5]

Internal Attempts at Reorganisation

Alongside of the Moscow activity, great efforts were being put in by the communists inside the country. Communists in jails came into contact with terrorists and succeeded in converting many of them to Marxism. By 1931, this conversion became general and there was a great demand for communist literature which was smuggled into the jails. Thus, within a short time many known members of the Anushilan Party and the Juganter Party (both terrorist organisations of Bengal) were weaned away from the path of nationalist resistance to Moscow's doctrines of proletarian revolution.

Alongside, a great stocktaking was also being undertaken. Early in 1933 a memorandum[6] was received in Bombay which was prepared by the communists accused under trial in Meerut, and was designed to be their swan song before conviction. It was evidently penned in the middle of 1932. This document had already been sent to Moscow for perusal. It contained a lengthy analysis of the causes of the Party's downfall. Amongst the causes set forth were neglect of provincial contacts, misleading reports to the Comintern, a prolonged factional fight in Bombay, the failure to submit the questions involved for arbitration and, finally, the Civil Disobedience campaigns of the Congress, which had presented the Party with very difficult problems.

The document made certain suggestions directed at reorganisation. It also dealt with matters outside the Party's immediate control. For example, it recommended that a substantial number of young men, about thirty to begin with, should be sent to Moscow for training. It was suggested that the Comintern send two representatives, preferably British, to organise and supervise the work of the Party in India. It was also recommended that the Comintern issue an 'Open Letter' to the Communist Party of India, analysing the mistakes of the past year, apportioning blame between different groups and giving a final decision on points of dispute.

This 'Open Letter'[7] did in fact appear in the *International Press Correspondence* towards the end of 1932. The letter is supposed to have emanated from the Communist Parties in China, Great Britain and Germany and dealt with precisely the subjects which the Meerut prisoners had suggested.

Great doctrinal value was attached to this Open Letter. It asserted that the development of the Indian Communist movement was being blocked by a state of discord and the existence of Party groups and stated:

'It must be thoroughly realized (and this will determine how seriously and consistently the communists stand by the illegal party and the revolutionary struggle) that the leading cadres of the party and the kernel of its organsiation must be in *an illegal position* and that mixing the conspiratorial and open apparatus of the Party organisation is fatal for the Party and plays into the hands of the Government provocation. While developing the illegal organisation in every way, measures must be taken for preserving and strengthening the conspirative kernel of the party organisation. For this purpose all kinds of open activity (in the press, meetings, leagues, trade unions, etc), special groups and commissions etc, should be formed which, working under the leadership of the Party committees, should under no circumstances injure the existence of the illegal nuclei.'

'To sum up, the slogan of an all-India centralised Communist Party, ideologically and organisationally united, a true section of the Comintern, fighting for the Platform of Action of the Communist Party of India and the programme of the Communist international, must become

D

the central slogan for gathering and forming the Party and for the struggle against the waverings, against a tendency of keeping to isolated circles, against toning down the struggle against national reformism and opportunist sectarianism, all of which hinder the victory of the working class.'

In the beginning of 1933 there were some signs of drastic reorganisation and of a regrouping of leaders and parties, seemingly with the object of excluding from further control of any of the party's activities those whom the report condemned. This outburst of enthusiasm was not, however, very long lived and by April 1933 the Party had apparently fallen back into the old rut.

Early in February 1934, a cyclostyled pamphlet made its appearance in Bombay and was secretly distributed throughout India under the authority of the Provisional Central Committee of the Communist Party of India.[8] This was a new thesis prepared by Dr Adhikari which was later reproduced in the *International Press Correspondence*, thereby receiving the blessings of the Comintern. This thesis represented a careful remodelling and assiduous polishing of the communist programme as a result of four years' constant consultation between Indian and British communists in India.

Alongside of this, work had been started to prepare a new statute of the Communist Party of India. It appeared in draft form in the *International Press Conference* of 11th May 1934, and was finally adopted with a few minor amendments.

It was at this juncture that the British Government in India decided that the Communist Party should be notified as an unlawful organisation under the Criminal Law Amendment Act of 1908 (as amended in 1932). It was recognised at that time that it might be difficult to obtain convictions against individuals under the Act, but it was hoped that the effect of the knowledge that the administration was declaring war on communism would be considerable and that the denial of facilities to function freely and openly would make the task of the communists more difficult. The Government of India's notification was followed by supplemental action on the part of Provincial Governments in the Punjab, Madras and Bombay.

Split in Trade Union Movement

The arrest of communist leaders in the Meerut Conspiracy case resulted in an improvement for a time in the field of industrial relations. Towards the close of 1929, however, the lessons of the Case were already beginning to be forgotten. The Tenth Annual Session of the All-India Trade Union Congress met in Nagpur in December 1929 with Pandit Jawaharlal Nehru in the chair. The speeches made and the resolutions passed at that session showed that communism was still very much a live force. The Pan-Pacific Trades Union Secretariat, the Workers' Welfare League of India in Britain and the League Against Imperialism, all three communist-controlled organisations, made a bid for the allegiance of the AITUC. Communists brought forward resolutions at this session demanding the affiliation of the AITUC with these three organisations.

The passing of these communist resolutions, which was secured by grossly inflated membership figures claimed by their Unions, brought matters to a head and the genuine trade unionists, who had been feeling uncomfortable at communist infiltration, separated from the AITUC and formed themselves into a distinct organisation called the National Trades Union Federation with thirty Unions, leaving the AITUC with only some twenty Unions. Thus came about the first split in the Indian trade union movement.

The communist elements were provided by this split with a still freer hand in what remained of the AITUC. Encouraged by this, the CPI again began to rear its head under the guidance of S. V. Deshpande and Mrs Suhasini Nambiar in Bombay and Abdul Halim in Calcutta. Early in February 1930 they were able to sponsor a widespread strike on the GIP Railway, one of the main State railways of India.

The fissiparous tendencies among the communists themselves were, however, at work in the trade union sphere also. As Secretary of the AITUC, the communist-dominated wing of the original organisation, S. V. Deshpande incurred considerable unpopularity by his refusal to convene the annual session in February 1931 according to schedule. The session was eventually held in Calcutta in the following July and the proceedings confirmed Deshpande's worst fears that he might be thrown out of office. The Congress was held under the presidentship of the radical militant nationalist leader, Subhas Chandra Bose, and it broke up in disorder when the communists found that the Credentials Committee had decided against them and deprived them of their fictitious majority. Deshpande's party left that meeting and later on the communists organised their own labour front called the Red Trades Union Congress. This disorderly session was a suitable climax to the disruptive tendencies which had been at work since March 1929 resulting in the course of two years in two splits. The strength of the Red Unions then began to decline, the Bombay Girni (Textile) Union membership falling from 50,000 to a mere 800 in 1932.

In the midst of these disruptive moves, communist leaders in jail were making plans for reorganisation which they put into effect when some of them were released in 1933. According to a thesis ascribed to Dr Adhikari, appearing under the title: 'The Communist, organ of the Provisional Central Committee of the Communist Party of India (Section of the Communist International)', the Red Trades Union Congress was to be revived, reorganised and strengthened. By this time most of the Meerut Conspiracy convicts had regained their freedom and all except Nimbkar began to work under the leadership of Dr Adhikari.

In 1934 the communists temporarily joined hands with the Royist group in the trade union movement and both of them gave a call for a country-wide strike of all textile workers. 23rd April was selected as the date for the outbreak of the first preliminary strike in Bombay to be followed by a sympathetic strike all over the country. On the appointed day, the strike began, and the response was overwhelming all over the country. Fourteen communists including Joglekar and Mirajkar were summarily arrested on 29th April, leaving Dr Adhikari to be the virtual dictator behind the scene, but he too was arrested later. After these arrests, the strike began to decline. The British Government in India then decided that the time had come to grapple with this movement.

The Communist Party was declared illegal, along with some dozen
Trade Unions under communist control and the Young Workers'
League. The CPI went completely underground.

Congress Socialist Party

It was against this background of the failure of the Communist
Party that the Congress Socialist Party was formed in 1934 by some
young and energetic men in the Congress. In the failure of the
Communist Party was seen the failure of the Left, particularly
during those days when Leftism was not very consciously separated from communism and the two were very badly mixed up in
the minds of many people. It was in order to fill the gap left by the
failure of the Communist Party that the Congress Socialist Party
was brought into being.

The programme of the Congress Socialist Party was drafted in
Nasik Road Central Prison through the year 1933 as a result of
discussions among a group of political prisoners participating in
Gandhi's campaign of Civil Disobedience. There were from the
start two clear tendencies discernible among the participants,
which continued to survive for well over a decade in the Party's
life and have not yet completely disappeared. One tendency, then
represented by Jayaprakash Narayan, was Marxist. Jayaprakash
Narayan had returned from America an intellectual adherent of
the Communist International. The other tendency, that of Democratic Socialism, was represented by M. R. Masani, who had been
a member of the British Labour Party and the ILP in his student
days in London. Neither side was prepared to make a surrender on
the doctrinal issue of democracy *versus* dictatorship of the proletariat. An uneasy compromise was made, which was to plague the
Party's existence for many a year to come.

There were, of course, from the start many temperamental
differences between the socialists and the communists. The influence of communist ideas had always been wider than the influence of the communist organisation. Many people have claimed
to be some sort of communists without belonging to the Communist Party. Similarly, Moscow has from the very beginning

attracted as well as repelled, both at the same time, the same set of people. Many people have admired Soviet Russia without wanting to be bound to her for anything more than inspiration.

The Congress Socialist Party had this sort of ambivalent attitude, which was reinforced by certain genuinely ideological reasons. The socialist leadership felt that Indian socialism must work out its own salvation, face and overcome its own difficulties and must not take its dictates from outside. Also, without being able to formulate it, they were – despite their allegiance to Marxism – deeply and increasingly influenced by Gandhism. While, perhaps, intellectually they accepted the Leninist theory that 'the end justifies the means', temperamentally and secretly, honesty and purity of means attracted them. These temperamental differences were later on to develop into major barriers.

To start with, due to the attraction of communist ideas, the Indian socialists passionately wooed the communists, despite the hostility of the latter who welcomed the CSPs birth by calling it 'Social Fascist'. That phase of co-operation logically belongs to the next period – after the Seventh Congress of the Communist International prescribed the tactics of United Front. But it happened that the socialists in their zeal for unity anticipated the Communist International's decisions and forced the communists to negotiate co-operation for limited tasks. The isolation into which the communists had fallen as a result of their own 'left-sectarian' tactics forced them to examine their tactics afresh. Besides, it is possible that Moscow had, as on the occasion of the Sixth World Congress, conveyed the contemplated change in tactics to the CPI even before the Seventh Congress met and formally adopted its resolutions.

Whatever the reasons, the socialists succeeded in persuading the communists to try out limited co-operation in the trade union field. In 1934 the following conditions for a united front were agreed upon:

'There shall be joint action by the All-India Congress Socialist Party, the All-India Trade Union Congress, National Trade Union Federation and the Red Trades Union Congress on specific issues, such as the

danger of another war, Government repression, the Joint Parliamentary Committee Report and other issues which may arise from time to time; the nature of joint action being holding of meetings and demonstrations, observing of "days" and anniversaries, issuing of statements and literature, etc.

'There shall be joint action only if the following conditions are fulfilled by parties to the joint action:

(1) There shall be no mutual criticism in speeches or by distribution of leaflets, at joint functions.

(2) There shall be no abuse of each other, nor imputations on the motives or honesty of either party.

(3) Before every joint action there shall be joint agreement regarding the terms of resolutions and slogans, carrying of banners and flags, and distribution of leaflets and literature.

(4) There shall be no advocacy of violence or non-violence by either part at joint functions.

(5) At joint functions there shall be no appeal for support to either party or to enrol members or to draw any exclusive advantage to either party.'

In the case of the Red TUC the following additional condition, as a sub-clause of (1) was agreed upon:

'Each party to the United Front Agreement (*ie*, the AICSP on the one hand and the Red TUC on the other) reserves to itself the right of genuine and honest criticism of the political principles and policies of the other from its independent platform.'

CHAPTER FOUR

Front Populaire
1935 - 1939

The next scene opens with the change of tactics announced by the Seventh World Congress of the Communist International which met in Moscow in the summer of 1935. The stiff, sectarian policy adopted in 1928 in the hope that capitalism was nearing its end had failed badly and crippled the communist movement everywhere. In every country communist parties had got badly isolated. This itself might not have mattered very much if it had not led to the rise of Hitler and the need to search for allies for Soviet Russia in the face of this danger. Hitler had come to power in Germany largely as a result of tacit communist support as against the Social Democratic and Centre parties implied in the slogan 'After Hitler our turn'. Stalin's early overtures to the Nazi Government having been rebuffed, allies had to be sought elsewhere and the stiff policy which frightened alternative allies had to be softened. Japanese aggression in Manchuria and China was another factor pushing Soviet policy in the same direction. Soviet Russia decided to enter the League of Nations and Litvinov became the great champion of Collective Security.

This need of the Socialist Fatherland called for a comprehensive change in strategy the world over. On 1st August 1935 the Seventh Congress of the Communist International met in Moscow. It is significant to note that the report on the colonial countries including India was made by a Chinese communist, Wang Ming, under the title 'The Revolutionary Movement in the Colonial Countries'. Wang Ming, dealing with India, reported:

'India is a classical colonial country with a relatively numerous proletariat and a considerably advanced demarcation of classes . . .
'Our comrades in India have suffered for a long time from "left"

56

sectarian errors; they did not participate in all the mass demonstrations organised by the National Congress or organisations affiliated with it. At the same time the Indian communists did not possess sufficient forces independently to organise a powerful and mass anti-imperialist movement. Therefore, the Indian communists, until very recently, were to a considerable extent isolated from the mass of the people from the mass anti-imperialist struggle. The toiling masses of India could not be convinced of the fact that the communists not only really desire to struggle themselves, but can also lead the millions in a struggle against the principal mortal enemy of the Indian people – British imperialism. In this connection, for a long time the small scattered groups of communists could not become a united, mass all-India Communist Party. By their sectarian policy and isolation from the mass anti-imperialist movement, these small communist groups objectively helped to retain the influence of Gandhism (the theory of Gandhi, who preaches passive resistance to British imperialism and who is actual leader of the National Congress in India) and national reformism over the masses . . .

'It was only recently that the All-India Communist Party, which has already taken shape, began to rid itself of its sectarian errors and made the first step towards the creation of an anti-imperialist united front. Nevertheless, our young Indian comrades, having taken this road, showed a great lack of understanding of the united front tactics. This may be borne out even by the fact that our Indian comrades in attempting to establish a united anti-imperialist front with the National Congress in December of last year put before the latter such demands as "the establishment of an Indian Workers' and Peasants' Soviet Republic", "confiscation of all lands that belong to the zamindars without compensation", "a general strike as the only effective programme of action", etc.

'Such demands on the part of our Indian comrades can serve as an example of how *not* to carry on the tactics of the anti-imperialist United Front. True, the Indian communists somewhat corrected their line later on and achieved, on the one hand the unification of the revolutionary and reformist trade unions and, on the other hand, an agreement with the so-called Congress Socialists for a struggle against the new slavish constitution . . .

'The Indian communists should in no case disregard work within the National Congress and the national revolutionary and national-reformist organisations affiliated with it, maintaining at the same time their complete political and organisational independence. Both within and without the National Congress, the Indian communists must consolidate all the genuine anti-imperialist forces of the country . . .'

This more gentle policy was rather difficult to follow for those who had been fed on sulphur-hot slogans. The significance of the new tactics and slogans was explained with the help of theory and analysis. It was pointed out that conditions on the eve of the threatening World War II were not the same as conditions on the eve of World War I. In 1914, the world was not divided between the world of capitalism and the world of socialism. In the thirties, Soviet Russia stood out as a bastion of socialism, supported by the world's organised working class, but a target of the imperialist offensive which was not there before. To sum up, the tremendous growth of anti-war sentiment among the broad massses of people, the left-wing swing and growing consciousness and unity in working class ranks, the existence of a number of capitalist States that for the moment wanted peace and the growth of the Soviet Union as a world power, opened up the perspective of uniting all democratic and peace-loving forces against the war instigators – the Fascists. This change in the 'objective situation' called for a change in tactics as well. Needless to say, the fight for the defence of the Soviet Union was also the fight against capitalism and imperialism.

It seems, however, that the full scope and meaning of the change was not fully understood by the Communist Party of India until the British Communist Party had intervened. R. Palme Dutt and Ben Bradley addressed a communication to the CPI entitled 'The Anti-Imperialist People's Front in India'. They said that the Indian national struggle had reached a critical point; that British imperialism had succeeded in imposing its slave constitution on India; that the first stage of the struggle against imperialism had failed and was in retreat; that the ever-worsening situation and the sharpening struggle of the masses called for more radical organisation and leadership; that this more radicalised leadership could only come forth as a result of the broadest possible anti-imperialist front. They said:

'Every Indian patriot will recognise that the first need for the powerful advance of the Indian national struggle, the key need of the present situation is the unity of all the anti-imperialist forces in the common struggle. This is the indispensable condition for the successful fight against the existing and ever sharpening reaction and oppression ... It is evident that all elements, including from among the Liberals, who are prepared to break with the co-operation with imperialism and accept the programme of the national struggle, are welcome to the common front ...'[1]

This plea was supplemented by a direct appeal addressed over the heads of the CPI by Palme Dutt and Bradley to non-communists under the title of 'An Open Letter to Indian Patriots'.[2]

This at last knocked understanding into the minds of the Indian Communist Party. The Politbureau of the CPI welcomed this statement and called upon the rank and file to implement the recommendations. 'The international situation demands acceptance of this policy', the Politbureau explained. It said:

'No political document has created so much stir in recent times as Dutt and Bradley's article, *The Anti-Imperialist People's Front in India*. No political document has evoked such unanimous and enthusiastic response from all the anti-imperialist elements ... Comrade Dutt and Bradley's article successfully applies to the actual circumstances prevalent in India the policy of united front adopted at the Seventh Congress of the Communist International and the decisions arrived at in that World Congress. It is generally recognised that the Seventh Congress was no mere Party Conference of the communists alone but one which had blazoned the path of heroic struggle and of certain victory for the entire world revolutionary movement of to-day. The concrete application to the present stage of the anti-imperialist movement in our country of the line of the Seventh Congress is a historic affair.'[3]

The Communists and the Indian National Congress

In India the years from 1935 to the outbreak of World War II in 1939 were years of comparative peace and some constructive advance. It is true that the Government of India Act of 1935 enacted by the British Parliament drew a lot of fire for retaining the Central Government in British hands while transferring power to

59

Cabinets responsible to elected Legislatures in the Provinces or States. Nonetheless, when elections under the new Constitution were called for, there was no boycott and in 1937 the Congress, which had emerged as the almost unchallenged victors of the elections, agreed to form cabinets in the States it had carried, while the Moslem League did so in the rest.

In this period, as throughout the history of the struggle for national independence, the Indian National Congress was its expression and embodiment. True, many small factions contributed their mite to the struggle, but they all became organic parts of the Congress. In turn, the Congress continued to be dominated by the colourful and unorthodox personality of Mahatma Gandhi. To be isolated from the Congress was to be isolated from the people, from the main expression of the people's political and cultural struggle. And yet this is what the communists had achieved as a result of their anti-Congress, anti-Gandhi programme prescribed by the Sixth World Congress of the Comintern in 1928. In fact, in 1934, a 'League against Gandhi' had been started. It did not succeed, but it alienated many people.

Now it had all to be changed. The Congress was to be wooed and the confidence of its leaders to be won. Slogans which gave provocation even when they embodied basic communist aims were to be eschewed and replaced by such slogans as were more acceptable to the Congress.

Yet these tactics did not conspicuously succeed, because the United Front tactics were not in the spirit of co-operation in a joint anti-imperialist struggle, but were calculated to isolate the national leadership from the rank and file and capture the larger organisation for Party ends. True, the Indian National Congress was no longer dismissed as a fascist or bourgeois agency of British imperialists; yet everything was done to belittle the rôle and inspiration of this movement. It was said that the National Congress was based not on the union of all elements supporting the national struggle but on restrictive individual membership with certain limitations of franchise and of a special ideology and creed which prevented it from embracing the broadest front of all who supported the national struggle; that the mass organisations, such as

Workers' and Peasants' unions and similar collective mass organisations constituting the most important force of the national struggle, were at present outside the National Congress; that only when all these forces were combined would the Congress become a 'real' anti-imperialist front embracing all genuine fighters for freedom. This, notwithstanding the fact that the total membership of all these 'mass organisations' put together was but a small fraction of that of the Indian National Congress. Explaining the rôle of the Indian communists *vis à vis* the Congress, Palme Dutt and Ben Bradley said:

'At this point the question will be asked what is relation of the National Congress to the anti-imperialist People's Front? Is not the National Congress, as many of its leaders claim, already the United Front of the Indian people in the national struggle? The National Congress has undoubtedly achieved a gigantic task in uniting wide forces of the Indian people for the national struggle, and remains to-day the principal existing mass organisation of diverse elements seeking national liberation. Nothing should be allowed to weaken the degree of unity that has been achieved ... We on the Left have many times criticised sharply the existing leadership and tactics of the National Congress. We have found many decisions and policies such as the calling of mass civil disobedience in 1934 ... the wavering in relation to imperialism ... the Delhi pact; the co-operation in the Round Table Conference ... disastrous to the true interests of the National struggle and equivalent to surrender to imperialism. We have traced the decisions and policies to the existing dominant bourgeois leadership whose interests often conflict with the interests of the masses and with the interests of the national struggle.'

They further explained that it was necessary to recognise that the National Congress as it existed was not the United front of the Indian people in the national struggle; that its constitution left out the broadest sections of the masses; that its programme of the struggle was defective; that its leadership could not be recognised as the leadership of the national struggle; that as it was, the leadership did not draw out and guide mass activity but rather acted as a brake upon it.

In spite of these defects, however, Dutt and Bradley pointed out, the National Congress could play a great and a leading part in the work of realising the anti-imperialist People's Front. It was even graciously conceded that the National Congress, by the further transformation of its organisation and programme and leadership, might itself become the form of realisation of the anti-imperialist People's Front. But it was the Communist Party that was to provide this transforming leadership from within.[4]

To implement this 'Trojan Horse' strategy, a minimum programme was decided upon and instructions were issued to individual communists on how it was to be pushed through. The Politbureau declared that 'individual enrolment is not a substitute for collective affiliation but only one of the means to intensify the agitation and strengthen the demands for collective affiliation, from inside the Indian National Congress platform in alliance with the INC rank and file and by mobilising them under our leadership on this and other allied immediate issues'.[5]

This agitation was not to be carried on from inside alone, but supported by agitation from outside. The circular said: 'The PB declares that this agitation from inside the INC is not enough. Our main emphasis should be on demanding collective affiliation etc, by mobilising all anti-imperialist mass organisations outside the INC. To demand collective affiliation and the acceptance of the minimum platform by the INC and refusing to go inside the INC will be taking up the traditional line of Royism becoming ineffective critics of reformism. It is only when independent activity outside the INC is intimately linked up with the work inside that the demand for collective affiliation will become irresistible and the formation of a united front with the INC and its local organisations become possible'.

The PB was very clear on these two tasks, for it again and again emphasises the need of combining the two tasks 'so as to produce the maximum results which will contribute to the building up of an all-embracing united front and the growth of the Party'. The circular said:

'The PB again warns all the members and organisations that on the plea of the united front, the movement outside the INC should not be neglected or thrown into the background of our activities. It is only in proportion of our independent activities that our work inside the INC will prove effective while it is also true that our work inside the INC will become to-day one of the most potent means of strengthening and extending the base of our independent Party.'

It was also decided that the application of the United Front tactics in relation to the Congress was not to be uniform but to differ from province to province, according to concrete circumstances. For example, in Bombay, where twenty per cent of the Congress membership was contributed by the proletariat and the class-struggle had reached a 'higher stage', tactics had to be different from what they should be in Calcutta or Punjab. To give an idea of the mind of the Communist Party:

'The Left is attempting to meet the efforts of the Right by appealing to the workers to join the INC and help them to fight the Right leadership and demand collective affiliation from inside the INC. If we oppose this effort of the CSP and Royists, we isolate ourselves even from the politically conscious section of the working class. If we remain neutral, we condemn ourselves to a position of political inactivity. The Left is enrolling the workers not through a mass campaign of meetings, demonstrations, etc, but by visiting them in their chawls (tenements). We should immediately enter into a pact with the CSP and Royists for joint enrolment of members on a joint platform of struggle for the united front policy from within the INC and for a struggle against the reformist policy of parliamentarianism and class-collaboration and repudiation of mass struggle . . .

'In Madras it should be possible to work inside the INC through the CSP which are on the whole Left. The task there is intensified activity through the CSP and not the question of building up contacts with the INC rank and file.'[6]

With this intensive education of the individual communists for the task of infiltration, a programme of appeal to the rank and file of the Congress was started. The communists said that they did not want the Congress to adopt the communist programme, but only to accept the implication of the Lahore Resolution on complete independence, but they complained that the Gandhian wing in the Congress had watered down all that had anti-imperialist content in it, that its mouthpiece, Sardar Vallabhai Patel, ridiculed the Kisan Sabhas (Peasant Federation). Characteristic of the appeals to the rank and file over the head of the leaders was the glorification of the mass struggle since 1920 which the communists had hitherto held in contempt, in contrast with the capitulating rôle of the rightist leadership in the face of the mighty mass struggle which frightened the leaders into a compromise with British imperialism.[7]

The 1935 Constitution

The basic idea in communist policy during this period would appear to be to develop internal pressure through the Indian National Congress and force the hands of the British Government to form an 'anti-fascist Peace Front' with Soviet Russia against Germany. The achievement of this purpose had to be linked with internal problems. The main political problem of those days was the attitude to be adopted towards the new Constitution embodied in the *Government of India Act* 1935, passed by the British Parliament according to which provincial autonomy was to be granted to popularly elected assemblies and cabinets in limited fields. The Indian National Congress was dissatisfied with the transfer of power being restricted to the States while the Central Government remained under British control. The Communist Party stood against the acceptance of this 'slave' constitution. A pamphlet dated 5th December 1936, issued by the Central Committee of the CPI under the title *Transform the Elections into Mighty Anti-Imperialist Demonstrations*, says:

'To-day the focal point of imperialist attack on India is the new constitution. To free ourselves from the new bondage should be the main flank of our political struggle. To concentrate all our forces, to mobilise all our energy to fight the slave constitution, that is the task which confronts us ... Transform the elections into a weapon to forge an anti-imperialist United Front! Form the United National Front against imperialism! Smash the New Constitution! ... Inquilab Zindabad!'

As an alternative it demanded the convening of a 'Constituent

Assembly', but it was made abundantly clear that the demand for a Constituent Assembly was a tactical demand. In an undated leaflet entitled *The United National Front* issued by Harry Pollitt, R. P. Dutt and Ben Bradley for the Central Committee of the Communist Party of Great Britain, the authors say:

'There can be no question of substituting the slogan of Constituent Assembly for the slogan of Soviet Power. It was Roy who advanced the slogan of Constituent Assembly against Soviets, against revolution ... Roy counterposes the slogan of Constituent Assembly to Soviets instead of counterposing it to the present slave Constitution, raising the illusion that the Constituent Assembly can fulfil the tasks of the Soviets.'

But all these appeals and slogans were of little avail. The failure of the communists was clear so far as the Congress was concerned. They could neither capture the Congress leadership nor make it accept their programme nor adopt their slogans by building internal pressure. It was clear that so long as Mahatma Gandhi's personality dominated the scene, the communists could not succeed so far as the Congress was concerned. So, less direct channels of winning and influencing the Congress were sought. These channels were discovered in the personalities of Pandit Nehru and Subhas Chandra Bose and in the newly formed but growing Congress Socialist Party under the leadership of Jayaprakash Narayan.

In fact, Pandit Nehru was being sought after by all, the Gandhians, the Communists, the Royists, the Socialists. Pandit Nehru, in turn, while he was friendly towards all, identified himself with none. Different appeals pulled in different directions. The emotional appeal of socialist slogans, admiration of the 'achievements' of Soviet Russia acquired by a study of Marxist literature, conflicted with his sense of realism and the influence of Mahatma Gandhi's personality. By and large, the latter predominated, but in the process a good deal was said about the Communist Party and Soviet Russia which made them not only acceptable but even popular in the minds of many people.

In their turn, the communists did their best to woo Nehru, offered him leadership of the United Leftist Forces and tried to divide him from his colleagues in the Congress Working Committee. One undated leaflet issued by the Central Party of the Communist Party under the title *'Down with Compromisers, Forward to the United Front'* said:

'The Congress Left led by Jawaharlal and the Socialist Party and mass organisations under communist and anti-imperialist leadership are striving for the United Front of the Congress with Working Class and peasant organisations in the form of Collective affiliation, for a programme of mass action combined with revolutionary utilisation of legislatures, for the transformation of the Congress into the Anti-Imperialist Front of the People.'

A long thesis dated 24th July 1936, published under the title *For the Anti-Imperialist Peoples Front: Long Live Soviet Hindustan* said:

'The bourgeois leadership is no longer united in its reformism, it is disintegrating. In his Presidential address Nehru's anti-imperialist voice stammered on some vital points, yet it was full-throated on several others, it was a clearer anti-imperialist call than had ever been made from the Congress chair. Nehru's was an approach which stood in opposition to all that the orthodox Indian National Congress leadership has stood for so far.'[8]

Communists and the Congress Socialist Party

The most important channel of infiltration was through the Congress Socialist Party, which was still young. R. Palme Dutt had already instructed the Communist Party to concentrate on the left-wing parties. He had advised that in order to realise the Anti-Imperialist People's Front and carry through changes in the organisation policy and work of the National Congress, it was essential that all left-wing elements in the Congress should be consolidated. 'The Congress Socialist Party can play an especially important part. It is of the greatest importance that every effort should be made to clarify questions of programme and tactics in the Congress Socialist Party', Palme Dutt and Ben Bradley wrote to the CPI in the letter already mentioned.[9]

Consequently, the Communist Party also decided to come to terms with the socialists. The Politbureau said that the Left was a tiny group and imperialism could any day wipe it out. But if the Left could build up a widespread, broad-based fighting front by drawing the masses into it, imperialism could never destroy it; on the contrary, its very growth would act as a check on the war preparations of British imperialism and when the war broke out it would be capable of giving battle to imperialism. Dutt and Bradley had told them exactly how such a mass movement could be built up.

The United Front tactics of the communists were greatly facilitated by the enthusiasm of Jayaprakash Narayan, the General Secretary of the Socialist Party, who had become an intellectual adherent of the Comintern during his years as a student in the USA. The reason for this attitude was the same as elsewhere – lack of understanding of communist tactics and intellectual surrender to Marxism. The Congress Socialist Party, from the beginning, wanted socialist unity, but considered it a 'vague phrase' if it were to be understood to include all those who called or considered themselves socialists. Instead, according to Jayaprakash, the problem of Socialist unity was 'the problem of the coming together in one party of all those groups and individuals who stand by Marxism'.[10] The Communist Party and M. N. Roy's group were regarded as two Marxist groups with whom such unity was possible.

The story of the United Front has been told most graphically and feelingly in two pamphlets, one a statement adopted by the CSP Executive on 9th August 1937, under the title of *The CSP, The Reds and Roy* and the other *Socialist Unity and the CSP* by Jayaprakash Narayan in 1941. Jayaprakash points out how the period till January 1936, was marked by the bitterest hostility on the part of the Communist Party and by ceaseless attempts at cooperation and unity on the part of the socialists. In January 1936, the Socialist Party met at Meerut, and, anticipating the change in communist tactics, decided to respond to the suggestion of a United Front with the Communist Party in furtherance of common objectives. The character of this Front was to be two-fold:

one, a United Front as between Party and Party and, two, going still further, admission of individual communists to membership of the Socialist Party to pave the way from United Front to complete merger and socialist unity. It is to be noticed that the gesture was purely unilateral. The opportunity was, however, avidly seized by the communists and by 1937–38 the CSP had two communists as Joint Secretaries and two others in the Executive Committee.

Through the channel thus opened, the communists started infiltrating not only into the Congress Socialist Party but also in its parent body, the Indian National Congress, and the All-India Kisan Sabha (Peasants' Union). Both open and concealed members of the Communist Party were thus given an opportunity to infiltrate into positions of importance in the national forces.

Among those who were thus given positions of vantage were Mr Sajjad Zaheer, who was made a Joint Secretary of the All-India Congress Socialist Party and a member of the All-India Congress Committee and who is now Secretary of the Pakistan Communist Party and was convicted in the Rawalpindi Conspiracy Case, Dr Z. A. Ahmed and Dr M. Ashraf, both of whom were appointed to important positions in the office of the All-India Congress Committee, Mr E. M. S. Namboodiripad, the present leader of the Communist Party in Kerala, who was made Joint Secretary of the All-India Congress Socialist Party, Mr P. Sundarayya, who was put in charge of the Andhra Socialist Party and is to-day the leader of the Communist Party in the Council of States, Mr A. K. Gopalan, who is leader of the Communist Party in the House of the People, Mr P. Ramamurthi, who is now Leader of the Communist Party in the Madras Legislative Assembly and was put in charge of the Madras Congress Socialist Party, and Mr P. Jeevanandam, who ran the Tamilnad Congress Socialist Party for the CPI till the United Front ended.

In the Punjab, the CSP was formed out of two distinct elements – the radical nationalists of the Naujawan Bharat Sabha and the dissident communists of the Kirti Kisan Party, which was the name under which the Ghadr Party, referred to in Chapter 2, functioned in the Punjab. The Kirti Kisan leaders functioned in the Punjab CSP as a faction and manoeuvred cleverly playing off the national leaderships of the CSP and CPI against each other to increase their own bargaining power against both.

Congress Socialist Party votes made these persons members of provincial and All-India Congress Committees. Besides, the membership of the Socialist Party gave the communists a cover also, for at that time the Communist Party was still illegal. This cover was also very valuable for them in building up their organisation.

Very soon, even in the very first year of the working of the United Front, complaints began pouring into socialist headquarters from all parts of India against the communists. The reports said that communists were claiming that they would not permit any other Party to entrench itself in the trade union movement.

Uneasy relations continued till the National Executive of the Socialist Party met in Patna in 1937, when the relations deteriorated still further. At this meeting, a statement of the Communist Party was read which caused great indignation. The statement said that the Congress Socialist Party was no Socialist Party and that it was to be used only as a platform. At this time the Socialist Executive Committee included four communist 'Trojan Horses' who denied their communist allegiance and also shammed shock and indignation at the 'discovery' of such a statement.

After this it was widely felt that there was no alternative but to expel the communists. In point of fact, however, nothing was done. On the other hand, by way of 'reorganisation', the Andhra Party was handed over to the communists by the General Secretary, Jayaprakash, and the Tamil Nad and Kerala Socialist Parties were allowed to be run by the communists. The comparative strength of the CPI in the South of India to-day owes not a little to the socialist naïvete of those years.

Some time later, another secret circular came to light. It was published by M. R. Masani, Joint Secretary of the CSP in September 1938, under the title *Communist Plot against the CSP*. This laid down in detail the tactics to be followed by the communists to capture the socialist organisation. The circular was dated 9th May 1938, and marked *Plan of Work*. It said that 'the exact nature of our work depends upon our present position inside the CSP units'. It said that to inspire confidence in the CSP leadership, and to keep the unity of the CSP, they would not from outside, for the time being, press the demand: 'all socialists inside the CSP' but that 'our comrades within the CSP would continue to popularise the slogan', and that 'in those localities and provinces where it is possible to include all socialists inside the CSP it should be done without fail and without making much noise about it'. Then followed an analysis of the success of infiltration in various provinces, the number of persons won over to communism and who would vote communist on specific issues. Specific tasks were detailed for communists in all provinces, depending on whether the communists were now in a majority or minority, whether they held responsible position in the executive or constituted the rank and file.

This time the circular was not even a shock, for it proved what the socialists already knew. Jayaprakash Narayan puts it in these words:

'For many comrades that circular was the last straw. Yet, the Executive again held its hand and allowed things to drift. Now it was no longer the ideal or hope of unity that decided the Executive. It was just reluctance to face an unpleasant task. Those were dark days for the Party, when lack of decision created a good deal of confusion and weakness. The enemies of the Party did not fail to profit fully by it . . . This policy of drift which was daily delivering the Party into the hands of the Communist Party drove some of the leading members of the Executive to resign. This produced great consternation in the ranks of the Congress Socialist Party, though it was welcomed by the Communist Party and its "Trojan Horses" and stooges.'[11]

When the Annual Conference of the All-India Congress Socialist Party was due to meet early in 1938, the communists, who were secretly functioning in the CSP, put out a draft Thesis for acceptance by the Party Conference over the signatures of S. S. Zaheer, Dinker Mehta (then Joint Secretary of the Congress Socialist Party and now Secretary of the Gujerat Communist Party) and S. S. Batlivala.

When the Conference met in Lahore with M. R. Masani as Chairman, things came to a head rapidly as a result of his Presidential Address, in the course of which he made friendly but firm criticisms of the Soviet dictatorship and the dubious policies it was pursuing in Spain and elsewhere, and stressed the necessity of adhering to democratic and clean methods for the achievement of a socialist society. Stung to action by an awareness of the clarification which the Presidential Address would produce in the ranks of the CSP, the communists decided to strike before the tide turned against them. They made an attempt at nothing less than complete capture of the CSP.

When the elections of the New Executive for the coming year came up, two lists were produced before the Conference. One was proposed by Jayaprakash Narayan, the Party's General Secretary and leader. This consisted of the old Executive with some alterations and gave the communists no less than one-third of the seats, including a couple of positions as Joint Secretaries. The communists produced their own list, which kept Jayaprakash in his position as General Secretary, but otherwise gave the communists a clear majority in the Executive. Jayaprakash and the authentic leaders of the CSP thereupon made it clear that if the communist list were accepted a split would become inevitable. It was only against the background of this threat that the Conference, by a narrow majority, voted for Jayaprakash's composite list, thus maintaining a precarious balance of power in the organisation.

The Lahore Conference of the CSP showed how near the communists were to capturing the entire organisation. None the less, it was not till two years later, in 1940, after the beginning of World War 2, that the CSP Executive at long last decided to expel all communists from the Party and break off the 'United Front' with the Communist Party.

Student Movement

The communists took advantage of the entry they were given in the national and socialist movements to infiltrate heavily into students' organisations. The All-India Students' Federation, which had till then been run by nationalist students including students attracted towards the Congress Socialist Party, now began to see a communist faction raise its head. The faction fighting to which this led culminated at the Third Session of the All-India Students' Conference which met in Madras on the last days of December 1937. On 1st January 1938, M.R.Masani, the Joint Secretary of the All-India Congress Socialist Party, who was in the Chair, had to dissolve the Conference as a result of communist indiscipline and a refusal to accept the rulings of the Executive Committee and of the President, which came in the way of their securing control of the All-India Students' Federation. The issue on which this indiscipline was committed was the communist students' refusal to accept the rejection of the credentials of the several delegates of their colour who came from Provincial Federations which had defaulted in payment of their financial dues and were under the Constitution debarred from voting. The voting itself was taking place on a communist resolution calling for greetings to, and solidarity with, Soviet Russia which the communists were attempting to push through despite the non-political and non-partisan character of the Students' Federation.

After the Conference was dissolved, a rump consisting of communists and their fellow travellers proceeded to hold a 'Conference' in which straight Party line resolutions were passed. This resulted in two students' organisations, each calling themselves by the name of the All-India Students' Federation. A few weeks later, the Communist Party, which realised that its student members had overplayed their hand, approached MrMasani and asked him to use his good offices to effect a rapprochement between them and the main body of students. In consonance with the United Front which the CSP then had with the Communist Party, Mr Masani acted as a mediator and persuaded the nationalist, socialist and non-party students to accept the communists back into the fold.

As a result of this compromise, the student movement in India continued to be plagued for several more years by communist factionalism and disruption until it at last split permanently between communist and non-communist groups.

Trade Unions and Other Fronts

During this period, the communists were able to make considerable headway in the trade union movement through the superficial unity that the efforts of the Congress Socialists had produced.

We have seen that the enthusiasm of the Socialist Party had forced the communists to come into a united front, at least on the trade union front, earlier even than the united front tactics adopted and prescribed by the Seventh Congress of the Communist International. The decision was forced on the communists because they were very isolated and they wanted a legal front to enable them to work. But with the adoption of the new line by the International, united front tactics became obligatory on the Indian communists.

Amusing though lurid light on the manner in which this Moscow decision was thrust down the throats of Indian communists is shed by the words of a communist leader about what happened in 1933, when the All-India Trade Union Congress met in Kanpur. Here are his own words:

'In 1933, the AITUC met at Kanpur. Old Party Comrades knew we had our own Red TUC and had condemned the AITUC as a reformist and reactionary body, which had to be smashed up. At that time our Party was rabidly sectarian. Joshi came from Bombay to Kanpur with the General Secretary's instructions – at that time Doc (ie, Dr G. Adhikari was the GS – saying that a handbill be issued exposing the AITUC as a pack of reformists and reactionaries. We had already one handbill of this nature. We had made 25,000 copies of another handbill to be distributed the next day in the open session. These handbills were brought to Joshi's place. Along with this there was an unopened packet containing *International Press Correspondence* in which we found a copy of the *Open Letter from the Chinese Party to the Indian Party* telling politely that we were left-sectarians. We looked at each other. What was to be done ? We burnt the whole lot of handbills. Then we came to Bombay and told the whole story to Comrades Doc and MRJ (Jhambekar). They also okayed our action.'[12]

On hearing from Moscow through the British Communist Party, the Politbureau asked itself on 24th July 1936:

'Will the proletarian forces become a solid front fighting united for the day-to-day demands of the workers? Will the proletariat succeed in establishing organic, direct relationship with the general anti-imperiaist movement? Will the working class in the course of the anti-imperialist struggle be able to assume its historic rôle as the leader of the anti-imperialist struggle . . .'

And it itself answered the questions:

'To the extent that we can successfully answer these questions in our practice we shall deserve to be called the Party of Lenin and Stalin. Comrades Dutt and Bradley have outlined for us the line of action by following which we can answer the above question in a way worthy of our name, Communist Party of India.'[13]

Conclusions

The successes of the United Front were in no way mean. The communists had infiltrated the ranks of the Indian National Congress. Through the patronage accorded by Pandit Nehru and the CSP they were able to influence to a certain extent the ideological content of the resolutions placed before the Congress at successive sessions.

Communist adherents and fellow travellers infiltrated into the Congress and came to occupy important positions. They succeeded in securing election to the PCCs and the AICC under the CSP umbrella. Those of them who were not members of the CSP then used the floor of the AICC and the PCCs for pushing the communist line of action. Most important of these persons were Mian Iftikharuddin, Swami Shahajanand and Indulal Yagnik. The amendments moved by them to Working Committee resolutions indicated the communist line. These were distinct from CSP amendments, except where agreed drafts were reached through the United Front machinery. This enabled Sajjad Zaheer, Ahmed, Ashraf and Iftikharuddin to build themselves up before an audience which they would otherwise have never reached. Iftikharuddin, in fact, was made President of the Punjab Provincial Congress Committee.

In relation to the socialists the communists were even more

successful. The success of the communists in boring within the Socialist Party was so complete that four 'founding fathers' of the Party, Achut Patwardhan, Rammanohar Lohia, Asoka Mehta and M. R. Masani, were forced to resign in 1939 from the Executive of the Party in order to bring the danger of communist infiltration openly to public notice. In a belated but generous admission of his error in permitting the communists to drive a wedge between the builders of the CSP Jayaprakash Narayan was later to write in 1941:

'The latter have tried to denounce Masani as a communist-baiter. He, of course, was nothing of the sort. What angered and frightened the communists was his organisational competence and soundness. He disagreed with the communists violently, but was prepared for honest cooperation with them as between two independent parties. But he was the first to see through their game of disruption and capture, played under the cover of unity. He was therefore early to demand the wholesale expulsion of the communists from the Party, not as an anti-communist measure, but as a counter-measure to their anti-Congress Socialist Party and capture tactics. Experience has completely vindicated Masani's stand.'[14]

CHAPTER FIVE

World War 2
First 'Imperialist', then 'People's'
1939 - 1945

Ushered in by the Hitler-Stalin Pact, World War 2 broke out on 3rd September 1939. In India, events moved fast following on the British Viceroy's proclamation declaring India a belligerent without consulting the Indian Legislative Assembly, Congress Cabinets in the States or even a national leader like Gandhi.

The All-India Congress Committee met and adopted a Resolution calling on the British Government to make an unequivocal declaration of their war aims and to provide a categorical assurance of Indian independence to enable the Indian people to join in the war effort against Nazi Germany. In the absence of any response to this offer of conditional co-operation, the Congress Cabinets in the States resigned from office in November 1939. Commencing with individual Satyagraha (passive resistance) against the war effort, the national resistance slowly broadened to the mass 'Quit India' campaign of 9th August 1942, which involved hundreds of thousands of arrests and threw up an underground resistance comprising of Congress and Congress Socialist leaders.

Stalin-Hitler Pact

The Stalin-Hitler Pact of August 1939 took the Communist Party in India, as elsewhere in the world, by surprise. Ever since 1933, when Russia had entered the League of Nations, she had been a passionate advocate of an anti-fascist policy. It had made the British look rank appeasers and betrayers of the democratic cause by contrast. Russia's Non-aggression Pact with Nazi Germany, however, transformed Hitler overnight from a fascist menace to a friend of peace. England and France became the imperialist war-mongers.[1] The Communist Parties of England and France, which had already openly promised support to a war against the fascist powers, were now ordered to change their line and oppose the war.

At first, the Indian Communist Party was also bewildered by the new alliance. For a time the leaders insisted that there must be an unpublished 'escape clause' in the Pact. They similarly could not believe a little later the first reports of the Soviet invasion of eastern Poland. But soon they were convinced that the new alignment was a brilliant piece of revolutionary strategy on the part of Stalin and enthusiastically supported it.

Whereas the British and the French Communist Parties found themselves in the difficult and treacherous rôle of opposing their national governments' war effort merely to suit Russia's convenience, the Indian Communist Party was favoured with a sympathetic internal situation. The communist condemnation of England for dragging India into an imperialist war against her will echoed every Indian patriot's sentiment.

It would have been much more embarrassing for the Indian communists to have had to support the war in case Russia had joined the allies against Germany, as in fact she did two years later. Till then, however, the Indian communists could pose as genuine revolutionists and anti-imperialists. They had already been professing to advocate an anti-war line before the war broke out.[2] This could conveniently continue and at the same time be exploited to strengthen the Party's influence with the masses.

This policy also happened to agree with the official policy of the Indian National Congress and of the Congress Socialist Party. By taking India into the war by a proclamation without consulting any Indians, even though the Congress was in office in the provinces at the time, the British Government had completely antagonised Indian nationalist sentiment. 'How can a slave India fight with any enthusiasm for the freedom of other countries?' was the question posed. The manifesto of 14th September 1939 issued by the Congress Working Committee, stated that a 'free democratic India will gladly associate herself with other free nations for mutual

77

defence against aggression and for economic co-operation'. It condemned fascist aggression in unequivocal terms.

But, in its anxiety not to embarrass the Allies, the Congress followed initially an extremely moderate policy in opposing the Government. This gave an excellent opportunity to the Indian communists to condemn the Congress for compromising with imperialist Britain and to pose as the real revolutionaries by advocating and sponsoring strikes and other impediments to the war effort.

Not only did the communists ride high on the tide of favourable public opinion in this period, but they became so confident as to believe that they alone could lead India to revolution and freedom and that they could scuttle the Indian National Congress and the Socialist Party altogether.

Since 1936 the communists had been working in the closest co-operation with the Congress and the socialists following the directive from Comrades Bradley and Palme Dutt of the British Communist Party, contained in their famous thesis, the *Anti-Imperialist People's Front in India*. In this they had been instructed to 'build the broadest possible front of all the anti-imperialist forces in the country on the basis of the Indian National Congress and support and strengthen it to this end'. With the outbreak of the war, however, this policy was suddenly reversed. Gandhi and Nehru were denounced as saboteurs of Indian independence and agents of imperialism. The Congress Socialists were described as henchmen of Gandhi for not sabotaging the Congress policy of 'compromise'. A virulent attack of calumny against the leaders of the Congress and the Socialist Party was started not with a view to inducing them to accept a more dynamic policy but to isolate them and to kill their influence with the masses. This policy was called 'united front from below', *ie* unity with the rank and file against the leaders.[3]

The communists did not succeed entirely because the rank and file of both the parties were too loyal and too sharp not to see the disruptionist game of their erstwhile comrades. But the communists did succeed in causing a split in the All-India Students' Federation and the All-India Kisan Sabha, which had been laboriously built up by the socialists. The All-India Trade Union Congress gradually became the preserve of the communists, with Mr N.M. Joshi serving as a convenient ally.

The Socialist Party, which had been working very hard for a united Left, finally saw the futility and the dangers of trying to work with the communists and decided to break the alliance. Mr Jayaprakash Narayan, who had been the chief advocate of co-operation, frankly admitted his mistake.[4]

The Socialist Party expelled all communists from its organisation. This decision was taken in the nick of time. A little delay, and the communists would have entirely broken the Socialist Party. As it was, while parting, the communists carried with them almost intact three of the best organised State branches of that Party – in Andhra, Tamilnad and Kerala in South India.

Attempts at impairing war production and the war effort through the fomenting of strikes and otherwise became part of communist routine. On 2nd October, soon after the outbreak of the War, the communists organised a strike in Bombay in which they claimed that 90,000 workers, mostly textile, participated. Forty mills remained closed as part of what was purely an anti-war demonstration.

The British administration in India was, for its part, taking counter-measures to deal with this threat. With the promulgation of the Defence of India Ordinance on 3rd September 1939, sporadic arrests of communists started. These became markedly more numerous from April 1940 onwards.

Similar action was taken against Jayaprakash Narayan and many other Congress Socialist spokesmen, who also were opposing the war effort on the ground that participation in an 'imperialist war' had been forced on the country by its British rulers. These socialist and communist *détenus* were largely concentrated in a detention camp at Deoli. It was there that the bulk of the communist functionaries were located when Hitler turned on Stalin on 22nd June 1941.

Hitler's invasion of Soviet Russia forced the latter into the democratic camp. This caused violent confusion in the Communist Party of India. Although some of the more shrewd leaders in the Deoli Detention Camp guessed that their policy would have to be revised in view of their urgent duty to rescue the 'Fatherland of Socialism' from the fascist onslaught, the underground leaders of the party clung obstinately to their anti-war position. In July 1941, the Politbureau published a pamphlet entitled *Soviet-German War* which justified the continuance of the same policy.[5]

'People's War'

For six months this anti-war attitude persisted amidst much debate and wrangling in the Deoli Detention Camp and outside till a letter from Harry Pollitt, Secretary of the British Communist Party, ordered a clear switch over. This letter was delivered to the communists in detention by courtesy of Sir Reginald Maxwell, the then British Home Secretary of the Government of India. Soon thereafter, the imperialist war became a 'People's War'. At the end of 1942, the Politbureau issued a new thesis condemning its own 'bourgeois nationalist deviation.'[6]

The new decision to support the war resulted in the gradual release by the British administration in India of the communist leaders from detention[7] and on 24th July 1942, to the lifting of the ban on the Communist Party itself, thus enabling it to function as a legal party for the first time after nearly a decade. It also meant, however, that the communists put themselves in the position of wartime allies of the British imperialist régime in India and in total opposition to the Indian National Congress, the Congress Socialist Party and the mass of public opinion.

Having fed on the strong current of anti-British and anti-imperialist feelings of the masses for two years it was no easy task for the communists to turn around to the same audience and convince it that British imperialism had overnight become a 'prisoner in the people's camp' and that the main enemy of India was no longer Britain but Germany and Japan. But the communists made a valiant bid to do so. With the British, who were prepared to exploit any offer of support, the communists negotiated a truce. Not only was the Party declared legal on 24th July 1942, but it was soon encouraged and given facilities to start a number of newspapers and associations, the one in the English language bearing the name *The People's War*. These did propaganda both for the war effort and for the Communist Party. Never has a political party consciously played a most unpopular rôle so deliberately.

At the same time that the communists turned from being anti-war to becoming pro-war, the Indian National Congress was being forced into a more and more desperate and uncompromising position against the war effort. In December 1941, Japan and America entered the war. Singapore surrendered to the Japanese in February 1942. On 9th March, Rangoon was seized. The Allied forces were in full retreat on all fronts. Japan was approaching the eastern frontiers of India. The morale of Indians was at its lowest. Nationalist opinion felt frustrated and impatient at not being able to participate honourably in the defence of the country. This made both America and China anxious. They saw the justice of the Indian demand. Chiang Kai-Shek publicly and Roosevelt privately put pressure on Winston Churchill to negotiate a compromise with the Congress before it was too late. Churchill was, however, by now confident of the ultimate outcome. He felt secure in the alliance of America and Russia. India's support was no longer indispensable. He yielded ground to the extent of sending Sir Stafford Cripps out to India to parley with the Indian leaders, but the proposals that Cripps presented were so limited and psychologically inadequate that every political party in India, including the Muslim League, the Liberals and the Harijans rejected them. There was complete unanimity in the country on this decision – but for one solitary exception. The Communist Party recommended that the Cripps' proposals be accepted. It attacked the Congress violently for rejecting them. It was the same Party which had earlier slandered the Congress for offering conditional support to the Allies and later for adopting the innocuous method of offering individual Civil Disobedience so that it might not impede the war effort.

Throughout 1941, individuals selected by Mahatma Gandhi had courted arrest by defying the official ban on propaganda against the war. Some 2,300 people were arrested, but that neither hurt the Government nor aroused any public enthusiasm.

81

In July 1942 the Indian atmosphere was choking with unrest, frustration, anger and a desire for change. With the failure of the Cripps Mission, all hope of compromise with the British had broken down. The Working Committee of the Congress met in Wardha on 14th July and resolved that unless India's minimum demands for freedom were met, the Congress would 'be reluctantly compelled' to start a campaign of mass Civil Disobedience.[8]

On 8th August, the All-India Congress Committee endorsed this decision in Bombay. But before the Congress could act on the resolution, in the early hours of the 9th all the Congress leaders were arrested. Simultaneously, the entire country broke out into a spontaneous revolt. The slogan 'Quit India' echoed through the length and breadth of the country. Despite severe repressive measures which the government took, India was shaken with violent demonstrations against the British. A powerful underground movement sprang up, led mostly by leaders of the Congress Socialist Party.

Against this national upsurge also the communists battled on the side of the British.[9] The underground resistance leaders were condemned as fifth columnists,[10] and the Party members often considered it their duty to spy on them and get them arrested wherever possible. They earned thereby the odium attached everywhere to traitors and police informers.

Since these charges have been denied by the communists, it becomes necessary to refer to an interview given to the press by S. S. Batlivala, a former member of the Central Committee of the Communist Party, in Bombay on 22nd February 1946, explaining the reasons for his severing his connection with the Party a little while earlier. 'I became thoroughly convinced' said Batlivala, 'that I could not trust the bona fides of my comrades or rely on them to work honestly in the movement for the achievement of Indian freedom. I also realised that there was no possibility of overthrowing the unholy leadership at the top by fighting inside the Party framework. I therefore decided to sever my connection with the Party.'

Batlivala then proceeded to refer to a confidential file of correspondence during years 1942, 1943 and 1944 between P. C. Joshi, the Party's General Secretary, and Sir Reginald Maxwell, Home Member of the British Government of India, which he had seen. According to him, that correspondence, if published, 'would conclusively prove that an alliance existed between the Politbureau of the Communist Party and the Home Department of the Government of India, by which Mr Joshi was placing at the disposal of the Government of India the services of his Party members'. Batlivala asserted that he had repeatedly called for the publication of this correspondence which had been kept secret even from members of the Central Committee so that the Party's ranks could be educated to the fact that 'the various political drives undertaken by the Party in the name of anti-fascist campaigns were a part of the arrangement which helped the Government of India to tide over certain crises.' Batlivala also wanted the CPI to declare publicly 'what contacts Mr P.C. Joshi had maintained through his confidential Party members with the Intelligence Department of the General Headquarters of the Army in India'.

Batlivala's statement then went on to make the serious charge that P.C. Joshi had 'detailed certain Party members without the knowledge of the Central Committee or the rank and file of the Party to be in touch with the Army Intelligence Department and supplied the CID chiefs with such information as they would require against nationalist workers who were connected with the 1942 struggle or against persons who had come to India on behalf of the Azad Hind Government of Netaji Subhas Chandra Bose'.

These charges were repeated by Batlivala in a letter to a columnist in the *Bombay Chronicle* weekly, which was published in its issue of 17th March 1946. In that letter, Batlivala went on to add that among the secret communications that had passed between the Party's General Secretary and the British authority in India, was one which 'offered to help retain the morale of the Indian soldier by performances staged by the Indian People's Theatre Association (a communist dramatic front) in the front lines in Burma and Assam – when sons and daughters of the soil will sing, dance and recite in the language of the sepoy himself with the aid of folk music – so that he will be convinced that he is fighting a patriotic war'. This offer, according to Batlivala, was 'made behind the back of the rank and file of the Party members as well as the IPTA Executive Committee members' but it was not accepted by the South East Asia Command to whom it was referred with Maxwell's strong recommendation. The reason given for the refusal was that 'the military authorities cannot entertain the idea of utilising the services of a political party for that purpose. Besides, we have our own ENSA organisation'.

The most serious charge made by Batlivala in his letter was that Joshi had, as General Secretary of the Party, written a letter in which he offered 'unconditional help' to the then Government of India and the Army GHQ to fight the 1942 underground workers and the Azad Hind Feuj (Indian National Army) of Subhas Chandra Bose, even to the point of getting them arrested. These men were characterised by Joshi in his letter as 'traitors' and 'fifth columnists'.

On the industrial front, the communists, using the control they exercised over the AITUC, similarly exerted their utmost to keep the workers out of the national unrest. The Party which had called for strikes, strikes and more strikes now demanded work, work and no strikes. Even though the mounting inflation and shortage of food and consumer goods was creating a great deal of dissatisfaction in labour ranks, they were asked to forget the class struggle, not to strike but on the other hand to work for increased production.[11] The peasants were similarly asked to shelve all their grievances and grow more food and surrender it all to feed the armies.

Apart from doing their best to sabotage the national movement for freedom, the Communist Party also tried to sabotage the national efforts at forging internal unity between the Indian National Congress and the Muslim League. These were the years when the idea of Pakistan as a separate Muslim State was beginning to find increasing favour with Mr. Jinnah's followers. Not only did the communists support the demand for Pakistan but went much further by saying that every linguistic group in India had a distinct nationality and was therefore entitled as they claimed was the case in the USSR, to the right to secede. This would have meant the total dismemberment of the country and its Balkanisation into a dozen or more independent States.[12]

For three years, from 1942 to 1945, practically every active Indian patriot and political worker was either in jail or underground. This gave an excellent opportunity to the communists to capture the labour, student, peasant and women's organisations run by them. The AITUC, the biggest labour federation of unions now became a pure communist 'front' masked only by the co-operation of Mr N.M.Joshi, its General Secretary. Party members also infiltrated into the All-India Women's Conference. Numerous other front organisations were created by the Party members in their non-Party capacity. These were supposedly purely cultural and literary and were able to rope in several popular but confused writers, artists and intellectuals. Amongst these new associations were the Indian People's Theatre Association, which joined the already existing Progressive Writers' Association and the Friends of the Soviet Union.

The communists were by 1944, both internationally and nationally, isolated and discredited. Their efforts to destroy the influence of Gandhi and of the Congress leaders since August 1942 had completely failed. Their approaches to Jinnah and the Muslim League had met with open and insulting rebuffs in spite of their acceptance of Pakistan and celebration of Pakistan 'Days'. They had lost support both among the peasants and the industrial workers. Their only influence was among upper class 'intellectuals' with whom it was fashionable to be communists, because of Russian military successes. Perhaps also, in pursuance of current Russian foreign policy, they had received instructions to liquidate their Party and to smuggle themselves back into the Congress, on the model of the American Communists who had then been instructed to follow the Browder Line. It was against this background that the release of Mahatma Gandhi in May 1944 found the communists playing up to him and rushing to him at this retreat at Juhu Beach outside Bombay with complaints against the Congress Socialist and other resistance leaders for betraying him and his non-violence while he was in prison. Even a private showing of the film *Mission to Moscow* was arranged for the Mahatma with a view to influencing him, but Gandhi was neither amused nor impressed. In December 1944, P.C.Joshi, the General Secretary of the Party, published a pamphlet entitled *Congress and the Communists*, seeking to re-establish the CPI's patriotic character. When, with the release of members of the Congress Working Committee in June 1945, the Congress resumed normal functioning, the members of the Communist Party were nevertheless declared to be ineligible for the membership of the organisation and were expelled from the Congress. The big lie had failed to obscure Gandhi's understanding of the Truth.

It must not be imagined, however, that even during this extreme of disrepute and isolation experienced by the Indian communists, there were not important nationalists who continued to associate with the communists in United Front organisations. Thus, a two-day conference in June 1944 in Bombay of the Friends of the Soviet Union (later named by the Government of India as a Communist Party Front), found Mrs Vijayalaxmi Pandit in the chair on the first day and Mr S.A.Brelvi, a Congress journalist, presiding on the second day. Mrs Sarojini Naidu, a member of the Congress Working Committee and a former Congress President, was at that time the National Chairman of the Friends of the Soviet Union.

CHAPTER SIX

National Independence
and the Calcutta Line
1945 - 1949

The end of the war found the Communist Party in India discredited and isolated. Its opposition to the nationalist impulse behind the 'Quit India' campaign and its war-time alliance with the British rulers of the country was not easily forgotten. The motivation behind its switch over from the slogan of 'Imperialist War' to 'People's War' had opened many eyes to the bonds that tied the destinies of the Party to the Kremlin. The general elections to the Central Legislative Assembly in 1945 showed that they could not carry a single constituency.

With the return from prison to public life of the Congress and socialist spokesmen and functionaries, the communists found themselves in full retreat on the peasant and student fronts alike. The All-India Women's Conference, towards the control of which they had made concentrated efforts, slipped out of their grasp. The 'cultural' organisations started during the war faded away into paper fronts.

In the trade union field, their monopoly of vocal leadership also came to an end. At the session of the All-India Trade Union Congress, the communists had the choice between agreeing to hand over possession of the apparatus to the nationalist and socialist organisers from whose hands it had been filched while they were in British prisons or 'underground', or to hold on and force yet another split in the chequered history of India's trade unions. The communists chose the latter path. Resolutions of a sectarian character denouncing the labour legislation enacted by the Congress controlled administrations at the Centre and in the States were passed. It was obvious that the methods of conciliation and arbitration, which formed the basis of such legislation, were not acceptable to the communists, who were determined to use the working class for their own political ends.

Both the nationalists and the socialists decided in course of time to form their own trade union centres – the one came to be known as the Indian National Trade Union Congress, and the other as the Hind Mazdoor Sabha (Indian Labour Association). Both of these soon outstripped in membership and eclipsed in importance the AITUC which became an empty shell in communist hands. Even their sole surviving ally, Mr N. M. Joshi, decided at that stage to step off their platform.

Between the end of the war and the transfer of power from British to Indian hands on 15th August 1947, there was a considerable amount of negotiating at the one end and of demonstrating on the other. There was a great deal of explosive excitement over the trials of the men of the Indian National Army which Subhas Chandra Bose had led in Burma and Malaya. There was the mutiny in the Royal Indian Navy which, for the first time, proved to the British that they could no longer rely on the loyalty of the armed forces. The communists were bewildered now. In many places, they opposed the popular demonstrations. Finally, they decided to ride with the tide and made a belated attempt at calling for a 'united front'.

From 1946, a change developed in the Central Committee of the Party. One group advocated the continuance of the war-time policy of restraining any mass activity of a revolutionary character. B. T. Ranadive, however, started agitating for a reversal in policy. He advocated a militant policy of violent insurrection and guerrilla activity. Some violent outbursts did occur in the Warali area in Maharashtra and in Travancore, resulting in the police opening fire. But these remained isolated incidents.

With the coming of independence and the partition of the country in 1947, as a result of a series of conferences initiated by the British Labour Government, came the end of the phase of communist exploitation or 'development', as phrase went, of the Indian struggle for freedom from foreign rule. The Communist Party – still under the leadership of P. C. Joshi – now decided to give support to the Nehru Government. Its enthusiasm for the Congress administration was now as great as had been its opposition to the Congress in the preceding phase. The communist fire was now turned on the socialists who were, ironically enough, now condemned for not supporting the Congress sufficiently.[1]

Even now, however, the tactic of support was not without certain limitations which revealed the motives underlying it. Thus, support was lent to Pandit Nehru, the Prime Minister, as against Sardar Vallabhbhai Patel, the Deputy Premier. The idea was to try and create a schism or split in the Congress ranks, in the unity and strength of which alone lay the hope of India getting the firm government it needed to face the overwhelming problems confronting the country immediately after its independence and partition. But for the strength of the Congress and unity in its ranks, India might have easily lost its independence and all hope of stability in the riots and massacres which followed partition on both sides of the border.

The Nehru Government enjoyed the support and blessing of the Communist Party of India for only a very short time. A shift then took place in the Russian policy and consequently in world alignments. The war-time honeymoon between the western democracies and the Soviets was drawing to a close.[2] In September 1947, A. Zhdanov in his speech at the Informatory Conference of representatives of a number of Communist Parties held in Poland, roundly attacked the Western powers as imperialist war-mongers, charged America specifically with aiming at world domination and posed Russia as the sole leader of the new democratic bloc desiring peace abroad and democracy and socialism at home. This new democratic bloc consisting of Russia, Yugoslavia, Poland, Czechoslovakia, Albania, Bulgaria, Rumania and Hungary also emerged now as the 'staunch champion of the liberty and independence of all nations, and a foe of national and racial oppression and colonial exploitation in any shape or form'.[3]

Details of communist policy as applicable to Asiatic countries were later decided on at the 'South East Asian Youth Conference' which was held in Calcutta from 24th to 27th February 1948. The Conference was outwardly sponsored by the World Federation of

Democratic Youth and the International Union of Students, but actually it was an important conclave of policy-makers, including men from Russia. At this conference it was laid down that the communist parties should initiate and lead violent insurrections and civil wars in the South and South-East Asiatic countries. Accordingly, uprisings followed in Burma in April, in Malaya in June and in Indonesia in September.

On 28th February 1948 was also held in Calcutta the second Congress of the Communist Party of India. There were 800 Indian delegates present and fifteen foreign delegates from Yugoslavia (then in the Cominform), Australia and Burma. Mr L. L. Sharkey, President of the Communist Party of Australia, and U. Than Tun, leader of the Communist Party in Burma, also addressed the conference.

The Calcutta Conference issued a Political Thesis which reiterated the Zhdanov interpretation of the international situation and held that 'though the bourgeois leaderships parade the story that independence has been won, the fact is that the freedom struggle has been betrayed and the national leadership has struck a treacherous deal behind the back of the starving people, betraying every slogan of the democratic revolution'.[4] It condemned the Indian socialists for openly preaching 'the illusion that socialism may be achieved by constitutional means' and called upon the communists to forge a 'Democratic Front' of all militant sections and honest revolutionaries to launch the final struggle to win real freedom and democracy.[5]

The newly elected Central Committee issued a statement condemning the draft Constitution of India as drafted by the Constituent Assembly.

The Communist Party was now purged of all 'reformist' elements and a period of such complete dictatorial control of the party and its policies followed such as even the communists in India had never known.[6]

Ranadive felt confident that the time was ripe and his was the responsibility to engineer the final revolution in India like the October uprising of 1917 in Russia. Shock brigades and guerrilla bands were organised and, with the orthodox Lenin-Stalin brand of dogma (as opposed to Mao's) as his guiding light, he initiated a programme of reckless violence and insurrection which aimed at the overthrow of the Indian Government.

The authorities were naturally watching the new developments closely. Within a month their machinery went into action. On 26th March 1948, the West Bengal Government declared the Party illegal and arrested a number of local leaders on the charge that they were arming the people to create revolution to capture power by violent means.

On 2nd April, the Bombay Government rounded up seven of the most important leaders, including Mr S. A. Dange, President of the AITUC and one of the Vice-Presidents of the WFTU, and Mr S. S. Mirajkar, President of the Provincial TUC, and detained them on grounds that their activities were dangerous to public safety and tranquility. The Government of Madras tightened its security measures and had to send troops to the disturbed areas in Andhra and Malabar. Leading communists were simultaneously arrested in all the States of India. These arrests were made under the existing Public Safety Acts (surviving under the old Constitution from before India became free) and without benefit of trial. Justifying the action, Mr Kiran Shankar Roy, who was the Home Minister in the Government of West Bengal, gave detailed reasons as follows:

'The Communist Party's long term plan is to wage a ceaseless campaign, open and underground, for the next six months, in preparation for a projected armed rising and a violent seizure of power.

'They are trying to collect arms at different places, some of which have been recovered in the recent searches. Secret bulletins of the Party seized by the Government show that the Communist Party, in its bid for power, is trying to organise countrywide strikes in the hope of paralysing the present Congress Government. They further show that armed mass risings all over India are the ultimate aim of the Party.'

The Government of Madras issued a pamphlet to describe the communist activity in that province. According to it, in rural areas the pattern was of tillers refusing to give any tax or produce on the plea that 'the fruits of their labour rightly belonged only to them'. The pamphlet accused the communists of terrorising people in outlying areas and setting up parallel administration. Land vacated by frightened landlords was distributed to cultivators by local workers of the Party. When revenue or police authorities later appeared on the scene they were beaten up. Besides there were several communist inspired and planned highway robberies and armed ambushes. The pamphlet concluded: 'They have stirred up class hatred and unleashed violence. They have strangled the productive machinery of the country by their policy of sabotage. They have challenged and attacked the very foundations of democracy and virtually declared war on the popular Government. They have used the peasant and labourer as pawns in their political game'. The Government of Bombay issued a similar pamphlet.

Sabotage, incendiarism, loot and murder became a daily feature of the Indian scene for the next year and a half. Several leaders escaped arrest and went underground to direct the agitation. The areas most affected were West Bengal, mainly Calcutta, Andhra and Malabar in Madras, Ahmednagar district in Bombay, the eastern parts of the UP, Amritsar districts in the Punjab, Manipur on the Indo-Burma frontier, and Hyderabad. Several State Governments banned the Party. They were West Bengal, Madras, Hyderabad and Travancore-Cochin. The Party was also banned in Indore and Bhopal States. In the rest of the country the Party enjoyed legal existence. By August 1949, the total number of communists under detention was about 2,500.

Inside the jails there were frequent clashes between the communist *détenus* and jail officials. There were several instances of hunger strike as well as violent outbreaks. In Sabarmati Jail in Bombay State, police had to open fire. Two persons were killed and forty-two injured, including police. In Cuddalore in Madras, one person was killed and more than eighty injured. In Dum Dum Jail also in Bengal, three were killed and eighteen injured. These, looking back on them, were minor prototypes of a technique now internationally well known as the result of the incidents in the prisoner of war camps in Koje island off Korea.

Communist agitation was dangerously strong in the rural districts of Telengana in Hyderabad. Here the communists had entrenched themselves before the Government of India took over the State in 1948. Over large tracts in Telengana the writ of the Government ceased to operate and any Government servant, Congressman or sympathiser of the administration dared to enter the area only with a price on his head. The Hyderabad Government issued a pamphlet called *Communist Crimes in Hyderabad* giving in detail the activities and cruel atrocities committed by the Party in this area. According to it:

'From 15th August 1946, to 13th September 1948, they brutally murdered nearly 2,000 persons, attacked 22 police outposts, seized and destroyed village records, manhandled a large number of village officials, burnt "chadris" and Customs outposts, captured 230 guns, looted or destroyed paddy and robbed cash and jewellery worth more than a million rupees . . . They attempted large-scale disruption of communications and lines of supply and transport and steadily and systematically adopted the technique of guerrilla fighting with the arms and resources at their disposal.'

The pamphlet gives a few instances of dastardly acts of murder as follows:

'More than 500 armed communists raided the village Peddavid, Huzurnagar Taluq, Nalgonda district, murdered ten villagers, including women and children and severely injured ten others. Children were thrown into the fire. Seventy houses had been set fire to and all of them were gutted. This incident was a reprisal as one of the villagers of Peddavid had previously given information to the police about the presence of Kot Narain, a notorious communist outlaw, in the neighbourhood . . . Sixteen people including a woman were kidnapped by communists at a place near Pengot and were taken to Lingagiri. The men were murdered and their bodies were set on fire. The burnt bodies were later found lying near Lingagiri border. There was no trace of the woman . . . A party of twenty-five communists entered the village Dharnipahad at night, caught hold of an aged Muslim woman, took her to the jungle and speared her to death.'

The Government of India issued a pamphlet called *Communist*

93

Violence in India. It detailed the communist guerrilla organisation and quoted extensively from Party letters, circulars and secret instructions to show how the party had declared virtual war against the State. It carried a long appendix giving details of communist violence State-wise. From the quotations we learn how the guerrilla bands were trained and shock brigades organised. They were instructed as follows:

'Every day practical exercises on silent killings must be done, one party attacking the police station and another defending; concealment, camouflage, taking cover both in day and night, crawling practice . . . The weapons dealt with are rifle, shot-gun, revolver, bombs, tommy gun and sten-gun . . . The activities of the guerrilla mean the raiding of police stations, zamindars' or jotedars' houses, sabotaging enemy communication lines, cutting of telephone and telegraph lines.'

The communist attempt at revolution was to culminate in a countrywide railway strike. It so happened that the railwaymen, through their All-India body, the Railwaymen's Federation, served the Government with a notice that they would strike if their grievances were not redressed. As a result of the negotiations, however, the Executive Committee of the Federation decided by a majority to withdraw the strike notice. But a minority led by the communists insisted the strike must take place on the appointed date which was 9th March 1949. Some of the railwaymen's unions dominated by communists, therefore, went ahead with strike preparations regardless of the decision of the Federation.

Once again the Government took swift action and rounded up all communists inciting the workers to strike. About 600 were arrested. A government spokesman in New Delhi explained that the action had been necessary because the strike was not a normal one but was designed to disrupt communications. He also stated that there had been contact between communists in India and those in Burma and that the Indian communists' plan to create chaotic conditions was part of a larger plan covering a wider region. On 28th February 1949, the Prime Minister said in Parliament:

'The Communist Party of India has recently concentrated on the issue of a general strike on the railways as well as in other essential services of paramount importance to the community. It has looked upon these strikes not from the trade union or economic point of view, meant to better the lot of the workers, but as a weapon designed to create a chaotic state in the country which, it is thought, would help the party to gain its other objectives, whatever they might be. It is deliberately seeking to create famine conditions by paralysing the railway system so that the foodstuffs should not be transported, the object being to create a general background of chaos, a breakdown of the administration and mass uprising.'

Anyhow, the scheduled 9th March came and went but there was no general strike. This failure perhaps more than anything else sealed the fate of the communist plan of revolution, besides exposing the weakness of the Party's hold on the rank and file of workers.

Notwithstanding this failure, the effort at industrial disruption proceeded. In the second half of the year 1949, calls were given in succession for an All-Bengal General Strike, a Calcutta Municipal Corporation Workers' Strike, an All-Bengal Jute Workers' Strike, a Madras Tramwaymen's Strike, a Coimbatoire Textile Workers' Strike, and finally on 2nd January 1950, for a one-day protest strike by textile workers throughout India. All of these failed to yield the results anticipated. The isolation of the communists from the working class was obvious for all to see.

While within the country the Communist Party battled to possess India, abroad the Russian organs also attacked virulently the Indian set-up. India was now considered Public Enemy Number Three, next only to the USA and Britain. The Indian Government was described as the main agent of Anglo-American imperialism in South-East Asia and the Socialist Party as agents of the reactionary bourgeoisie. In his *New State in India's Liberation Struggle*,[7] A.N.Dykov, Doctor of Historial Sciences, explains at length as follows:

'In June 1947, the Communist Party of India also was not able to give a correct evaluation of the Mountbatten Plan and characterised it not as an imperialist manoeuvre but as a certain step forward. It did not immediately understand the treachery of the leadership of the National Congress and counterposed its Right to its Left wing as though the latter was a progressive one. Therefore, it called upon the masses to rally round Nehru and assist him to get rid of Patel. All this shows that illusions about the unity of national interests and the influence of the Congress were still strong not only among the backward peasantry and the petty bourgeois masses, but also among a certain section of the working class and that the Right opportunist mistakes had not been overcome within the Communist Party.

'It was only in December 1947, that the Communist Party of India gave a correct estimate of the Mountbatten Plan as a new imperialist manoeuvre and characterised the Nehru Government as a whole as a government of the Indian big bourgeoisie; which had entered into an agreement with British imperialism and formed an alliance with the Indian princes and landlords.'

Characteristic of this open hostility towards the Indian Government displayed by the countries of the Soviet bloc were the messages that passed between Mao Tse-tung and the Communist Party of India. On 12th October 1949, B.T. Ranadive, the Party's General Secretary, sent the following message of greetings to the victorious Chinese communist chief:

"Dear Comrade Mao Tse-tung,

'On behalf of the Central Committee of the Communist Party of India, I send you and through you to the people of China, our warmest greetings on the occasions of the formation of the People's Government of China. The formation of the People's Government signalises the final victory of the Chinese people against the enemies and enslavers of China – the American imperialists and the clique of Kuomintang reactionaries. This great and historic victory seals the doom of foreign imperialism and its national agents on the continent of Asia, and opens the prospects of the immediate liberation of the peoples of Asia. It changes the balance of forces on a world-scale and constitutes a decisive turning point in the world struggle for peace, democracy and Socialism. In liberating themselves the people of China have inflicted a decisive defeat on the common enemy of the peoples of the world – American imperialism – and have advanced the cause of world liberation.

'The toiling masses of India feel jubilant over this great victory.

They know it hastens their own liberation. They are inspired by it to fight more determinedly and courageously their battle for ending the present régime and establishing the rule of People's Democracy.

'I wish to assure you and through you the people of China that the Nehru Government which pursues a policy of hostility to the Chinese people and still continues its recognition of the bankrupt Kuomintang Government, does not represent the wishes and the will of the people of India. The overwhelming majority of the Indian people decisively stand for friendship and co-operation with the great Chinese people. The Nehru Government on the other hand follows the dictates of the Anglo-American imperialists, who wish to build India as a bastion of reaction against China. The Anglo-American imperialists carry on their nefarious conspiracies in Nepal and Tibet under the cover offered by the Nehru Government. Thus the Nehru Government is directly advancing the game of the enemies of the Chinese people.

'I wish to assure you and through you the people of China that the Communist Party of India will unmask all the anti-Chinese intrigues that the Nehru Government might hatch under the dictates of the American imperialists and rally the people to defeat them.

'The Central Committee of our Party has asked me to convey their special tribute and greetings to Comrade Chu Teh and the members of the Chinese Liberation Army who have upset all imperialist plans by their quick military victories. The great military skill of Comrade Chu Teh and his associates and the valour, courage, and self-sacrificing spirit of the members of the Liberation Army confounded the American advisers of Kuomintang and shattered all hopes of prolonged resistance by Kuomintang forces.

'The Central Committee of our Party salutes the great Communist Party of China and its leader Mao Tse-tung on the occasion of its historic and world-shaking victory. The victory scored by the Communist Party of China is the victory of Marxism-Leninism, of the Stalinist Line. The Communist Party of China and its great leader, Mao Tse-tung, have demonstrated once more the invincible power of Marxism-Leninism.

'And finally allow me, Comrade Mao Tse-tung, to congratulate you on the occasion of your election as the President of the People's Republic of China.

'Long Live Comrade Mao Tse-tung!

'Long Live the Communist Party of China!

'Long Live the Fighting Unity of the Chinese and Indian People!'[8]

G

Mao Tse-tung on his part cabled the full support of the Chinese people to the Indian communists in their 'struggle' and expressed the hope that the day was not far off when India too would be liberated by the Communist Party from the oppression of Anglo-American imperialism and its Indian lackeys. This message was all the more noteworthy against the background of the early recognition accorded to the Mao régime by the Indian Government.

CHAPTER SEVEN

Again the United Front
1950 - 1951

The story of these two years stretches from the new directive of the Cominform to the CPI on 27th January 1950, to the general elections at the end of 1951. Its importance lies in the fact that it was a period during which the international apparatus, by constant and consistent pressure, rescued the Party from the legacy of its own previous *dictat* of the Zdhanov line in February 1948 and refurbished it as an effective and well-financed instrument of intervention in India's first elections on the basis of universal franchise. The events of these two years laid the foundation for the present position and policies of the Indian communists and provide a clue to future developments.

It was clear as the CPI entered the year 1950 that not only had the revolution of Ranadive's conception not come off but the Communist Party had suffered a severe blow and set back. It had alienated public sympathy and the organisation was reeling under Government repression and started cracking up.[1] On 25th February 1950, the Deputy Prime Minister and Home Minister of the Union Government, Sardar Vallabhbhai Patel, came before the provisional Indian Parliament with 'a Bill to provide for Preventive Detention in certain cases'. Sardar Patel urged the House to pass the Bill on the very day of its introduction as a matter of emergency. If this was not done, some of the most dangerous communist agents in India, who were guilty of violence, would be let loose as a result of proceedings then pending before the High Court in Calcutta. All three readings of the Bill were, in the result, rushed through the House, though not without a note of warning being sounded by certain members. Thus, Mr M.R. Masani asked the House to face the fact that this measure contemplated 'a far reaching encroachment on the rights of the individual citizen' and was liable to expose Parliament to 'the most serious misconstruction' if adequate expression was not given 'to the sense of reluctance and disquiet with which Parliament was enacting such a piece of legislation'. He urged that the Bill, which was a 'hasty improvisation', should be replaced at the earliest possible moment by 'a more principled and well conceived, well thought-out measure which does not shirk the issue, which goes to the root of the mischief and which frankly takes its stand for the defence of democracy against totalitarian aggression from within or without'.

In his reply to this plea, the Home Minister conceded that it was with a heavy heart that he had introduced this measure. He agreed that the Bill required 'to be closely examined whether a better substitute of a more or less permanent nature based on specific principles can be brought in or not'.[2]

Internally, the Party entered the year 1950 facing a split, despite purges. Externally, it found Russia once again changing her tone and policy towards India.

The Communist Party conceded that its membership had dwindled from 90,000 in 1948 to 20,000 and it admitted a drop in the membership of the All-India Trade Union Congress, which it controlled, from 700,000 to 100,000. The plight of the peasant and student organisations run by the Party was even sadder. The condition of the Party by the end of 1949 and its miserable state during the two years of 'militancy' have perhaps been best described by P. C. Joshi, the ex-secretary of the Party, who was condemned in 1947 for his reformist policies and was temporarily expelled from the Party in December 1949.

In a pamphlet called *Views*, Joshi wrote:

'I think my comrade holding the present situation to be a revolutionary situation is not only unable to use the evidence of his own eyes and ears but is guilty of repudiating Lenin's own definition of the same.

'Of all our sectarian mistakes this has been the most disastrous, for it has led to the adoption of tactics suited to an insurrectionary or semi-insurrectionary situation. The result has been that the masses have not responded to our calls and our comrades have landed themselves into the terrorist mire . . .

'The Party has ceased to function as an organisation. Every single organisational principle of the Party has been done to death in cold blood ... *Provincial Committees are being reshuffled in an unprincipled manner by a fiat from above ... Comrades are expelled without charges being communicated to them ... If some comrades or some units take a determined stand ... they are purged.*

'Month after month membership has become less and less active till to-day a tiny percentage is in action.

'Passivity, frustration, demoralisation constitute inner party morale.'[3]

Ranadive, however, was so sure of his line that he even considered it his duty to call Mao Tse-tung to account and tell him that he was not a good Marxist. This was in reference to a thesis put forward by Ranadive some time in the middle of 1949, opposing a trend within the Party towards 'right' deviation urging collaboration with a section of the peasantry and soft-pedalling of the proletarian dictatorship. In the course of this thesis[4] Ranadive made bold to write: 'Some of Mao's formulations are such that no communist can accept them. They are in contradiction to the world understanding of the Communist Parties ... Why do the Chinese have to go through the protracted civil war ? Just because the leadership of the Chinese Communist Party at times failed to fight for the hegemony of the proletariat and bringing the majority of the mass in alliance and under the leadership of the proletariat, because it followed tactical policies which led to disaster'. He condemned outright Mao's theories as 'horrible and reactionary', 'Titoist deviations' ' against every tenet of Marxism-Leninism' and did not think they could contribute in any way to the policies of the Indian Communist Party.

By the end of 1949, the USSR was clearly changing its line towards India. Vehement criticism of the Indian National Government gave way to softer rebukes. It was decided to make capital out of India's foreign policy of neutrality and twist it to suit the Cominform design of pulling India out of the Anglo-American bloc and into the Russian orbit. This change in Russian foreign policy was not confined to India but applied to all the newly freed Asian countries. Thus the Indonesian Republic was extended prompt diplomatic recognition on its establishment in January

1950, although only a few days earlier *Izvestia* had attacked the 'reactionary Hatta-Soekarno group'. A protracted quibble with Pakistan over the exchange of diplomatic missions was brought to an end and Mr Liaquat Ali Khan, Prime Minister of Pakistan, was invited to visit Moscow. India's new Ambassador was granted the much coveted interview with Stalin which Mrs Pandit, his predecessor, had been refused.

It is possible that, with China brought safely within the Soviet orbit and the Moscow-Peking Axis poised for a new phase of expansion in East and in South-East Asia, the prime necessity had become one of blocking such attempts at regional groupings and measures for collective security as would be the normal reaction to such a policy of expansion. What was perhaps being attempted was to detach from such acts of solidarity countries away from the immediate firing line and to lull them into a false sense of security by gestures of the kind mentioned above.

Cominform Directive

At the same time the Cominform issued through its organ published in Bucharest *For a Lasting Peace, For a People's Democracy*, of 27th January 1950, a new directive to the Indian Communist Party. The background to the Cominform weekly's article of 27th January 1950 was later disclosed to the CPI by R. Palme Dutt. According to him, the CPGB, which was concerned in giving all assistance within its power to the Indian Communist Party from its very inception, was gravely concerned over the development of the CPI's policy during the past two years. The CPGB had tried to hold its hand and had even forbidden any public discussion of the CPI's plight by Indian communists in Britain. When, however, the document of the CPI entitled *Strategy and Tactics* appeared containing an extraordinarily slanderous attack on Mao Tse-tung, the CPGB realised that a situation of the utmost gravity had been reached by the movement in India as well as for the international movement. In order to avoid any impression of trying to discipline the Indian Party, the CPGB had provided an analysis to the Cominform journal *For a Lasting Peace, For a People's Democracy*, and made certain proposals to it. This in turn resulted in the appearance in that journal of the editorial of 27th January 1950, which, according to Palme Dutt, proved to be helpful in ensuring a rapid change in India without any material damage to the prestige of the CPI and gave it the necessary stimulus to correct itself.

The article in the Cominform journal authoritatively announced that the path pursued by Mao Tse-tung and the Chinese communists was the only correct path for colonial and dependent peoples. It pointedly quoted the call of the Chinese communist Liu Shao-Chi that India must follow in the footsteps of China:

'The path taken by the Chinese people . . . is the path that should be taken by the people of many colonial and dependent countries in their struggle for national independence and People's Democracy . . . The mass movement of the peoples in the colonies and semi-colonies, the movement that unfolded after the war and developed into an armed struggle, forced the British imperialists to make a tactical retreat. A sham independence was bestowed on India. But the interests of British imperialism remain "sacred and inviolable." The Mountbattens have departed but British imperialism remains and, octopus like, grips India in its bloody tentacles . . . In these conditions, the task of the Indian communists drawing on the experience of national liberation movement in China and other countries is naturally to strengthen the alliance of the working class with all the peasantry, to fight for the introduction of urgently needed agrarian reform and – on the basis of common struggle for freedom and national independence of their country, against the Anglo-American imperialists oppressing it and against the reactionary big bourgeoisie and feudal princes collaborating with them – to unite all classes, parties, groups and organisations willing to defend the national independence and freedom of India.'

Working out the strategy for this policy of a United Front, the Cominform article directed:

'The Peace movement which has already begun with a broadbased character must be developed throughout the country along the line laid down in the resolution of the Information Bureau of the *Defence of Peace and the Struggle against Warmongers*. It must become the pivot of the entire activity of the Party and the mass organisations. It is our duty to merge the struggle for national liberation with that for peace, tirelessly exposing the anti-national and treacherous policy of the Congress and the League Governments which have become direct lieutenants of the British and American imperialists and are seeking to make India a base of war against the USSR, the People's democracies and the liberation struggles of the peoples of Asia.'

The kernel of this new *dictat* was quoted in a statement of the Editorial Board of the *Communist*, the monthly journal of the CPI for February–March 1950:

'(1) The working class must unite with all classes, parties, groups and organisations willing to fight the imperialists and their hirelings and to form a broad, nationwide front headed by the working class and its vanguard, the Communist Party, the Party equipped with the theory of Marxism-Leninism, the Party that has mastered the art of revolutionary strategy and tactics, that breathes the spirit of revolutionary irreconcilability of the people, the spirit of proletarian organisation and discipline in the mass movement of the peoples; (2) a decisive condition for the victorious outcome of the national liberation struggle in the formation, when the necessary internal conditions allow it, of People's Liberation Armies under the leadership of the Communist Party.'

It further admitted:

'The editorial article is thus a sharp reminder to the Communist Party of India and in Pakistan of the great lag which exists between the mighty advancing forces in the entire colonial world led by their Communist Parties and the Indian people's liberation movement led by the Communist Party of India . . .

'This lag is explained by the fact that while fighting reformism, which acted as a brake on the unleashing and the bold leadership of the struggle of the workers and the toiling masses, the Party Centre committed certain errors in dogmatist and sectarian directions, which restricted the scope of those struggles and prevented the mobilisation of the broadest masses in the same.'

Ranadive immediately acknowledged his mistake and was enthusiastic about the new directive, but the Party refused to have him any more. In June 1950, Rajeshwar Rao, leader of the Andhra group, was elected Secretary. Ranadive was condemned as 'the initiator, executor and dogged defender of the Trotsky-Tito type of left-sectarian political line'. The Politbureau was reconstituted. Perhaps in reply to a thesis propounded by Dange, Ghate and A. K. Ghosh, the Politbureau issued in June 1951 a lengthy policy statement which admitted regretfully: '*The tradition of our party, specially since the "People's War" period, has been to swing like a pendulum from one extreme to the other . . . We woke up suddenly like Rip Van Winkle at the end of 1947 to jump into left sectarianism which has brought the Party and the mass movement to the present plight of total disruption*'. Issued as a draft to be placed before the Central Committee for discussion, this voluminous statement consisted of fifteen chapters.

In general the thesis was that during the post-war period two camps had crystallised in the international field – the first being the camp of peace and democracy and socialism headed by the USSR and the second the camp of imperialistic reactionaries headed by the Anglo-Americans. The Congress Government was following a foreign policy dictated by the Anglo-Americans and was dependent on them for armaments. According to the thesis, the four cornerstones of India foreign policy were: (1) Support to the camp of imperialism, spoken of as the camp of democracy; (2) alignment with the Anglo-American bloc; (3) hostility towards the Soviet Union and (4) dreams of military domination and political hegemony in the South-East Asia region. In pursuance of these objects, the Indian Government was actively participating in the war preparations of the Anglo-Americans.

The achievement of Indian independence was explained as an intrigue of the British who, in the face of a revolutionary situation, had 'conspired into a deal' with the Congress and League leaders and established puppet régimes in India and Pakistan. The three years of Congress rule had not brought any essential change in the dependent colonial and slave agrarian economy of the country. The Constitution had been framed to perpetuate the sanctity of unbridled monopolist and landlord exploitation. In the result, the class struggle was ripening at such a pace that the Communist Party had no option but to choose between armed resistance and abject surrender.

The whole set of existing relations in India made it incumbent that armed struggle should be the principal form of struggle. This would be different from the classical form of general political strike and armed uprising. It would be a peasant war under the leadership of the proletariat summarised by Mao in the words 'guerrilla warfare'. No hard and fast rules could be laid down as to where and when and how the armed struggle should be launched. But whatever the immediate issue might be – whether that of food or otherwise – it was to be linked with the question of land and power to the people.

Unfortunately, at such a critical juncture, the Party stood disrupted politically, organisationally and financially. It had not, however, been destroyed. The main task was to build up a mass party capable of playing a historic rôle in building the People's Democratic Front and standing at the head of the armed 'guerrilla' struggle.

The People's Democratic Front was to be a united front of workers, peasants, petty bourgeois and middle bourgeois and the parties that represented these classes, based on the immediate programme of the Communist Party and on the fight for its realisation.

For the purposes of forming such a front, non-Congress parties in India were to be divided into four main categories: (1) genuinely anti-imperialist parties and groups, consisting of the forward bloc, the Workers' and Peasants' Party, the Revolutionary Socialist Party and the United Socialist Organisation; (2) pro-imperialist parties and groups under a 'left' cloak, such as the Socialist Party of India; (3) Congress, with the different factions and groups which are working from inside or outside the Party, and (4) communal reactionary parties, such as the Hindu Mahasabha, Rashtriya Swayam Sevak Sangh, Muslim League and the Akali Dal. The Communist Party would contact the parties in the first group and enter into a united front with them. There was no question of forming a united front with the second group. The third group, viz, the Congress, was in a state of flux and should be watched carefully. A bitter fight against the fourth group would have to be waged.

In the field of labour, where the AITUC had become weak, the

Party workers should infiltrate into the INTUC and the Hind Mazdoor Sabha and seek to disrupt them under the slogan 'one union in each factory and industry and one national TUC affiliated to the WFTU'.

The communist-controlled All-India Kisan Sabha was to be strengthened but, under cover of this, Party workers were to concentrate surreptitiously on forest and mountainous regions which could be developed into future 'guerrilla' bases.

The petty bourgeois, which was being ground down by Congress rule and now stood disillusioned about independence, was to be tackled by exposing its non-Marxist leadership. Professional intellectuals were to be approached under the slogan of 'peace' and civil liberties. The demand of the middle bourgeoisie for the protection of small industry was to be supported, and the formation of linguistic provinces advocated.

A formal apology was now tendered by the Politbureau of the Party to Mao Tse-tung for the 'utterly wrong, irresponsible and slanderous criticism made against him by the old Politbureau' and the resolution criticising him was withdrawn unreservedly.

But neither Mao nor Rajeshwar Rao could arrest the deterioration within the Party or pull off the revolution, which was now to be of the Chinese pattern. Ranadive staked all his hopes on the proletariat. Rajeshwar Rao pinned his faith on agrarian upheavals – a series of Telenganas throughout India. But Telenganas did not breed except in certain restricted areas in Tripura, Manipur and Assam.[5] Indian communism continued to slump in sheer frustration and despondency. A secret circular of the Politbureau dated 16th September 1950, took note of the internal conflicts and differences of opinion and said:

'This emergence of the opposing political trend and other intermediary opinions and divergence of views has its repercussions on the organisational functioning of the Party which was already on the verge of collapse and in a state of chaos due to past mistakes of the Party leadership. A state of semi-paralysis leading to lack of mass activities is now the general picture inside the Party, though exceptions are also there. Since the last CC (Central Committee) meeting in May, the inner Party crisis has further accentuated and it has assumed the most acute form

leading to organisational deadlocks and extreme financial crisis at all
levels of the Party organisation.'

Finance

The financial position of the Party appears to have been genuinely
unsatisfactory. In West Bengal wholetimers and underground
workers could not be given their pay for several months. Some
'dens' in Calcutta had to be given up through inability to pay
arrears of rent. In Madras and Assam too there was a deficit in
Party funds. Great difficulty was apparently felt in Bihar in maintaining the underground apparatus due to want of money. In
Orissa, the Provincial Committee described the collection of
funds as 'primarily a question of existence'. In Jaipur, the Party
office was locked by the landlord due to failure to pay rent. Party
headquarters decided to sell surplus property, rent out surplus
rooms, not to issue new publications, to give or hire on commission
the New Age Printing Press, to retrench workers in the Press.
Mashal weekly suspended publication. Attempts to collect funds
for the defence of the Telengana communist under-trial prisoners
brought no substantial returns.

In West Bengal also, the financial position of the Party appeared
to have deteriorated. The Manager of the *Swadhinta* tendered his
resignation as a protest against the failure to meet bills. The West
Bengal leaders issued directives to underground members to come
out into the open and make arrangements for their own maintenance as the Party was not able to subsidise them any further. In
Delhi, wholetimers did not receive their pay for two months. In
Madras, however, with the release of A. K. Gopalan from prison,
the position of the Malabar Party showed some improvement as
a result of purses amounting to Rs 32,000 donated to him.

CPGB Intervenes

The Party was at this stage being constantly guided by instructions received from R. Palme Dutt and the Communist Party of
Great Britain through various contacts, including Indians who

managed to visit England under various pretexts, such as health or business. According to an important letter despatched at this time by R. Palme Dutt on behalf of the CPGB, the chief mistakes committed by the CPI during the past two years were: (1) denial of the essential character of the national democratic revolution as anti-imperialist and anti-feudal and failure to realise the semi-colonial position of India; (2) linking the democratic revolution with the fight for socialism and proletarian revolution; (3) the revision of the agrarian strategy and tactics of Marxism-Leninism, adoption of the Slogan 'Nationalisation of the Land' and the consequent treatment of the entire body of rich peasantry as a hostile force; (4) sectarian treatment in trade union activities and the refusal to effect unity between the different labour organisations; (5) the rejection of the Chinese experience for India, culminating in the denunciation and criticism of a whole series of other parties and especially of Mao Tse-tung and the Chinese Party, and (6) violation of inner party democracy.

According to the CPGB, in view of the havoc caused by the Trotskyist-Titoist left-sectarian policies which had brought the Party to the point of liquidation nothing short of a Party conference which could elect a new leadership could restore a healthy situation. Those responsible for these Trotskyist-Titoist trends should be tried and removed from responsible positions in the Party.

The call for armed struggle, when the Party organisation was weak and disrupted, would only lead to new suicidal adventures which would further decimate the already depleted cadres of the Party. There was no doubt, however, that ultimately, after a period of recuperation and rebuilding of the Party, the revolution in India must take the form of armed struggle. The Central Committee appeared to have mechanically applied the experience of Andhra to other parts of India where the movement had not reached the same level. Instructions in regard to the 'China Way' were not to be taken too literally.

The CPGB further opined that it was urgently necessary for the CPI, on the basis of the correction of policy indicated in the editorial of the Cominform weekly of 27th January 1950, to re-establish its position as rapidly as possible as the spokesman of the Indian masses and of all oppositional forces on all issues and thus build up a national front. The CPI had distorted the meaning of the Cominform editorial by assuming that it had been asked to pursue the Chinese path by adopting armed struggle as the main form of struggle and by building broad-based anti-imperialist fronts. Left sectarianism had run its full course and was no longer a serious danger. There must be special care taken, however, to guard against the swing over to the other extreme at this stage, namely to right-wing opportunism, legalist illusions or surrender of the leading rôle of the Party.

The CPGB also criticised the lack of attention to, and political leadership on, such current burning political issues as Korea and 'the Nehru-Stalin proposals'. According to R. Palme Dutt, there were no illusions about the fact that the Nehru Government represented the interests of monopolist big business, but that did not mean that the Nehru Government or the Indian bourgeoisie would aways support Anglo-American imperialism. There were two trends in the Government of India, one represented by the Patel Group which wanted to identify itself with the Anglo-Americans, and the other led by Nehru, which was conscious of the greatness of China and of the fact that war with China might mean India's doom. By reason of such opposing trends, India was following a vacillating foreign policy. Its stand on Korea and the Atom Bomb was progressive, and the CPI should exploit it and mobilise great popular pressure to see that such progressive policies were implemented.

In regard to *Cross Roads* the CPGB commented that, since this organ had to play a double rôle as the Party organ as well as a 'broad left-wing' organ intended to appeal to a non-Party public, it had not been able to do justice to either task. The Party should therefore establish its own organ for Party members and enable *Cross Roads* to present itself as an organ of left-unity addressed to a non-Party public and serving to build up a democratic front, whose organ it would progress to be while still run under the direction of the Party.

The CPGB criticised the CPI for making no reference to the

coming All-India elections, the first on adult suffrage, in the documents sent by it abroad. Immediate preparations must be made for these elections. The legal position that the Party still enjoyed should be fully exploited by extending the press and publications of the Party to gain more legality.

Palme Dutt opined that Joshi was a successful General Secretary from 1935 to 1947, when he worked out the United Front tactic successfully. Reformist mistakes were natural in such a context and Joshi, like many others, had not been able to guard against them. The Second Party Congress had rightly dealt with the situation, but the tendency as there expressed has gone too far and Joshi's criticism of the Central Committee's activities as expressed in his *Views* was substantially correct.

Towards the end of 1950, India was also visited by several international communist representatives, whom the Party took a lot of interest in popularising in India. D.N.Pritt, the British lawyer, while he was in India ostensibly in connection with defence of the Telengana accused, was fully utilised to boost communist morale and the Soviet régime. He went as far as to say that there was more freedom in Soviet Russia than in Great Britain, that the Soviet system of justice was better than in any capitalist country, and that conditions in the Soviet labour camps were better than in jails in other countries.

Central Committee Meets

The instructions from the British Communist Party, along with other material, were circulated to Party members and units and, some time in December 1950, the Central Committee of the Party met. At this meeting, important organisational changes on the lines suggested by the CPGB were initiated. It was admitted at the meeting that political and organisational differences had virtually paralysed and reduced the Party to a state of passivity at a time when mighty events were taking place at home and abroad. This situation had caused deep concern to communists both in India and internationally. There was such an even balance of forces between the two groups led by Rajeshwar Rao and Dange that neither group felt strong enough to take the responsibility of leading the Party. There was an awareness that these sharp differences could be solved only by obtaining guidance from the international communist leadership. Meanwhile, all that was possible was to make organisational changes with an eye to prevent further disruption pending receipt of detailed instructions from international headquarters.[6]

The CPGB's advice that all leaders of the left sectarian trend should be removed from their position was followed by removing S. Lahiri and holding an enquiry against Ranadive and four other members of the Politbureau. The case of P. C. Joshi was to be reopened and a fresh trial given to him. It was further agreed that: (1) the unity of all left parties should be built and strong propaganda should be conducted for the early holding of the general elections and for the full restoration of civil liberties; (2) unity amongst working classes should be developed; (3) a policy of mobilising the people for peace according to the decisions of the Warsaw Peace Congress should be worked out and a resolution on Korea should be adopted; (4) every effort should be made to defend the cause of the Telengana fighters, and no Party member should demand in the press the cessation of the struggle; (5) all Party members who had been unjustly expelled during the period between the Second Congress and June 1950, should be readmitted and P. C. Joshi's case should be reopened; (6) the Bombay and Maharashtra committees should be reconstituted; and (7) provincial conferences should be convened at the end of about three months and the Party Congress in about six months' time.

The Central Committee meeting did not appear, however, to have stabilised the position. Allegations continued to be bandied.

The net result of all these months of discussions was that no firm Party line could yet be chalked out. The main trends, one in favour of armed struggle and the other against, persisted. It became obvious that unless the Third Party Congress actually materialised and the keenly awaited instructions were received from the international apparatus, there was little prospect of the Party functioning as a united body. Meanwhile, the Party made tentative moves towards securing legality and facilities for functioning freely during the election campaign.

Groping Towards Legality

On 17th September 1951 the Communist Party issued a statement in Bombay which challenged the Government of India to withdraw the Preventive Detention Act[7] and stop following a repressive policy against the Party members. In return the Party promised to give up terrorism and act as a legal party employing constitutional means to contest for power. The Communist Party statement said:

'Let him (Rajagopalachari) have the ban on our part withdrawn in all those states where it exists; let him give up the practice of detention without trial; let him release political prisoners; let him end the military police terror in Telengana and other areas. He will then find us working openly as any other political party and join other democratic parties, organisations, groups and individuals, in a mighty democratic movement against his government and their bosses – Anglo-American imperialism and Indian reaction.'

Rejecting the plea of the Party, on 10th March 1951, Mr C. Rajagopalachari the Home Minister, said in Parliament:

'If the men who have grouped themselves and practice terrorism and sabotage in the name of communism will not merely issue challenges and make conditional offers of adopting peaceful and open political life, but will back profession with practice, we could take the risks involved in trusting them. Past conduct cannot just be wiped out by the simple press statement . . .

'Three leading Indian communists issued to their comrades a statement on 23rd September 1950 explaining the Communist Party's policy. It is categorically stated therein that the party should put the peasant movement progressively on the rails of the armed struggle, and that in agrarian relations they should, by mass mobilisation and direct action, as in Telengana create armed forces in rural areas and strong bases for their operation. It is further categorically stated therein that there is no question of liquidating Telengana but that on the contrary it

H

is a question of raising the movement in the rest of the country to the level of Telengana.

'The Politbureau of the Communist Party of India issued a policy statement on 15th November 1950 in the following terms: "Finally it is necessary to clearly grasp the truth that the armed struggle has become the principle form of struggle in the present agrarian revolutionary stage that our national liberation movement has grown to". It was added that simultaneously they should "adopt and co-ordinate all other conceivable forms of struggle such as economic and political strikes, demonstrations, agricultural labour struggles, signature collections for peace pledges and election contests".

'An important foreign communist who was invited to advise the Indian Communist Party gave the following opinion in December 1950: "It is the task of the Communist Party to skilfully utilise the stand of the Nehru Government on questions like Korea and the atom bomb. Regarding the armed struggle, as we have stated in our letter, we do not deny that ultimately the revolution in India will and must take the form of an armed struggle. It is hardly to be debated".

'It is thus clear that we cannot accept declarations and challenges but must await facts . . .

The Preventive Detention Bill was duly ratified and revived for another year by the Indian Parliament with a few modifications.[8] Under it the Executive could detain a person in jail on suspicion provided his case was considered by an Advisory Board within ten days of the arrest. The recommendations of the Advisory Board were to be binding on the Executive.

The communists continued to pose as martyrs and lay low, leaving it to the people to draw their own conclusions. Thus the correspondent of the *National Standard*, Bombay, reported from Lucknow in the issue of 15th February that:

'Prominent Communist leaders, who for over a year have been underground to escape arrest, have "discovered" themselves, and are now seen moving openly in towns. Warrants against them have been cancelled. Communist activities in this State have been at a standstill for a long time, and communists no longer constitute a danger to public peace in the Government's eyes.'

Yet on 21st February, the Home Minister took the Parliament and the country by surprise by announcing that there had been a communist uprising of very serious dimensions in Manipur and Assam, on the vital north-eastern frontiers of India, but that the situation was 'under control'.[9]

Mission to Moscow

While this manoeuvring for electoral facilities was proceeding, Moscow had taken radical measures for checking the fissiparous tendencies in the Party and setting it on its own feet. A commission consisting of S. A. Dange, Ajoy Ghosh, Rajeshwar Rao and Basava Punniah, representing both the major trends in the Party, was invited to visit Moscow in order to seek guidance and clarification. Accordingly, these four went 'underground' to Moscow and returned to India some time early in 1951 with an important document which was described as the Tactical Line (Appendix A). This was presented to the Politbureau and evidently some members of the Central Committee as a document of basic theoretical significance, a thesis on the theory of revolution, in the Indian context, for the entire period. So secret was this document considered that most of the members of the Party were kept in ignorance of its very existence.[10]

In any event, the document, claiming as it did the alleged authority of Stalin and Molotov, secured the assent of leaders of different groups within the Party and in it they were able to see the light by which to steer their future course of action.

This document emphatically says that without an armed revolution the present régime in India cannot be replaced, that armed revolution will be a combination of partisan war in the rural areas and armed workers' risings in the cities. The entire work of the Party, in Trade Unions, among the peasants and in the Legislatures was to lead, step by step, to this ultimate goal. The two opening paragraphs of the document entitled 'Not Peaceful But Revolutionary Path' come straight to the point:

'The immediate main objectives set forth in the Draft Programme of the Communist Party of India are the complete liquidation of feudalism, the distribution of all land held by feudal owners among the peasants and agricultural workers, and achievement of full national independence and freedom. These objectives cannot be realised by a peaceful, parliamentary way. These objectives can be realised only through a revolution, through the overthrow of the present Indian State and its replacement by a People's Democratic State. For this the Communist Party shall strive to rouse the entire peasantry and the working class against the feudal exploiters, strengthen the alliance between the working class and the peasantry, a broad nation-wide United Front of all anti-imperialist classes (including the national bourgeoisie) sections, groups, parties and elements willing to fight for democracy and for freedom and independence of India.

'While resorting to all forms of struggle, including the most elementary forms, and while utilising all legal possibilities for mobilising the masses and taking them forward in the struggle for freedom and democracy, the Communist Party has always held that in the present colonial set-up in India and in view of the absence of genuine democratic liberties, legal and Parliamentary possibilities are restricted and that therefore the replacement of the present state upholding the imperialist-feudal order by a People's Democratic State is possible through an armed revolution of the people'.

'Partisan war', the document continues, 'must be one of the major weapons in our armoury as in the case of all colonial countries. But this weapon alone cannot ensure victory. It has to be combined with the other major weapons, that of strikes of the working class, general strike and uprising in the cities led by armed detachments of the working class. Therefore in order to win victory of the popular democratic revolution, it is absolutely essential to combine two basic factors–the partisan war of the peasants and workers' uprisings in the cities . . .

'With hundreds of streams of partisan struggles merging with the general strikes and uprising of the workers in the cities, the enemy will find it impossible to concentrate his forces anywhere and defeat the revolutionary forces but will himself face defeat and annihilation. Even inside the armed forces of the Government the crisis will grow and big sections will join the forces of revolution . . .

'As the crisis matures, as the unity, consciousness and organisation of the masses grows, as strength and influence of the Party develop and as the enemy resorts to more and more ruthless measures to crush the agrarian movement, the question of when, where and how to resort to arms, will be more and more forced on the agenda. As the question is of immense practical importance it is absolutely necessary that the Party will be able to give a clear and unambiguous answer to it . . .

'It is also necessary that, while utilising all legal possibilities, the existing illegal apparatus of the Party is strengthened enormously'.

The thesis then goes on to postulate, apart from political and economic crises, the following preconditions to success: (1) Partisan warfare after adequate preparation in 'topographically suitable areas'; (2) 'The need of proximity of friendly states across the border which would asure the partisans of a safe and friendly rear'.

Armed with this weapon, the Indian communist leaders set to work and prepared a Policy Statement which could be made available to their rank and file and to the general public without impairing the conditions of legality which were so essential on the eve of general elections. That Policy Statement, which was published in May 1951, turned out to be nothing but a clever rehash of the Tactical Line document, following closely the reasons and directives but omitting what could not be published for reasons of expediency or legality. Even what it omitted to say was only thinly veiled. This was adopted, as we shall see presently, with very minor amendments at the All-India Party Conference in October, 1951.

A few extracts from this document[11] show how closely the public Policy Statement followed the secret Tactical Line:

'The Communist Party has adopted a programme, in which it says that it "regards as quite mature the task of replacing the present anti-popular and anti-democratic Government by a new Government of People's Democracy" . . . "Who should form such a Government? The programme says that it will be created 'on the basis of coalition of all democratic, anti-feudal and anti-imperialist forces in the country" . . . There are a large number of people who think that this Government can be replaced by a People's Democratic Government by utilising the parliament ushered in by the new Constitution . . . "Even the most hardened liberal would now feel ashamed to maintain, let alone the Communist Party and other democrats and revolutionaries, that this Government and the classes that keep it in power will ever allow us to carry out a fundamental democratic transformation in the country by parliamentary methods alone. Hence, the road that will lead us to freedom and peace, land and bread, as outlined in the Programme of the Party, as to be found elsewhere . . ."

'For a time, it was advocated that the main weapon in our struggle would be the weapon of general strike of industrial workers, followed by countrywide insurrection as in Russia. Later, on the basis of a wrong understanding of the lessons of the Chinese Revolution, the thesis was put forward that since ours is a semi-colonial country like China, our revolution would develop in the same way as in China, with partisan war of the peasantry as its main weapon . . .

'After a long discussion, running for several months, the Party has now arrived at a new understanding of the correct path . . .

'We are essentially a colonial country, with a vast majority of our people living on agriculture. Most of our workers also are directly connected with the peasantry and interested in the problem of land . . .

'That makes the struggle of the peasantry of prime importance . . .

'The CC finds that drawing upon the Chinese experience in this way and to come to such a conclusion would mean neglecting to look to other factors of the Chinese Revolution and also neglecting to look into our own specific conditions . . .

'We cannot fail to take note of the fact that when the Chinese Party began to lead the peasantry in the liberation struggle, it had already an army which it inherited from the split in the Revolution of 1925 . . . We cannot fail to note the fact that China had no unified and good communication system, which prevented the enemy from carrying out concentrated and swift attacks on the liberation forces. India is different in this respect from China, in that it has a comparatively more unified, well-organised and far-flung system of communications . . .

'India has a far bigger working class than China had during her march of freedom . . .

'Further, we cannot fail to note the fact that the Chinese Red Army was surrounded and threatened with annihilation again and again until it reached Manchuria. There, with the industrial base in hand, and the great friendly Soviet Union in the rear, the Chinese Liberation Army, free from the possibility of any attack in the rear, rebuilt itself and launched the final offensive which led it to victory. The geographical situation in India in this respect is altogether different . . .

'This does not mean that there is nothing in common between us and China, excepting the stage of our revolution and its main tasks. On the contrary, like China, India is of vast expanses. Like China, India has a vast peasant population. Our revolution, therefore, will have many features in common with the Chinese Revolution. But peasant struggles along the Chinese path alone cannot lead to victory in India . . .

'It can thus be seen that while the previous line of reliance on the general strike in the cities neglected the role of the peasantry, the subsequent one of partisan struggle minimised the role of the working class . . .

'Both the lines in practice meant ignoring the task of building the alliance of the working class and the peasantry as the basis of the United National Front, ignoring the task of building the United National Front, ignoring the task of putting the working class at the head of this Front in the liberation struggle . . .

'The working class, relying on agricultural workers and poor peasants, in firm alliance with the peasantry, together with the whole people, leads the battles in towns and rural areas to liberation, to land and bread, to work and peace . . .

'This understanding will also show to comrades that the main question is not whether there is to be armed struggle or not, the main question is not whether to be non-violent or violent. It is our opponents who pose for us the question whether our creed is violence or non-violence. Such a poser is a poser of Gandhian ideology, which in practice misleads the masses, and is a poser of which we must steer clear. All action of the masses in defence of their interests to achieve liberation is sacrosanct . . .

'But one action history does not sanction and that is individual terrorism . . .

'The question that now remains, and an important one, is: we have got the path and the perspective, but what now ? . . .

'It would be gross exaggeration to say that the country is already on the eve of an armed insurrection or revolution, or that civil war is already raging in the country . . .

'Equally wrong are they who see only the disunity of the popular forces, only the offensive of reaction, and advocate a policy of retreat in the name of regrouping of forces . . .

'Because insurrection and civil war do not exist, some would like to move and work as if they are living in a democracy with rights and liberties and nothing need be done to protect the Party and the leadership of mass organisations from onslaughts of the law run mad . . .

'We have to realise that although the masses are getting fast radicalised and moving into action in many parts of the country, the growth of the mass movement has not kept pace with the growth of discontent against the present Government and its policies and methods. To ascribe this to repression alone would be wrong. This weakness of the mass movement is due, above all, to the weakness of our Party and the division in the camp of progressive forces . . .

'It must be understood that because of the vast expanse of our country, because of the uneven development of the agrarian crisis and of the working class and peasant movement, and the uneven state of organisation and consciousness of the peasant masses and the influence of the Party, the peasant movement will not develop at the same tempo everywhere and different forms of organisation and struggle will have to be adopted, depending on the maturity of the crisis, the degree of unification of the peasant masses and their mood, the strength and the influence of the Party and other factors . . .

'All these tasks call for the most intense, patient and daily work among the masses, continuous agitation on our basic programme and immediate, simple demands of the people, a concrete working out of such demands for every section of the people according to general and local conditions, practical leadership of mass struggles, a combination of various forms of struggles, and a systematic building up of a network of mass organisations . . .

'One of the key tasks that faces us in defence of the people is that of building of the peace movement . . .

'We must bring into the consciousness of the people that while we support any move of any class or group including this Government for preserving peace, yet we must not forget that this Government, under the influence of imperialist warmongers, landlords and profiteers, follows not a consistent and honest policy of peace but plays between America and England to gain from their rivalries and also plays between the peace-loving countries and warmongers. Such inconsistency must be overcome by the action of the masses . . .'

The Party Programme made a detailed analysis of the situation in India; India was still a dependent semi-colonial country. The keys to military and naval defence were held by the British. Four years of the Nehru Government had belied the hopes of the masses in every respect. The people were convinced by their experience that the Congress Government was pledged to the protection and preservation of British capital, parasitic landlords and the princes. Promises made to the people had been broken in all spheres. Civil liberties had been suppressed. After making this analysis, the Politbureau declared that its immediate objective was the first stage of revolution in a semi-colonial country and that, in view of the backwardness of the economic development of India and of the weakness of the mass organisations of the workers, peasants and the toiling intelligentsia, the Party did not find it possible to carry out immediately a socialist transformation in the country and was therefore not demanding the immediate establishment of socialism. The Politbureau, however, regarded as quite mature the task of replacing the present anti-democratic and anti-popular government by a new government of People's Democracy, created on the basis of a coalition of all democratic anti-feudal and anti-imperialist forces in the country, capable of effectively guaranteeing the rights of the people.

The practical tasks to be carried out by the new 'People's Democratic Government' would be:

In the field of State structure, assuring the sovereignty of the people, unhampered freedom of conscience, speech, press, assembly and strike, the recognition of the right of all nationalities to self-determination, the reconstitution of the present artificial States into national States, and the replacement of the police by a people's militia.

In the field of Agriculture, confiscation of land from the landlords without compensation and distribution to the peasants.

In the field of Industry, protection of national industries against competition from foreign goods, living wage for the worker, an eight-hour day and a forty-four hour week.

In the field of National Independence, severance from the Commonwealth, confiscation of all factories, banks, etc, owned by foreigners.

In the field of Foreign Policy, India needed peace and peaceful development and the chief enemy of peace and advocate of an aggressive war now was the United States of America. India should stop 'carrying on a suspicious play between the two international camps' and 'flirting with the United States of America' and form a united front with the peace-loving countries. India should also stop wrangling with Pakistan and conclude a firm alliance of friendship and mutual assistance with her and Ceylon.

The claim made by the communists that the Draft Programme and the Statement of Policy had the support of the international communist leadership was undoubtedly well founded in view of the knowledge later available of the secret Tactical Line. Proof of international backing was to be found in the prompt publication of the Draft Programme in the Cominform Journal of 11th May and the publication of the Statement of Policy in the Cominform Journal of 15th June, within a fortnight of its issue in India.

At the meeting of the Central Committee held in May 1951, at the conclusion of which the policy statement was issued, Rajeshwar Rao, who had succeeded Ranadive in June 1950 as General Secretary of the Party, resigned as Secretary.

The Central Committee decided that the Politbureau itself should function as the Secretariat of the Central Committee and appointed A. K. Ghosh as the Secretary of the secretariat. It was announced that an All India Party Conference would be 'convened shortly for concretising the programme and effecting necessary changes in the Central leadership of the Party'. The Central Committee resolved to readmit P. C. Joshi to the Party.

Implementation of New Programme

The second half of 1951 was marked by efforts to reorganise and rebuild the Party machine which had cracked under the stress of internal dissentions. Provincial Conferences were held in most States and delegates elected to an All-India Party Conference.

Controversies still continued, however, between Dange and his followers who wanted the adoption *in toto* of the Party's Draft programme and policy as approved by the International Communist Movement, and A. K. Gopalan who was understood to have expressed the view that the Draft Programme might be amended if found necessary before final acceptance. The personal rivalry between these two men for Party leadership appeared to be coming to a head. This might have accounted for Dange's sudden appearance before a Magistrate in Bombay on 17th August 1951 after having been 'wanted' in connection with a prosecution pending against him for several months.

The Commission appointed to investigate into the conduct of Ranadive and other former members of the Politbureau submitted its recommendations during this period and the Central Committee decided on suspensions ranging from six months to a year. Action against B. T. Ranadive and G. M. Adhikari, the former heads of the Party, was however deferred until they had clarified certain points put to them. The charge of Trotskyite-Titoite connection against them was withdrawn.

An attempt to appropriate Independence Day, 15th August, became manifest in 1951. The Party Secretariat called for demonstrations all over India on that day 'to expose the real nature of the rule that the Congress has imposed in the country during the four years of its rule' and to pledge themselves to destroy its rule. An appeal to defeat Congress candidates in the ensuing elections was made on that day, at meetings in various parts of the country. The public response to this attempted misappropriation of a patriotic occasion was, however, very disappointing.

The Secretariat of the CC of the CPI welcomed the Indian Government's decision not to sign the Japanese Peace Treaty at San Francisco. It regretted, however, that the Indian Government did not come out openly against the stationing of American troops and did not propose immediately to press for the immediate return of Formosa to Communist China. It asserted that these omissions and clarifications were not accidental and indicated the 'powerful pull of reactionaries who wanted the country to fall in line with the Anglo-Americans'. The Secretariat also argued that the Indian Government should have been represented at San Francisco and joined hands with 'the forces of peace' to oppose the American draft treaty. 'The forces of democracy and peace in India' were therefore asked to bring pressure on the Indian Government.

By October 1951, dissensions in the Party were to a large extent ironed out resulting in the holding of the All-India Party Conference, the reorganisation of the Politbureau and the Central Committee and the finalising of the policy and programme of the Party. Provincial units of the Party were instructed to rebuild the organisation and regain mass contact.

All-India Party Conference

The All-India Party Conference was held 'underground' in Calcutta for six days from 11th to 15th October 1951. Thirty-two out of forty-four delegates attended. Andhra, Assam, Orissa and Madhya Pradesh were not represented.

A new Politbureau, with A. K. Ghosh as General Secretary and S. A. Dange, Jyoti Basu, Muzzafar Ahmed, P. RamaMurthy, E. M. S. Namboodiripad and one member from Andhra, was set up. Sixteen members of the CC (consisting of twenty-one members) were unanimously elected, leaving five seats to be filled later. Among these were Z. A. Ahmed, S. S. Yusuf of UP, Y. D. Sharma of Delhi, Sohàn Singh Josh of Punjab, Ranen Sen of Bengal, S. Y. Deshpande of Bombay, A. K. Gopalan of Kerala, Romesh Chandra of *Cross Roads*. A Central Commission was set up with S. V. Ghate, K. C. George, Dr B. K. Basu, Karyanand Sharma, K. Satyanarayan, while the Agit-Prop Committee consisted of S. A. Dange, S. V. Deshpande, Sardar Jafri, Romesh Chandra and Victor Kaul of *Cross Roads*. Those elected reflected an increase in the influence of urban working–class leaders like Ghosh, Dange and Ghate, alongside of adequate representation to rural areas where armed guerrilla struggle had been launched.

The draft Programme and Statement of Policy placed before the Party in May were adopted after minor amendments had been made. B. T. Ranadive's defiant explanation and mild self-criticism were not accepted but a move for his expulsion was unsuccessful. The Andhra Party having accepted responsibility for his good behaviour, Ranadive was suspended for two years. Similarly, Dr G. M. Adhikari was suspended for one year.

The Conference resolved to congratulate the Telengana fighters but considered it inadvisable to continue guerrilla warfare. It authorised the new Central Committee to announce the unconditional withdrawal of the struggle and to contact the Hyderabad State Government to permit communist functionaries to tour the region to implement this decision and to release all *detenus* there. The Andhra CP had already abandoned guerrilla activities.

The Conference decided that the Constitution Committee should be appointed by the Politbureau to revise the Constitution of the Party and make it less bureaucratic.[12]

The printed programme issued by the Politbureau was adopted by the All-India Conference. This was nothing but the draft Programme of May 1951 with very minor amendments.

After the Conference, Dange held a press conference in Calcutta on 19th October where he stated that the question of violence and non-violence as a creed did not arise and that the masses could resort to an armed uprising if they so desired in certain circumstances. Dange claimed a Party membership of 30,000 in India.

Terrorist Activities

Since an outstanding feature of communist activity throughout the years 1950 and 1951 was the remarkable way in which the campaign of violence in Telengana, Andhra, Tripura and Manipur went hand in hand with a campaign for 'Peace', a reference to this two-faced policy becomes essential.

In Telengana, communist terrorism in the latter part of 1950 continued unabated. Between October and December 1950, there were no less than 344 serious incidents, including 96 murders, 151 attacks on the police and military, and 82 attacks on the home guards and village officials. The police killed during that period 223 communists and arrested 143. They recovered 57 guns, 3 SBMI guns and 12 rifles, along with ammunition and explosives. Towards the end of 1951, there was a decrease in terrorism.

In Tripura, a number of villagers were kidnapped, some of them being forced to work for the Party; others who were not suitable for such work were released.

In Manipur, the communist Irabat Singh contacted communist leaders in Burma to arrange for the training of Red Guards from Manipur and for the deputation of certain Burmese communists to function in the State. Seven decoities in the month of July 1951 alone yielded the communists Rs 42,947, while another in August gave them another Rs 1,000.

'Peace'

Alongside of this campaign of terror, the Peace Movement was intensified. In order to broaden the basis of the All India Peace Council, a Special Convention was fixed to meet in Bombay on 28th and 29th October 1950. For the purpose of organising the Second All India Peace Congress, a preparatory committee consisting of Dr M. Atal as President, Mr Krishna Chander as Secretary, and Dr Mulk Raj Anand, K. A. Abbas, K. M. Joglekar, R. K. Karanjia (Editor of *Blitz*), Romesh Thapar (Editor of *Cross Roads*) and four others was formed. Slogans given by the World Partisans of Peace were duly reiterated.

The Joint Secretary of the All India Peace Committee wrote to the communist Jambhekar in Prague that they had been able to collect 671,089 signatures on the Stockholm Peace Appeal by November 1950.

The efforts of the Communist Party to obtain the support of other 'Leftist' Parties in their 'Peace' propaganda met with some success, the Forward Communist Party, the Forward Bloc and the Workers and Peasants Party extending their co-operation. At an All Peace Conference held in Delhi on 19th November, Pandit Sunderlal, an old Congressman and former devotee of Gandhi, claimed that Lenin and Stalin were greater lovers of peace than Mahatma Gandhi.

The Cominform did not, however, appear to be satisfied by these efforts. Jambhekar, Indian 'representative' on the Permanent Committee of the Partisans of Peace, wrote from Prague that the World Bureau had decided to render 'guidance' to the All India Peace Committee through their personel representatives. One of these emerged in the person of Pablo Neruda, *alias* Neftali Reyes, the Chilean poet in exile and a member of the World Peace Committee, who utilised the facilities to visit the country granted to him to meet communist cells in the country.

The Second All India Peace Congress was planned to meet in Delhi in March 1951. This Conference was, however, banned in Delhi and the Government of India decided that foreign delegates would not be allowed to enter India in any event. The refusal to allow foreign delegates appeared to have caused considerable concern among the communists. It would appear that this decision upset the idea of holding a session of the Central Committee of the CPI at the same place as the Peace Congress and of obtaining suggestions on the Party's organisational problems from the foreign emissaries attending the Peace Congress. That Congress was thereupon held in Bombay instead. Four hundred delegates met in Bombay under the banner: 'India can halt War'. The Convention endorsed the appeal for a Five-Power Pact of Peace issued by the World Peace Council in Berlin in February 1951.

A notable feature of this Convention was that the known communists kept scrupulously in the background and put forward prominent members of the Congress Party, artists and writers. Speaker after speaker got up to insist that he was not a communist. It was decided that Peace Committees should be organised with instructions to infiltrate into the ranks of all parties in every State, district and village.

Immediately following the Peace Congress, an Indo-China Friendship Association was inaugurated by the same people, but as if from a different platform.

Despite all these activities, self-criticism continued. The Politbureau stated in a circular that the peace movement in India had been suffering from both left and right deviations and stressed the need for avoiding sectarianism. 'At the same time', it added, 'some of the Party workers had betrayed wrong and opportunist tendencies, and had looked upon the Nehru Government's foreign policy as almost a genuine peace policy'. It explained that 'Nehru's foreign policy is essentially a policy of manoeuvre between the main enemy of peace, America, and its partner, Britain, on the one hand, and peace-loving countries on the other. Nehru fears the consequences of a world war and therefore advocates a policy of "moderation", of not going "too far". At the same time the Indian Government continues to be an active member of the British Commonwealth which is a partner of American imperialism in aggressive wars'. Therefore, the Politbureau directed that 'the peace movement, while supporting all those specific acts of the Government which hamper the plans of the warmongers, *eg* Nehru's declaration against the atom bomb and the vote against American proposal to denounce People's China in the UNO, must also simultaneously point out the half-hearted and vacillating nature of the Government's policy, and wage a determined battle to mobilise mass opinion in favour of a consistent peace policy'. It categorically stated that the peace movement was not a pacifist movement, but a fighting movement for concrete action in defence of peace, and hence it 'must fight against all attempts to sow hostility against the Chinese People's Republic. It must explain to the people how the liberation of Tibet is not a threat to peace, but a decisive blow against the instigators of war, and uphold the heroic action of the Chinese volunteers who, by smashing the plans of the American warmongers to enslave the Korean and Chinese peoples, strengthened the cause of world peace. The Peace movement must also wage a determined battle against slanders against the Soviet Union'.

The All India Peace Committee continued to receive international direction. The Secretary of the World Peace Council informed Krishnan Chander, the Secretary of the All India Peace Committee, that the Indian peace movement was making quick progress and as such it (World Peace Council) intended to employ a political staff of a Secretary and two or three others from India in the World Peace Council at Prague. The Indian Committee, was, therefore, requested to submit a list of candidates for consideration. The Secretariat of the World Federation of Democratic Youth had also decided to organise a competition for the collection of signatures between India and Indonesia. The Women's International Democratic Federation had directed India and Pakistan to take special interest in the forthcoming International Conference for the Defence of Children. The international Festival Committee for the Berlin Youth Festival informed the Indian branch that fifty free passages would be issued to the delegates from India.

United Front

Separate treatment of United Front activities of the Party is called for by reason of the long and persistent campaign by the international communist movement to switch the CPI on to that track.

The Central Committee of the party at its meeting in December 1950 stated in its resolution on 'United Front' that the Congress Government 'stands completely exposed before the masses'. As a result, there was an urge in all Leftist parties and elements to unite under a broad common programme of replacement of the present Government by a Democratic People's Government, pledged to the adoption of socialist measures at home and alignment with 'Progressive' countries abroad. The Communist Party of India, therefore, called upon all Democratic and anti-imperialist parties to come together on the basis of an agreed programme and to unite to fight for the realisation of the common objective, and build up united mass organisations such as Trade Unions, Kisan Sabhas (Peasant Unions), Student Unions. To establish contact between the various parties and groups and to establish a machinery for joint work were among the immediate tasks that should be undertaken. While the Communist Party envisaged the possibilities of enlisting the support of 'many honest and sincere people in the Congress', the Right-wing leadership of the Socialist Party was to be left severely alone.

This greater emphasis on the unity of the 'Left' was obviously inspired by the pressure of the CPGB which wanted the CPI to develop a broad national anti-imperialist Front, which had become the cornerstone of Moscow's policies in the countries of Asia. The Cominform Journal had indeed described this as one of the three basic tasks.

Despite all this prompting and prodding, the United Front did not appear to make much headway. The Socialists continued to be opposed to the United Front, and Aruna Asaf Ali, who had developed communist tendencies, was removed from membership of the Socialist Party. Smaller Marxist groups like the Forward Bloc and the Peasants' and Workesr' Party did, however, join up.

The application of the slogan of the United Front in so far as it affected specific sections of the people, such as workers, peasants, students and the Services may now briefly be reviewed.

Trade Unions

In a circular to all party units *On the Key Tasks of the Trade Union Front and Trade Union Unity*, the Central Committee had at the end of 1950 expressed the view that, though a few legal possibilities still existed, repression by the authorities was increasing and was likely to be further intensified and therefore, while exploiting the legal possibilities with care and tact, the revolutionary trade unions

I

should orientate towards illegal trade unionism as the principal form of organisation. It advised that economic and political strikes should be so conducted as not to give scope to the authorities to smash and annihilate the fighting capacity of the classes, but to conserve, preserve and nourish its fighting forces so as to deliver powerful blows at the enemy at the opportune and crucial moment. It had pointed out that it was difficult to give all-embracing directions and had directed the local leadership to act with initiative and adopt flexible and elastic tactics with good judgment, depending on the situation at a particular place.

At the same time, it had stressed that the working classes must realise that, without overthrowing the imperialists and their native stooges in India, no fundamental betterment of the workers' situation was possible. The perspective was not of a general strike and the capture of the cities leading to armed rebellion in the rural areas, but just the opposite. The perspective was armed guerrilla resistance in rural areas linked with and based on agrarian revolution, the gradual establishment of liberated bases and the setting up of liberation armies for the purpose of finally overthrowing the government.

Criticising the views of those, including R. Palme Dutt, who held that the four principles of the Chinese path, namely the building up of a united front, ensuring the leadership of the Communist Party in that front, building up a Communist Party equipped with the theory of Marxism and Leninism, and the setting up of liberated bases and people's liberation armies, wherever and whenever possible, were to be taken independently of the rest and should as a rule be taken in the order in which they had been mentioned and that armed struggle should come last and at a very remote date, the Central Committee held that all these four principles were inseparable and formed an integral part of the whole and must be followed simultaneously. Whilst recognising that differences existed between conditions obtaining in China and India, it held that those differences were secondary and auxiliary and could not affect the fundamental character of the struggle.

This circular, which had been issued by the Central Committee, which included members of both the Rajeshwar Rao and Dange groups, indicated that most of the leading Indian communists were not thinking of giving up violent activities.

Since neither the INTUC nor the Hind Mazdoor Sabha was prepared to contemplate unity with the AITUC, the only progress made in this field was in relation to a splinter group based on Calcutta called the United Trade Union Congress. At a Working Committee meeting of the All India Trade Union Congress in Calcutta, the communists admitted their responsibility for disruption in some of the trade unions and promised to give up left-sectarianism in future. Twenty-five resolutions, which included ratification of a formula for unity with the UTUC, were passed and a committee was set up for working out a concrete programme for joint day-to-day work by the All India Trade Union Congress and the United Trade Union Congress.

From April 1951, the new communist line for trade unions became more defined and clear. An intensive programme for a 'popular front' was on the order of the day. Consequently, 'left' trade unions were asked to merge and the call was made for only 'one union in each industry'.

Efforts were made to infiltrate into the All India Railwaymen's Federation and this took the form of the 'dissolution' of the communist-controlled All India Union of Railway Workers. Regret was expressed by the communist-controlled unions and re-affiliation to the AIRF solicited. The leadership of the AIRF, under Jayaprakash Narayan, the socialist leader, however, saw through the game and opposed the readmission of communist unions. The communists decided nontheless to continue their efforts to get back with the help of non-socialist functionaries in the organisation.

The Politbureau circulated to party workers instructions on a railway strike to the Bengal Provincial Organising Committee. Support was to be given to the strike ballot and unity demanded. The Politbureau, however, warned that 'due care must be taken not to sacrifice all the cadres in the campaign and to guard their safety including that of the unexposed members in the workshops'. How best to combine safety and activity was left to the discretion of the local branches.

Though the importance of the peasantry as the main backbone

of the communist cause had been stressed, attempts made to revive the activities of the defunct All-India Kisan Sabha appeared to be lacking in punch. Bankim Mukherji was authorised to reorganise it as an open and legal body.

Students

A great deal of attention was devoted to students and youth under constant spurring from the International Union of Students and the World Federation of Democratic Youth.

Attempts were made to put new life in the moribund Party front, the All India Students' Federation. These took many forms. Thus, two Chinese students, Miss Wang Chi and Miss Wang Yu-Lu, came to India under the pretext of attending a non-party medical conference in Madras. They attended two receptions given to them by the communist students in Madras, and subsequently attended the Punjab Students' Federation Conference at Jullundur on 9th February, where they stated that the situation and the objective conditions in India were similar to those in China and presented a similar challenge to the students. They presented books, photographs of Mao Tse-tung, a banner of peace and some cash to the Punjab Students' Federation on behalf of the International Union of Students and the Union of Students in Poland.

The International Union of Students sent a request to the AISF to send an observer to the next Executive Committee meeting to be held in Peking round about May 1951 in addition to the Indian Executive member, Miss Sushila Madiman.

A competition was organised between the AISF and the Indonesian Students' Organisation. Badges of honour were offered for those who collected the largest number of signatures.

The International Union of Students invited an Indian delegation a hundred strong, including a cultural squad and a sporting team, to be sent to the World Youth Festival in 1951 in Berlin. A permanent delegate to the International Headquarters was also invited.

The International Festival Committee of the 'Third World Festival' launched an 'International Solidarity Fund' to finance the expenditure of the delegates from colonial and dependent countries so as to enable them to attend the festival in large numbers. The Fund was expected to provide free passage and free stay in Berlin to some of the delegates who might not be able to afford it.

The All India Students' Federation, in its turn, issued a circular endorsing the decision of the Berlin session of the World Peace Council starting a world-wide agitation for the signing of a 'pact of peace between the five great powers' and that of the International Conference of Teachers, Scientists and Cultural Workers to bring about closer cultural co-operation amongst the different nations and people. It stressed that a signature campaign for the Five Power Peace Pact was the best means of mobilising all sections of the organised and unorganised youth in India.

The President of the Third World Festival of Youth and Students for Peace suggested to the National Festival Committee in India to set up a solidarity fund and collect donations for the international fund which would aid the oppressed youth in the 'colonial and dependent countries including Latin America, Africa, Middle East, South-East Asia, the Far East and the Republican Spain, Portugal and Greece'. In order to step up the collection of signatures for the Berlin appeal, the Secretariat of the International Union of Students promised to invite those students who would collect a large number of signatures as guests to the Berlin Festival and pay for their expenses. Dissatisfied with the progress made, arrangements appeared to have been made for the deputation of Moss, a well-known communist student from Britain, to study the situation in India and advise the AISF.

At a meeting of the AISF held in Delhi from 1st to 3rd June and 7th to 11th June 1951, a resolution was passed appealing to students not to join the National Union of Students, which it was proposed to establish as a non-political non-partisan body representative of Indian students. When, however, preparations for the election of delegates to the Convention of the NUS went ahead briskly, the communists decided to try and disrupt the Convention by getting some of their activists elected as delegates. The election results showed that they were able to elect hardly a score of young men and women.

When the Convention met in Bombay with M. R. Masani as Chairman of its Reception Committee and with Pandit Nehru and Mr Jayaprakash Narayan, the Congress and Socialist chiefs on its platform, it was obvious that the communist attempt to render the Convention abortive was doomed to failure. All the same, it took three gruelling days to get the constitution and statutes of the organisation adopted and the office-bearers elected, in the face of unflagging communist attempts to obstruct the work and break up the Convention. In the end, the communist group walked out of the Convention.

The Friends of the Soviet Union, an outstanding Communist Party front, turned its attention to the economic sphere. It considered the incorporation of the promotion of Indo-Soviet trade and economic co-operation among its aims and seemed to have come to the conclusion that real friendship was best based on economic ties.

The Politbureau issued a circular entitled 'Friends of China Societies' calling for the establishment of these fronts. Party workers were asked to establish provincial and district committees and call for closer alliance between Indian and Communist China, and thus bring pressure to bear on the Indian Government.

The Secretariat of the Central Committee issued a statement protesting against the 'outrageous frame-up called the Rawalpindi Conspiracy Case' and also gave a call for India-wide agitation to save the communist leaders who had been accused in that case. A Rawalpindi Case Fair Trial Committee, with Dr Mulk Raj Anand as Chairman and Mr Rajani Patel, Barrister-at-Law, as Secretary, was set up in this connection.

Infiltration into Services

Attempts by communists to suborn the loyalty of the lower ranks of the armed forces and the police took the form of cyclostyled leaflets in Urdu and English appealing to the police and to the troops to desert their offices, murder their officers and join the Communist Party. In Hyderabad, a Telugu pamphlet entitled

Appeal to the Military and Police issued by the Area Committee of the Hyderabad State Committee was found in circulation.

In Tripura, the communists succeeded to some extent in suborning the loyalty of the police and the military by a combination of persuasion and threats. Many sepoys complained that members of their families were being harassed in order to force them to join or to help the communists.

In Delhi, workers were exhorted to infiltrate among the troops and try to convert soldiers, and the Russian and Chinese examples were held out.

Opulence

Once the programme dictated by the international organisation in the beginning of 1951 had been accepted and the Party leadership transformed, there were manifestations that the financial position of the Party began to mend. No doubt, a certain amount of money was raised in India itself. Thus, in Pepsu the Lal CP managed to collect funds for buying arms. A hundred rupees per plough were reported to have been collected in the Eastern districts resulting in a considerable amount.

It was obvious, however, that the money locally raised could account for only a fraction of the funds that were now being expended on the maintenance of a huge army of paid functionaries throughout the country. As the time for polling in the General Elections approached, startling signs of the Party's sudden opulence became visible. In the State of Andhra, this took the form of a fleet of cars and jeeps used for campaigning purposes and later the purchase of an expensive rotary printing plant for starting a daily in the Telegu language. It was widely asserted that, except for the ruling Congress Party, the Communist Party had more funds available for the election campaign than any other in India.

CHAPTER EIGHT

General Elections

At the end of 1952, the Union of India had its first general elections. For the first time in the nation's history, every man and woman over twenty-one years had a vote in determining the country's government and destiny. The electorate numbered about 176 million – the largest in the world – a great part of it illiterate. There were 90,000 polling stations, 224,000 polling booths, 620 million ballot papers.

The Communist Party geared itself to meet this opportunity and challenge. As has been described in the previous chapter, the Party had been smitten with dissensions till the end of 1950 but it had managed in the first half of 1951 to patch up the differences in its ranks and put up a show of unity on the basis of the United Front Programme outlined by the Cominform Journal and R. Palme Dutt on behalf of the international movement. The Draft Programme and Statement of Policy which the Party issued after the re-constitution of the Politbureau was the plank on which the Party entered the campaign for the general elections scheduled to take place towards the end of the year. On 6th August, the CPI issued its Election Manifesto. The change of policy implicit in these documents was endorsed by the Conference of the CP held in Calcutta in October 1951. From then on, the new Politbureau and Central Committee saw to it that the entire energies of the party units throughout the country were harnessed to the election campaign. Muzzafar Ahmed had already been selected as President of the Central Election Board. Later, when Dange emerged from the 'underground', he was appointed Secretary of the Election Board in place of Jyoti Basu.

Perhaps at this stage it would be worth while dealing in some detail with some of the main planks in the communist platform for the general elections.

Land

Land reform has been claimed to be one of the main planks of the communist programme in India and the slowness in achieving agrarian reform has constituted one of the strongest and most plausible grounds for communist propaganda against the Congress administration since the achievement of independence.

India to-day undoubtedly presents a sorry spectacle of a predominantly rural economy unable to support itself. The causes are numerous. To enumerate only a few, methods of cultivation are antiquated; holdings are small and uneconomic; draught and flood are regular visitors; and irrigation is confined to somewhat limited areas. The land is burdened with a vast population of landless labourers many of whom are surplus. The peasant in general lacks the incentive to grow more food and the finance to invest in the land to increase its yield.

The Congress administration have been committed to the abolition of absentee landlordism and the elimination of intermediaries between the State and the tiller of the soil. The pace, however, has been slow. There has been difficulty in raising the funds with which the dispossessed landlords are to be compensated. The State has found this burden too heavy to bear and the peasants have shown unwillingness to share it.

The Draft Programme of the CPI considered the agricultural problem to be of primary importance. It was necessary, according to the draft programme, 'to hand over landlords' land without payment to the peasants and to legalise this reform in the form of a special land law; to ensure long-term and cheap credit for the peasants to enable them to purchase agricultural implements and the necessary seeds; to ensure long-term and cheap credit to small artisans to enable them to purchase raw materials, etc, and carry on their manufacture and trade; to ensure government assistance to the peasants in the improvement of old and the building of new irrigation systems; to cancel debts of peasants and small artisans to moneylenders; to ensure adequate wages and living conditions to agricultural labourers'.

Commenting on this rural programme in *Discussion Pamphlet* No. 1, published by the CPI, Prakash (the author) said that: 'basic agrarian reform is the core and content' of the anti-feudal and anti-imperialist revolution which the Party envisages as being necessary to free India. If the communists get power, they promise land will be handed over to the peasants and agricultural workers without payment. Peasant debts will be cancelled. No compensation will be paid to princes, big landlords and jagirdars whose property will be confiscated. The small landlords who own only a few acres will be helped to rehabilitate themselves or compensated where necessary. The peasant who gets land will not have to make any payment for it. Those landlords who want to be cultivators will get their due share of land like all peasants.

As regards the capitalist landlords who, in certain parts of India, own thousands of acres of land, adequate land will be left to them to pursue capitalist farming. The rest will be distributed among peasants and agricultural workers. The revolution will not harm the rich peasants. They, too, to some extent suffer from feudal exploitation and from usury and will therefore gain from the revolution. Agricultural workers will be given land wherever possible. Those who cannot be immediately provided with land of their own will get adequate wages and will be ensured human conditions of life.

The communists admit, however, that these reforms as contemplated will not effect a socialist transformation in the country. Two factors according to them constitute the impediment: (1) the backwardness of the economic development of India, and (2) weakness of the mass organisations of workers, peasants and the toiling intelligentsia.

Elucidating the point, Prakash asked in this *Discussion Pamphlet*: 'What has organisation and consciousness to do with possibility of establishment of socialism? Further, could India have established socialism even if she had strong organisation of workers and peasants?' In his opinion, socialism cannot be established immediately in a country with a backward economy. 'This is indisputable. Nevertheless, what *socialist measures* can be carried out in a country, to what extent *steps towards socialism* can be taken – the answer to this depends not only on the nature of the country's economy but also on the stage of consciousness and organisation of the masses'.

'Even in an advanced capitalist country, the rapidity with which the victorious People's Democracy will be able to carry out socialist transformation will depend on the consciousness and organisation of the working class, its capacity to master the technique of administration and management, its capacity to organise production efficiently.

'This is even more true in a backward colonial country. Nationalisation of land, which though itself not a socialist measure, is a big step towards socialism and towards the organisation of collective farming, cannot be carried out to-day and should not be attempted, not because our economy is backward, but because the peasant masses are not conscious of its need and cannot be organised on its basis . . .

'This does not mean that the People's Democratic State will not adopt any socialist economy owned by the State, a sector which will be of a socialist nature. This sector will consist of the properties of imperialists, feudals and national traitors to start with, and will gradually extend its scope depending on the needs of the people, and the growth of organisation and consciousness of the working class and other toiling masses and their unity.'

The Election Manifesto promised:

'The Government of People's Democracy will be a Government of all democratic parties, groups and individuals representing workers, peasants, middle classes and the national bourgeoisie, the bourgeoisie that stands for genuine industrialisation of the country and for the freedom and independence of India . . .

'It will cancel peasants' debts and transfer all lands and implements of landlords and princes, without payment to the landlords, without any price to the tillers of the soil, taking care to provide for the poorer sections of landlords and without harming the interests of the rich peasant. Agricultural workers will be assured adequate wages besides land. Freed from feudal exploitation and with their demand for land satisfied, the peasantry will be able to increase production of food and raw materials, build dams and irrigation works, stop flood with their vast man-power, feed the cities and towns and change the very face of the country as they are doing in China.'

Industry

Turning to the field of industry, the most prominent item of the communist programme was the confiscation of all foreign concerns and capital without payment of compensation. It was the contention of the communists that the economy of India was still run and controlled by British, American and other foreign imperialist interests. This thesis was elaborated by A. M. Dyankov in his *New Stage in India's Liberation Struggle*. The Election Manifesto elaborated this thesis as follows:

'Britishers continue to own or control our mines, our plantations, our oil wells and refineries, our jute mills, many of our engineering works and other concerns. They control our foreign trade, our banking and finance. With their investment of 600 crores of rupees and through their managing agencies, they get millions of rupees as profits and hold our economy in their death-grip, throttling all development, keeping us backward and dependent, refusing to supply us with capital goods with which we could develop our industries. They looted our people of goods and services worth 1,600 crores (Rs 16,000 million) in the war years promising to pay them back which they never did. They scaled down the sum to less than half and refused to release even the balance in accordance with our own requirements. They framed the Colombo Plan, the avowed aim of which is to keep India backward and dependent – a market for British goods, a source for cheap raw materials and cheap labour.

'To all this, to this continued hold of Britishers on our economy, to this colossal looting and swindling of our people, to this continued colonial status of India, the Nehru Government has been a willing party. Instead of confiscating British capital in India, it has begged the Britishers and Americans to invest more capital and assured them that they can ship out the profits. It has refused to break the tie with the British and Americans or even establish close trade relations with the democratic countries who could supply us with the capital goods we need.'

According to this Manifesto, a People's Democratic Government would 'break with the British Empire . . . (and) confiscate and nationalise all British capital in India . . . It will develop the industries of India with the aid of the nationalised capital and by enlisting the co-operation of the private industrialists who will be assured legitimate profits and protection of their interests'.

The Draft Programme of the Party further set out that

'we do not advocate at this stage of our revolution, the nationalisation, *ie*, confiscation by the State of all key industries as one of the items of our programme. We only stand for the confiscation of the properties of the British imperialists, feudals and national traitors'.

As communists,

'we stand for the abolition of all forms of exploitation of man by man, of all class distinction. But we know that our country is far from communism yet, far from socialism even. Hence, without renouncing our ultimate goal for a moment, we place before our people, those which we consider to be the immediate tasks, the tasks without carrying out which we cannot take even one step forward. And we fight against the present government not because it is not introducing socialism but, because by the selfish interests of the landlords, princes, imperialists and financiers linked with them, it is refusing to carry out even what it pledged itself to do.'

Perhaps the most important reason which is not mentioned for the adoption of such a modest programme was to win over the support of the majority of the Indian people to join in the 'United Front'. The Party was prepared to compromise even with the Indian 'vested interests' if they would work with the communists to overthrow the present Government and help the communists to get into power. The programme therefore was deliberately such as to command the widest possible support. It cannot be said that it failed altogether in its object of confusing and placating certain sections of the Indian bourgeoisie.

Linguistic States

The Indian States of to-day have in their contours survived from British times. Their boundaries, which were drawn for administrative convenience, include in several cases more than one linguistic group. The State of Bombay, for instance, has three language groups – Marathi, Gujarati and Kanarese.

Almost all parties in India, including the Indian National Congress, have in the past accepted the principle that the States into which the country is divided should be reconstituted on a linguistic basic with a view to giving each of these groups the fullest scope for developing its distinctive literature, thought and culture. There has been a very marked reluctance on the part of the Congress administration to avoid rushing through with this reform inspired by the fear that it might lead to an accentuation of already existing fissiparous tendencies. It is recalled that the origin of Pakistan also lay in the cry of a distinct Muslim culture and its right to free development.

Communist advocacy of the linguistic redistribution of States differs somewhat from that of other parties and is in a way much more far reaching. The communist theory is that each linguistic unit constitutes a separate nationality and that India is in fact a multi-lingual and multi-national State. The communists therefore demand not merely a readjustment of boundaries, but also that each State should be given the right of self-determination and even of secession, as they claim is the case in the USSR. It was on the basis of this theory that the CPI had throughout supported the Muslim League demand for a separate State, culminating in the vivisection of the country. Writing in the *People's Age* of 3rd August 1942, Mr B. T. Ranadive had this to say:

'What is the progressive essence of the Pakistan demand? The application of the principle of self-determination to certain nationalities in India. Muslims in certain areas do form a distinct nationality bound together by common culture, history and tradition. In consonance with the demands of justice and fair play, they must have the completest liberty to build their own life, liberty sanctioned by the *right to form a separate State if and when they chose.*

Unification of India cannot be built except on this basis of complete freedom of nationalities to accede.'

The theory is of course based on the alleged position in the USSR. Writing on the same subject in the issue of 19th March

1944, of *People's War*, Sajjad Zaheer, now Secretary of the Communist Party in Pakistan, had said: 'This is precisely the lesson we learn from the USSR. There the establishment of socialism, having eliminated the very basis of exploitation of man by man, and of oppression of one nation by another, it has been found that the tie which keeps the nationalities of the USSR together is the right to secede from the Union vested in each of the fifteen Constituent Republics. Even though each Republic has now got the right to keep its own national army and control its own foreign relations, it does not mean disintegration but a further strengthening of the bonds of unity between the free nations of the Soviet Union.'

In India, however, unity was destroyed; it led to partition and since then there has been no peace between the seceders (Pakistan) and the parent country. One trembles to think of what would have happened if every linguistic group had also asserted the right of secession. There would by now have been no India, but another Balkans.

A.M. Dyakov gave a rather detailed analysis of the Indian communist stand on the question of linguistic units in his *New Stage in India's Liberation Struggle*. According to him, the Congress had not created linguistic provinces because it would strengthen the anti-Congress and the so-called 'democratic elements' in some of these provinces. He also claimed that 'it is only the Communist Party of India which has put forward the slogan of a consistently democratic solution of the national question, *ie*, the right of all the nationalities of India to self-determination, including the right to secession and the formation of independent States'.

The Election Manifesto of the Communist Party promised in consequence that

'It will form national states by the abolition of the princely states and reconstruction of the present provinces, grant them wide powers including the right of self-determination, and create a united India by the voluntary consent of the nationalities and tribal peoples. It will grant regional autonomy to tribal people and national minorities wherever possible.'

Constitution

The Communist Party disapproves of the Indian Constitution on the ground that it is not democratic enough. The draft Programme of the CPI discussed these shortcomings as follows:

'In order to come forward as a Government of the people, after spending millions of the people's money on wrangling in Legislative Houses (1) the Government produced what it calls a democratic constitution and in terms of that constitution calls upon the people to elect a Government of their own choice and realise the fundamental rights given under the Constitution . . .

'While it is a fact that universal adult franchise now exists in the Constitution of India and it can and will be used by the people, it is a deception of the people to say that elections alone under this Constitution can end the landlord-capitalist rule in the country and the imperialist hold over its life. Adult franchise serves to gauge the maturity of the working class and the people and is formally an element of democracy but it cannot express the true will and the true interests of the exploited masses so long as land is not the property of peasants but that of landlords, so long as the power of landlords and capitalists holds the people in subjugation in fields and factories, so long as the power of capital over the press and means of propaganda drugs the people with lies, so long as the power of money utilises religious and caste frictions and rivalries to divide and to weaken the people, so long as the bureaucrats and the police ban political parties, suppress civil liberties and even imprison without trial even the elected representatives of the legislatures for their political opinions and for their honest work.[2]

'It is also a deception of the people to say that under the new Constitution the masses or the Government elected by them can work their way to freedom and happiness. The Constitution guarantees no rights to people which are enforceable in any way or which are not subject to violation by the emergency autocratic degrees of the bureaucracy, which is irremovable and inviolable. The right to strike, to living wage, to work and rest for the working class salaried employees is not guaranteed and made enforceable. The land of the landlords and the properties and incomes of the dethroned or enthroned princes are made inviolable. The landless peasants can have land, it appears, only if he can buy it or compensate the landlord for it . . . Thus, while the strangle-hold of landlords, princes and imperialists on our economy, land and capital is guaranteed by this Constitution[3] not a single item of the life and liberty of our masses is guaranteed, beyond stating them as pious illusory wishes.[4] The Constitution is not and cannot be called a true democratic constitution but is the constitution of a landlord-capitalist state, tied to foreign imperialist interests – mainly British.'

The Communist Party's suggestions in the field of State Structure were as follows:

'(1) The sovereignty of the people, *ie*, the concentration of power in the country in the hands of the people. The supreme power in the State must be vested entirely in the people's representatives who will be elected by the people and be subject to recall at any time upon a demand by the majority of electors, and who will constitute a single popular assembly, a single legislative chamber.

'(2) The restriction of the rights of the President of the Republic, in virtue of which the President and persons authorised by him will be deprived of the right to promulgate laws, which have not been passed by the legislature.

'(3) Universal, equal and direct suffrage of all male and female citizens of India who have attained the age of eighteen years in all elections to the Legislative Assembly and to the various local government bodies, secret ballot, the right of every voter to be elected to any representative institution, payment to people's representatives, proportional representation of political parties in all elections.

'(4) Local government on a wide scale and with wide powers through People's Committees. The abolition of all local and provincial authorities appointed from above.

'(5) Inviolability of person and domicile, unhampered freedom of conscience, speech, press, assembly, strike and combination; freedom of movement and occupation.

'(6) Equal rights for all citizens irrespective of religion, caste, sex, race or nationality; equal pay for equal work, irrespective of sex.

'(7) The right of all nationalities to self-determination. The Republic of India will unite the peoples of the various nationalities of India not by force but by their voluntary consent to the creation of a common state.

'(8) Reconstruction of the present artificial provinces or States with the dissolution of Princely States into the national States according to the principle of common language. The tribal area or areas where the

K

population is of specific composition and is distinguished by specific social conditions or constitutes a national minority will have complete regional autonomy and regional governments.

'(9) Introduction of progressive income-tax in industry, agriculture and trade and maximum relief in taxation for workers, peasants and artisans.

'(10) Right of the people to receive instruction in their own national language in schools; the use of national language in all public and State institutions. The use of Hindi as an all-India State language will not be obligatory.

'(11) The right of all persons to sue any official before a People's Court.

'(12) Separation of the State from all religious institutions. The State to be a secular State.

'(13) Free and compulsory primary education for the children of both sexes up to the age of fourteen.

'(14) Replacement of the police by militia. Elimination of the mercenary army and other punitive forces and the establishment of a national army, navy and air force for the defence of India, closely linked with the people.

'(15) The establishment of the People's health service with a wide network of medical centres and hospitals all over the country, designed to liquidate the centres of cholera, malaria and other epidemic diseases in the country.'

Foreign Policy

In the communist view, the foreign policy of India needs to be tuned in to that of the Soviet democratic bloc since they are the only protectors of world peace and progress. Laying down the 'foundations of foreign policy of India', the draft Programme of the CPI stated:

'India needs peace and peaceful development. She is interested in peace and economic co-operation with all States. In this respect, Britain is not an exception if she only proves capable of carrying on economic co-operation with India on the basis of full equality. India is not interested in the spurious play between peace and war, between partisans of peace and advocates of aggressive war, carried on by the present Indian Government.

'The chief enemy of peace and advocate of an aggressive war is now the United States of America, which has rallied round herself all the aggressive countries. This camp of war is facing the camp of peace which includes such states as the Soviet Union, the Chinese People's Republic and other countries of People's Democracy. Instead of joining hands with the partisans of peace against the aggressors and branding the United States of America as chief aggressor, the Indian Government is carrying on a suspicious play between those two camps, and is flirting with the U S A, thus facilitating the struggle of aggressors against peace-loving countries. What India needs is not play between peace and war, but a united front with peace-loving countries and friendship with them.'

The Election Manifesto of the Party went on to criticise Nehru's so-called independent policy of neutrality and stated:

'A Government tied to imperialism . . . cannot pursue an independent and progressive foreign policy, a genuine policy of peace. The issue of war or peace dominates the whole world to-day. It is the key issue facing every country, every people . . . Our people want to be free and independent. They want foreign troops to withdraw from all countries so that all countries may be free and independent. They want to establish close friendship and fraternal relations with their great neighbour China that after years of slavery and degradation has freed herself and is building a new life for her people. They have been thrilled by the epic struggle of the Korean people who defied the might of the American imperialists and defended their country in face of overwhelming odds. They hate the British imperialists who ruled us for hundreds of years and sympathise with the people of Malaya who are fighting against the same enemy. Our people love and respect the Soviet Union where the workers and peasants have freed themselves from all exploitation and showed to all people the path forward. They know that on every issue the Soviet Union has upheld the cause of the colonial people fighting for freedom.

'Our people want to live in friendship with the people of Pakistan and settle the issue of Kashmir by peaceful and democratic means which will enable the people of Kashmir to decide their own destiny without interference from imperialist powers that dominate the U N O . . . The Nehru Government took the issue of Kashmir to the U N O and paved the way for the machinations of the imperialists who have created a most dangerous situation of tension between India and Pakistan . . . The reactionary communalists, who hold power in Pakistan and who are taking conspiracy cases (a reference to the Pakistan Conspiracy case against army generals and communist functionaries[4]) to murder the best sons of the Pakistani people, have utilised the situation, to pose as defenders of the sovereignty and independence of Pakistan and mislead the Pakistani people.

'Instead of deposing the Maharaja of Kashmir, introducing genuine agrarian reform, giving land to the peasants, expelling the UNO arbitrator, removing the issue from UNO and making concrete proposals to end the military partition of Kashmir to enable the entire people of Kashmir to decide their destiny freely and jointly, the Nehru Government has followed a policy of seeking aid from imperialists, who want India and Pakistan to remain at loggerheads so that both may be weakened and the strategic area of Kashmir may be used for war against the Soviet Union and China.'

'Above all', said the Manifesto, 'our people love peace and hate war'. But the policy of the Nehru Government was not a policy of peace. It was a policy of manoeuvre between the camp of Peace and the bloc of warmongers. It was therefore most disappointing to the leaders of the Peace movement in India.

The CPI promised that, if returned to power at the general elections, 'it will fight for a pact of peace between all the great powers of the world, for prohibition of the atom bomb, for progressive disarmament, for the withdrawal of all foreign troops from all countries and the right for every nation to be free and independent. It will establish a pact of friendship and alliance with Pakistan, Ceylon and Nepal'.

'The foreign policy of the government must be a policy of joining hands with countries and forces that are upholding the cause of peace and of independence of all nations. There can be no neutrality in the battle between peace and war.'

Despite this strong criticism, however, the communists fully exploited the advantages to them of the foreign policy of the Indian Government. The failure of the United Nations forces effectively to defeat the Chinese Communist aggressors in Korea and the appearance of Chinese communist troops on India's frontiers with Tibet were used by the communists to try and intimidate members of the middle classes. Thus, after building up a picture of the inevitable triumph of the Soviet-Chinese bloc in the coming days,

Blitz (Bombay), a fellow-travelling journal, of 20th January 1951, had this to say in regard to an interview given by a lady who was the Vice-President of the Progressive Group in Bombay in which she had suggested that India's foreign policy should be re-orientated so as to align the country with the Democracies: 'She may not perhaps realise that shrewd observers consider this unsolicited démenti as evidence of her playing into the hands of the American propagandists. God forbid she may not live to regret these words'.

The effects of communist military successes in the Far East and in Tibet would not have perhaps amounted to much if they had been encountered by dynamic democratic leadership furnished by governmental leaders. As it happened, however, such pronouncements as came from these quarters did little to counteract the atmosphere in which the Communist Party in India could thrive. Thus, when spontaneous indignation was expressed throughout India at the Chinese communist invasion of Tibet in the face of definite assurance given to the Indian Government, the first wave of popular resentment was dispelled by an interview given on 30th October 1950, by the Prime Minister to *Reuter's* Diplomatic Correspondent, Sylvain Mangeot, in the course of which he expressed the view that the Chinese attack on Tibet was not the expression of any aggressive intentions but was based on a real, though unjustified, apprehension entertained in Peking that the USA was bent on destroying the new régime in China. The Prime Minister also declared later that the developments in Tibet constituted no threat to India's own security.

The Indian Prime Minister's contribution at the Commonwealth Conference and the reports of his statements in London and Paris roused *Blitz* of 13th January 1951, to an enthusiastic editorial entitled 'Brave Nehru,' in the course of which it wrote:

'The worst critics of the Prime Minister must confess that Jawaharlal Nehru played ball – and played it magnificently – with the cause of Peace, Progress and, above all, Asia, at the so-called "Commonwealth", Conference. We did not want him to go to London at all. We warned him of the "war trap" that was being set for him by more than one stooge of the New American Empire in the "British" Commonwealth. We knew that the Indian famine and the Kashmir crisis would be used to bribe, bully or blackmail the Prime Minister into a western war against Russia, China and Asia. Frankly we were afraid that Nehru might become an unwilling tool of this thieves' kitchen brewing the war broth and allow himself to be induced to play the rôle of an Indian or Asian Bevin. We are happy to confess that, far from playing such a rôle of a stooge, Nehru, in his own way, has helped the cause of peace in London. He fought – and probably destroyed – the American plot to declare China as aggressor in the Korean War. He is also said to be responsible for scuttling the American move for economic sanctions against China. He is reported to have carried a majority of Commonwealth nations with him on the issue of the recognition of the Peking Government both inside and outside of the UNO ... We congratulate Prime Minister Nehru without reservation, on the success of his London Mission.'

India's refusal to sign the Japanese Peace Treaty at San Francisco and her refusal to vote for the 'Peace Through Unity' resolution adopted by the UN General Assembly at its 1951 Session similarly provided grist to the communist mill.

It was reported that during the election campaign there were instances of the communists quoting in their own support statements by Pandit Nehru and Ambassador Panikkar eulogising the 'achievements' of the Chinese Communist régime.

The Communist Alternative

In the Election Manifesto the Communist Party posed itself as the alternative to the Congress régime:

'Five years of Congress rule – four of them after the attainment of "freedom" – have brought our country and our people to the verge of disaster ... What lies at the root of these miseries? Congress leaders claim they have ended foreign rule, they have stopped the looting of our people by the British imperialists ... Each one of these arguments is false, each one of these assertions is a lie. The leaders of the Congress have not won freedom for our country. They have betrayed our freedom struggle. They have allowed the foreigners and the reactionary Indian vested interests to plunder and loot our people just as they did in the past. They have themselves joined in the loot.'

The Manifesto proceeded to describe the Nehru Government as

a 'Government of Landlords and Monopolists', a 'Government of Lathis (batons) and Bullets' and then gave its picture of the alternative:

'The Government of People's Democracy will be a Government of all democratic parties, groups and individuals representing workers, peasants, middle classes and the national bourgeoisie, the bourgeoisie that stands for genuine industrialisation of the country and for the freedom and independence of India . . . Basing itself on the power of the people and guided by their interests a people's Democratic Government will solve all the problems that face our country, harness its vast natural resources and manpower for the regeneration of India, for the transformation of India into a free and democratic, happy and prosperous country, paving the way to a Socialist society, free from all exploitation of man by man.

'We have before us the glorious example of China which under a government of People's Democracy has registered an advance that has amazed the whole world. It has freed the peasants from feudal shackles and increased food production by ten million tons. It is fast building its industries and roads, stamping out epidemics, spreading education in the remotest areas. It has liberated women from countries of bondage, put an end to national animosities and united the people as they have never been united in their entire history. China, enslaved by foreign imperialists, robbed by her corrupt native rulers, backward and dependant has given place to a new China – free and strong, a mighty world power, an inspiration to the entire people of Asia. All this has been done in less than eighteen months. And it should not be forgotten that China was more backward than India, had to support a far bigger population and its economy was shattered by decades of war and devastation . . . What the people of China did we can also do. The ending of the present régime and the establishment of a People's Democratic Government of India would mean the beginning of a new era for our people.'

Cominform Support

In its issue of 31st August 1951, the Cominform journal, *For a Lasting Peace, For a People's Democracy*, published in full with banner headlines the election manifesto of the CPI. This was the first time since the reconstitution of the Central Committee in

May 1951 that a document released by the CPI was published verbatim, thus signifying the approval of the Cominform to the new leadership and policies of the CPI.

The Cominform journal similarly published with banner headlines an article by A.K.Ghosh entitled 'The Communist Party in India in the struggle for the United Democratic Front, for a People's Democratic Government'. This article reiterated the earlier analysis of the CPI.

The satisfaction of the Cominform with the behaviour of the Indian Party was also evidenced by the publication in the Cominform journal of a report issued by the CPI of its Party Conference and by the greetings and good wishes of the CPGB which were sent to the CPI wishing it success in the general elections. In their message, Harry Politt and R.Palme Dutt opined that the election manifesto of the CPI had demonstrated the correct path for the Indian people to follow.

The communist conduct of the election campaign showed that the fullest use was to be made of this opportunity to popularise the Party programme, recruit members, strengthen mass contact and build up a united front. The All-India Cultural Conference for Peace scheduled for November was postponed till the new year. A Conference of the All-India Students' Federation was similarly put off. *Cross Roads* was to be made an important organ in the election campaign and Party workers were instructed to push up its sale to 20,000 copies a week.

In one of his election letters to Party members, the General Secretary of the Party advised against the frittering away of resources by contesting a large number of seats. Concentration on a few seats so that results could be achieved was advised.

The unexpected success of candidates of the communist sponsored United Progressive Bloc in Travancore-Cochin was fully exploited in communist publicity material. *Cross Roads* hailed the 'pioneers' who had defeated the Congress and called the 'bluff of Jayaprakash Narain, Asoka Mehta and Company'. These early successes undoubtedly boosted communist morale in other States.

A surprising factor of the election campaign were the immense resources the CP were able to mobilise during the elections. In the last days of the campaign, the Party was able to put in the field, both in cities and villages, a fleet of jeeps, motor cars, station wagons and trucks fitted with loudspeakers and generators. This was particularly marked in Andhra. It issued millions of handbills, posters and booklets of all sizes. Large sums of money were also spent by the Party on payment of volunteers and workers engaged in electioneering. Obviously, not all this money was produced by contributions raised in India.

United Front

The CP knew, however, that even with these resources they could hardly expect to win the elections single-handed. They began to look round for parties with whom they could make common cause to overthrow the Congress régime. They expressed their willingness to negotiate with any and every party which was willing to deal with them.

The first round of talks was between the CPI and other 'leftist' parties, such as the All-India Forward Bloc (Marxist), the Kisan Mazdoor Praja Party (KMPP), and the United Socialist Organisation (USO). The communists proclaimed that if the 'left' forces could come together, the election programme of the CPI could be somewhat amended in order to make it acceptable as the programme of the 'left democratic front'.

In the result, electoral blocs were formed in various provinces. In Bombay and Maharashtra, the CPI achieved an alliance with the Bombay Kamgar Kisan Party and what were described as 'left' socialists, who had broken away under the leadership of Mrs Aruna Asaf Ali from the Socialist Party but had not yet openly announced their adherence to the CPI.

In Orissa, the United Front was formed with the United Socialist Organisation.

In Pepsu, a United Progressive Bloc was formed in which the CPI and the Lal (Red) CP participated.

In Punjab also, the United Progressive Front included the Lal CP.

In Delhi, a United Progressive Bloc was formed consisting of the CPI Forward Bloc (Marxist), Lal CP, and the Left Socialists.

In Tamilnad a United Democratic Front was formed as a result of alliance with the KMPP, Dravida Kazaghom, Tamilnad Toilers' Party and the Commonweal Party to defeat the Congress.

In Travancore-Cochin, the formation of the United Progressive Bloc covered the KMPP, the Kerala Socialist Party and the Revolutionary Socialist Party.

In Bihar, a United Left election alliance committee was formed.

In Assam, an election committee was formed with representatives of the Forward Bloc, the Revolutionary Socialist Party, the Revolutionary Communist Party of India and the Gurkha League.

In Hyderabad State, the United Front consisted of the Democratic People's Front, the League of Socialist Workers, the Sahakari Kamgar Paksh, the Hyderabad Trade Union Congress and the Scheduled Castes' Federation.

In Tripura, a United Front consisting of the CPI, Forward Bloc Gana Mukti Parishad was formed.

In West Bengal, there was a general agreement between the CPI, the Forward Bloc (Marxist) and the Bolshevik Party, but here the KMPP refused to join hands with the communists in the elections.

The only major organisation on the 'left' that did not respond to the communist call for a united front was the Socialist Party of India. In the result, it incurred a considerable amount of vilification from communist quarters. Personal attacks were made against the leaders of the Party. Thus Mr Jayaprakash Narayan and Dr Rammanohar Lohia were accused of being bribed with dollars by American capitalists.[5] They were also attacked for making an alliance with Dr Ambedkar, the leader of the Scheduled Castes' Federation in Bombay. This was described as a reactionary and unholy alliance notwithstanding the fact that the Communist Party had themselves sought a united front with the same 'reactionary' organisation.

As the campaign developed, the efforts of the Communist Party were as much directed to isolating the Socialist Party and preventing other groups from joining with it as to drawing them within its own orbit. Once a small group was drawn into the United Front, the keenness of the communists appeared to diminish with the result that, as the campaign advanced, cracks became evident within the Front itself in provinces like Maharashtra, Bihar and West Bengal.

In the building up of this United Front and the attack on its opponents, the CPI had the support of Moscow and of the Cominform. On 27th October, Radio Moscow, broadcasting in Hindustani, read extracts from an article written by A. K. Ghosh, the General Secretary of the Party, which said *inter alia*:

'The right wing leaders of the Indian Socialist Party are the biggest hinderance to the formation of a united front against imperialism. These leaders have established contacts with all those powers which are against the Soviet Union and the working class. The socialist leaders are openly supporting the interventionist policy of the Americans in Korea.'

There was some uneasiness in the communist ranks about an attempt to down the Socialist Party even *vis-à-vis* the Congress. In order to meet this, the General Secretary of the CPI, in a circular letter to Party members, refuted the argument advanced by some communists that the CPI should support the socialist party in order to oust the Congress, just as the CPGB had supported the Labour Party as against the Conservatives. This analogy, according to A. K. Ghosh, was false. He argued that the analogy was false because in Britain the Labour Party represented the organised working class, and for the maintenance of the unity of the working class it was necessary that the 'extremely small Communist Party' should suport the former's candidates, while in India the Socialist Party, despite its claim, did not represent the organised working class. He stated that the party would not support many of the Socialist Party candidates who had nothing to do with either socialism or with any progressive ideology, and had been given the socialist ticket only because of their local influence. The communists would not also support the 'extremely right-wing reactionary section' which denounced left unity, declared that it preferred Congress victory to the victory of communists, and which was the avowed enemy of the Soviet Union and the People's China and the supporter of the Anglo-American Bloc. An exception, however, was made with regard to some of the socialist candidates who were democrats and had a good record of 'suffering and sacrifice in the cause of the people' and were looked upon by the working class and the peasantry as their champions. Such candidates should be supported if the party had not come to any local electoral agreement with the other candidates.[6]

The actual nomination and polling in the General Elections which took place in turn in various States resulted in a small incident which is perhaps not lacking in significance. In one of the urban constituencies in Bombay City for Parliament where Congress, socialist, communist and scheduled castes candidates contested the elections, Mr Asoka Mehta, General Secretary of the SPI, lodged an objection under a provision of the Constitution of India to communist S. A. Dange's nomination to the House of the People on the ground that members of the CPI, who owed their allegiance to a foreign power, should be debarred from contesting elections. The provision in question lays down that no one who owes loyalty to a foreign state shall be entitled to vote in or contest an election. The returning officer, who was faced with this intriguing situation, overruled the socialist objection on the ground that he did not have before him sufficient proof in favour of Mr Mehta's contention.

Results

The results of the elections undoubtedly reflected a major communist success. The communist bloc of twenty-three in Parliament came second only to the ruling Congress Party. In several of the State Assemblies also the Communist Party emerged as the second largest party and was the leading opposition group. Detailed results of the election to the House of the People showing the votes polled by various parties, the percentage of votes secured and the seats won are given in the first table on the following page.

The second table shows the results State-wise showing the number of votes polled by the CPI, both for the State Assemblies and for Parliament, as against the total votes polled by all parties.

The third table shows the seats secured by the communists both in the House of the People and State Legislative Assemblies in various States as against the total number of seats available.

Election to House of the People
Seats Won and Votes Polled by Parties

Parties	Valid votes polled	Percentage to total valid votes polled	Seats won
Congress	47,528,911	44.85	362
Socialist	11,126,344	10.50	12
Kisan Mazdoor Praja Party	6,158,782	5.81	9
Communist Party of India, and People's Democratic Front	4,712,009	4.45	23
Jan Sangh	3,236,361	3.05	3
Scheduled Castes Federation	2,501,964	2.30	2
Ram Rajya Parishad	2,094,811	1.98	3
Krishikar Lok Party	1,498,488	1.40	1
Hindu Maha Sabha	1,046,263	0.91	4
Forward Block (Marxist)	988,272	0.90	1
Revolutionary Socialist Party of India	393,984	0.37	2
Forward Block (Ruikar)	133,936	0.13	
Revolutionary CPI	86,245	0.12	
Bolshevik Party	25,792	0.02	
Other Parties*	7,678,662	7.27	26
Independents	16,845,494	15.90	41

* *Other Parties include: Bihar:* Jharkhand Party 3, Lok Sewak Sangh 2, Chotanagpur Santhal Parghanas Janata Party 1, *Bombay:* Peasants' and Workers' Party 1, *Madras:* Tamilnad Toilers Party 4, Commonweal 3, Madras Muslim League 1; *Orissa:* Ganatantra Parishad 5, *Punjab:* Akali Party 2; *Hyderabad:* Peasants' and Workers' Party 1; *Pepsu:* Akali Dal 2; *Travancore-Cochin:* Travancore -Cochin Tamilnad Congress 1.

Name of State	Parliament		State Legislative Assembly	
	Number of votes polled by CPI*	Total votes polled by all Parties	Number of votes polled by CPI*	Total votes polled by all Parties
Assam		2,647,127	69,431	2,448,890
Bombay	14,383	11,528,291	67,036	11,123,388
M. Pradesh	29,422	7,192,591	24,460	6,997,489
W. Bengal	720,304	7,613,932	800,961	7,442,697
Punjab	261,623	4,992,339	221,119	4,974,234
Orissa	211,303	3,705,393	206,939	3,670,275
Madras	1,780,301	19,928,519	2,591,923	19,974,801
Bihar	39,272	9,901,452	108,671	9,544,439
UP	59,699	17,074,957	155,869	16,791,139
M. Bharat	24,716	1,953,571	39,600	1,987,622
Hyderabad	1,367,404	4,854,862	1,086,111	5,202,142
Rajasthan	5,490	3,525,964	17,181	3,258,640
Pepsu		1,475,112	63,238	1,354,835
Mysore	73,322	2,824,427	25,116	2,745,515
Saurashtra		762,706	7,791	953,765
Travancore-Cochin		3,490,466	**	3,398,173

* Party affiliation given as at the time of nomination.

** As the Party was under ban, communists filed their papers as Independents.

Name of the State	State Assembly	House of the Peoples
West Bengal	28/238	5/34
Madras	62/375	8/75
Hyderabad (PDF)	42/175	7/25
Travancore-Cochin (UFL)*	32/108	4/25
Orissa	7/140	1/20
Punjab	4/126**	
Assam	1/108	
Bombay	2/315	
Pepsu	2/60***	
Mysore	1/99	

Electoral Colleges
Tripura	13/30	2/2
Manipur	2/30	

* As the Party was under ban, the communists filed their papers as Independents.

** Excluding two members elected on LCP ticket.

*** Excluding one member elected on LCP ticket.

The electoral advance made by the communists in the Union Parliament needs to be put in proper perspective. Taking an overall picture, it needs to be borne in mind that the CPI and the People's Democratic Front, which was its auxiliary, did not get more than 4.45 per cent of the total polled votes. As against this, the Socialist Party which got only twelve seats as against the twenty-three of the communist bloc, and the KMPP which obtained only nine seats, polled respectively 10.50 per cent and 5.81 per cent by contrast. The Communist Party, therefore, was in reality the fourth in order of support given by the electorate, taking the country as a whole.

So far as the different States are concerned, the CP won a total of 170 seats in the various State Assemblies. It is to be remembered that the communists concentrated their efforts in certain selected pockets where they had some influence. In one way, this was a sign of weakness as it was an acceptance of the fact that over the larger area of the country they had scarcely any following. On the other hand, it was an indication of their strength because it showed that wherever they had concentrated they won seats. Thus, in Madras State, the communists won sixty-one seats, of which forty-one were from Andhra region alone. Again, out of these forty-one seats, thirty seats were secured only from three districts on the borders of Telengana – namely Kistna, Guntur and Godavari districts. In Hyderabad State, of the forty-four seats won by the United Democratic Front, no less than thirty were from three districts namely, Warangal, Karimnagar and Nalgonda where communist violence had been particularly intense right from 1948 up to the elections. Elsewhere in the State they did extremely poorly. Again, in Travancore-Cochin the main successes of the CPI came in well established pockets. In Tamilnad, out of fourteen seats carried by the communists, no less than six were from Tanjore alone.

While it may be conceded that communist successes in Madras, Travancore-Cochin and Hyderabad States were impressive, a very different story was told by many other States in the country. Thus, at the other end of the scale, in a major province like the UP, the Communist Party put up forty-two candidates but failed to carry a single seat and polled less than one per cent of the votes cast.

Many explanations have been given of the comparative successes achieved by the CP. One of these is that, as the *Times of India* wrote on 25th January 1952, with particular reference to Travancore-Cochin States, 'The vote for the United Front (CP dominated) was not entirely a genuine vote for the Left, but also in some part a vote of protest against the Congress in the States'. In other States also there was undoubtedly the advantage that the Congress administration's unpopularity resulting from maladministration and a measure of corruption provided. In Telengana and elsewhere, where communist violence had provoked police retaliation, the unpopularity of the police as a result of excesses committed also came as grist to the communist mill. In spite of the fact that the communists themselves were responsible for causing the policeman to hit back even in self-defence, communist propaganda donned the mantle of heroism and martyrdom. In Hyderabad, at a public meeting, a communist leader was questioned: 'Don't you think it futile to think of capturing power through violence and stray armed assaults on officials of law and order?' To this the communist spokesman replied: 'I know you do not capture power by murdering a policeman but your act will provoke the police to retaliate against many persons, even some of them innocent, and the result will be that they will all have a grudge against the administration, which eventually strengthens the CP'. The act of the Government of India in releasing communist *detenus* specially in the South and in Hyderabad and withdrawing warrants against those who had gone underground just on the eve of the elections played directly into communist hands by giving their emergence a sense of drama and of heroism which would have been lacking either if they had been released earlier or not at all.

Leaving aside such negative factors as food shortage and the unpopularity of the administration, however, there were undoubtedly certain positive factors which made for the specific success of the Communist Party as against other opposition groups. One of these factors undoubtedly was the hard and concentrated effort put in by the communist organisation. Another was the fact that they had more money to spend per constituency contested than any other party in India. Undoubtedly, however, the biggest factor in support of communist propaganda was the illusion about the Utopian conditions believed to be prevalent in Soviet Russia and Communist China. The naïve people in the villages had depicted to them in poetic terms conditions in those two countries somewhat in the manner of the famous Persian couplet carved on the arch in the Diwan-i-Khas in the Red Fort in Delhi which runs: 'If there is a heaven on earth, it is this, it is this, it is this'. The Indian communists went round the countryside promising to re-

L

produce in India, as in Soviet Russia and Communist China, a land flooded with milk and honey. In this, they were considerably assisted by the statements made by the Indian Ambassador in Peking and high ranking domestic opponents of theirs.[7]

Another aspect of Congress propaganda that helped the communists was the dead set made by leaders of the Congress Party against what was described as the evil of communalism, meaning Hindu revivalism. Writing after the elections, a leading commentator, *Insaf* wrote in the *Hindustan Times* (Delhi) of 30th January 1952:

'Perhaps the communists would not have had such a good start if Mr Nehru had not wasted his energy fighting shadows. Communalism and feudalism, which he treated as the chief enemies, died with the British and whatever was left of them was destroyed by Sardar Patel's genius.'

Perhaps it would be of interest to cite a few opinions expressed by communist sources themselves explaining their successes and failures. One of the leading communist leaders surveyed the scene after the elections at a private meeting of the Party in Bombay in January 1952. His general conclusion was: 'In the elections the Congress won. Though the Right socialists and the SCF formed a United Front, they were defeated. We are also defeated'. This had reference to the failure of S. A. Dange and Asoka Mehta, the communist and socialist candidates who both lost to the Congress in the working-class area of Bombay City.

'From the elections,' continued the spokesman, 'we come to the conclusion that the labour class and middle class are not willing to follow us unreservedly. They are divided. This is the conclusion that we can draw from the votes cast for us and the socialists. Thus, the middle class of Dadar cast 9,000 votes for us and 11,000 for Atre (Socialist). At Lal Baug and Parel (working class area), half the votes were cast for us and half for the Socialists. From the voting at Walkeshwar and Mahaluxmi (bourgeois and petty-bourgeois), it seems that the petty capitalists are also divided. One group does not agree with the reactionary leadership of the Congress, but its creed is not yet formed for a separate leadership. The middle classes are not willing unreservedly to acknowledge labour leadership. The small capitalist is, however, prepared to fight against the big capitalist. Since 1942, the workers have gone under the leader-ship of the capitalists . . .

'What should we do after the election? A number of new workers are now collected behind the United Front. Now the question before them will be which party they should join. These workers should first learn Marxism. For this purpose we are starting a labour college . . .

'Our programme is to defeat the Congress, to expose the reactionary leadership of the Socialists and to organise a "democratic front".'

The CPI emerged from the election campaign with both its legal and illegal apparatus strengthened. Every opportunity and local issue had been mobilised to strengthen the mass contacts of the Party. The elections had provided a breathing space and an opportunity for organisation after a period of disaster, destruction and defeat. Contact with the masses had been revived and a large number of Party workers recruited. In communist circles the claim was made that, at that rate, by the middle of 1952 the CPI would have the same following and the same organisational strength which it had possessed on the eve of its acceptance of insurrection-ary methods in February 1948.

There was one respect in which the end of the elections found the communists already facing a set-back. That was in regard to the solidarity of the various United Fronts that they had formed. Perhaps this was inevitable. The United Front had, in almost all cases, been a conglomeration of disparate elements lacking any basis of common policy and programme but united in their anta-gonism in the ruling Congress Party. Once the purpose was served, that basis began to evaporate. Part of the responsibility, undoub-tedly, was of the communists. In accordance with their usual methods, they tried to dominate the United Fronts and thus created a reaction against themselves. This break-up was, however, delayed in some cases by the hope that the United Front could secure power. In Madras and Travancore-Cochin States, there was no clear majority for any Party and the communists hoped, by widening their coalition, to make it possible for a communist-dominated cabinet to take office. For some weeks, the situation in both States was obscure. The directive from the Congress head-quarters to eschew a coalition helped to strengthen communist hopes. In the end, however, such coalitions were formed in both the States with the result that the Congress Party, assisted by a few allies, was able to produce a clear majority and Congress cabinets soon took office. Once this stage was reached, the schism between the communists and their allies in Travancore-Cochin became public property, with a spate of charges against the communists made by RSP and KSP leaders and rejoinders made by the communists. In Madras State, a similar trend started with the defection from the United Front of the Commonweal Party and the Tamilnad Toilers' Party and later developed into a situation where even the two basic parties to the Front, namely the communists and the KMPP, parted company as a result of a pact to merge into one big party made by the national headquarters of the Socialist Party and the KMPP.

CHAPTER NINE

Parliament and Other Fronts
1952 - 1953

The general elections at the end of 1951 had provided an excellent opportunity to the Communist Party to enlist sympathisers, restore mass contact and revitalise the Party which now emerged as the main opposition to the Congress in the Union Parliament and in the State Legislatures of Madras, Travancore-Cochin, Hyderabad and West Bengal.

This unexpected success boosted communist morale. The Politbureau of the Central Committee, which met in Bombay in March 1952, issued a statement commending the tremendous swing of the people towards the Communist Party and the spectacular victory of the United Front as a vindication of the Party's policies.

Among the immediate consequences of the elections one was that the centre of gravity appeared to be shifting from Bombay to the South. The Party headquarters were moved from Bombay to Madras with a centre consisting of A. K. Ghosh (Secretary), C. Rajeshwar Rao (Andhra), P. Ramamurthy (Tamilnad) and Ravi Narayan Reddy (Telengana) to control the day to day operations of the organisation. Along with the Party headquarters, the journal *Cross Roads* was also shifted to Madras. This concentration on the South aimed not only at increasing the pressure on the 'weak State governments' of the South but at preparing the ground for a territorial base, such as was Yenan in China, in time to come. The Cominform journal started writing as if South India were not a part of India but a separate political unit.

Fundamental Attitude to Parliament

Before proceeding to analyse in some detail the actual policies adopted by the Party both at the Centre and in the States, it may be worth while recalling the basic communist attitude to Parliament and parliamentarianism on which the day to day policy of the communists was to be reared:

'Communism repudiates parliamentarianism as the form of the future ... it repudiates the possibility of winning over the parliaments, its aim is to destroy parliamentarianism. Therefore it is only possible to speak of utilising the bourgeois State organisations with the object of destroying them ...

'... Work within Parliaments which consists chiefly in making revolutionary propaganda from the Parliamentary platform, the denouncing of enemies, the ideological unification of the masses, who are still looking up to the parliamentary platform, captivated by democratic illusions, especially in backward territories, etc., must be fully subordinated to the objects and tasks of the mass struggle outside the Parliaments ... if the communists have the majority in the local Government institutions, they must (1) carry on a revolutionary opposition to the bourgeois Central authority; (2) do all for the aid of the poor population (economic measures, establishment or attempt to establish an armed workers' militia); (3) point out on every occasion the barriers which the bourgeois State power puts against really great changes; (4) develop on this basis the sharpest revolutionary propaganda without fearing a conflict with the State authorities ...

'Boycotting the elections or the Parliaments, or leaving the Parliament, is permissible, chiefly when there is a possibility for an immediate transition to an armed fight for power.

'... A communist representative, by decision of the Central Committee of the CP is bound to combine legal work with illegal work. In countries where the communist delegate enjoys a certain inviolability, this must be utilised by way of rendering assistance to the illegal organisations and for the propagation of the Party ...

'Each communist must remember that he is not a "legislator" who is bound to seek agreements with the other legislators, but an agitator of the Party, detailed into the enemy camp in order to carry out the orders of the Party there. The communist member is answerable not to the wide masses of his constituents, but to his own Communist Party – legal or illegal.

'The communist representatives should ... never forget that only those are worthy of the name of communists who not in words only but also in deeds are the mortal enemy of the bourgeois and its social-patriotic flunkeys.'   (Statutes of the Communist International)

The new line of United Front having brought rich dividends in the course of the elections, the communists now surveyed the new and crucial field of legislative activity against this background set for it by the international organisations. To start with, the Party opined that a 'uniform policy for all States is not possible because of the differing strength of the Party in the various States'.[1] One thing was clearly understood: that under no circumstances would the Party agree to the formation of any parliamentary front which would restrain the Party from expressing its views on the floor of the Legislatures. The people must be reminded constantly that it was the CPI which was the defender of the people. The Party would, however, try to build up such United Fronts as would, while reflecting an agreed minimum programme, at the same time allow freedom for independent expression outside the area of such agreement. Communist members would not therefore merge in any bloc. 'Care should be taken that the Party does not lose its identity in any State'.[2] There was nothing, however, to prevent an understanding being reached with other parties on specific issues.

Varied Techniques

A distinctive technique was prescribed in the case of the Southern States where, in the absence of a clear Congress majority, the possibility of infiltrating into office was not barred. There the achievement of a majority which could assume the reins of office became the prime concern. Thus, in Madras State, the Party was prepared to merge in the United Democratic Front, and even to authorise Mr T. Prakasam, leader of the KMPP, to act as leader for the specific purpose of fulfilling the requirements of the Constitution by producing the majority which would satisfy the Governor of the State that his duty lay in calling the leader of the UDF to form a cabinet. On the other hand, it was agreed that, in the absence of such a government being formed, the UDF was to function only as a co-ordinating committee on agreed matters allowing each party to function independently and that the UDF when in opposition would not have its own disciplinary rules.

In the case of Travancore-Cochin and Hyderabad also, the

communists would function within the United Left Front and the People's Democratic Front respectively in the hope of widening these fronts to secure a majority.

The Party agreed that in the event of communists forming or participating in a government in any State, their aim would be to introduce agrarian reforms in order to show that the communist government was more useful to the people than Congress ministries had been. Simultaneously, the communists were to try to win over the Services and to plant their own men in the administration so that, even in the event of the cabinet being dismissed, communist infiltration in the Services would be permanent.

In developing a parliamentary strategy, the Party was aided actively by the Cominform whose journal *For a Lasting Peace, For a People's Democracy* wrote on the subject in the opening months of 1952. Thus, in its 8th February issue in an article entitled 'For Peace and Friendship between Peoples' the Cominform laid down: 'The great historical duty of the Communist and Workers' and Peasants' Parties in the present period is to prevent the imperialists from deceiving the people, from hurling them into the abyss of a new war ... There is no more important task for all peace partisans than the all round exposure of the intrigues, manoeuvres, demagogy and vilification of the imperialists and their mercenary press and their right-wing Socialist and Titoite lackeys'.

For some time the position in the States in the south was obscure. But the picture as it ultimately emerged was that of the Congress Party, with the assistance of allies, achieving majorities in the State Legislatures of Madras, Travancore-Cochin and Hyderabad and forming administrations which showed every sign of being stable. From then on, the solidarity of the United Front started cracking visibly.

Among the political allies they lost, the most notable were the Praja Party elements in Madras and elsewhere which had merged with them in a bloc under the name of 'The United Democratic Front' and which in December 1952 broke away to join with the Socialist Party in forming the Praja Socialist Party. Similarly, the 'United Front of Leftists' the Stalinists had formed with the

Kerala Socialist Party and the Revolutionary Socialist Party in the State of Travancore-Cochin resolved itself in October 1952 into its constituent elements, leaving behind temporarily a trial of bickering and mutual recrimination. The only accessions of strength on this level that came the way of the communists anywhere in India were the merger of the 'Left' Socialist group led by Mrs Aruna Asaf Ali at the end of 1952, and the merger, by the middle of 1953, of the Kamgar Kisan Party in Bombay State. A survey of the purely parliamentary scene would therefore indicate, if anything, an intial set-back to communist efforts to widen their orbit.

Union Parliament

In so far as the Union Parliament was concerned, P. Sundarayya and A. K. Gopalan, Party leaders in the Council of States and House of the People respectively, called a conference of 'non-Congress democratic members of Parliament' on 13th May 1952, to discuss with the communists the formation of a United Democratic Opposition on the basis of a common programme.[3]

The minimum programme provided by the CPI envisaged:

'Abolition of all special powers of the President of the Republic relating to declaration of an emergency and promulgation of ordinances;
    'Withdrawal of India from the Commonwealth;
    'Confiscation and nationalisation of all British-owned factories, banks, plantations and other interests;
    'Abolition of restrictions on freedom of speech, press, association;
    'Right to strike;
    'Abolition of the principle of detention;
    'Abolition of the compensation clauses in the Constitution which prevent the radical agrarian reforms from being carried out;
    'Immediate formation of linguistic States, adjusting the boundaries of existing States on the principle of common language;
    'Abolition of princely States (areas which constitute national minorities will have complete regional autonomy);
    'Foreign Policy: Removal of British officers and so-called advisers from our armed forces and financial and economic key posts;
    'Gurkha forces not to be allowed to be recruited for the British Army;

'Military budget to be cut down by fifty per cent;

'Withdrawal of Kashmir question from UN. No foreign intervention in Kashmir to be allowed. Sending away of UN military advisers from Kashmir;

'No acceptance of foreign loans and so-called political aid with strings attached to it;

'Industry: Protection to national industries against the competition of foreign goods and developing the national industries.'

In this attempt, however, they did not have much success in that neither the Socialist Party nor the KMPP was prepared to join the front.

Perhaps certain pronouncements of communist leaders did not do much to inspire confidence in their adherence to constitutional methods. Thus, A. K. Gopalan, leader of the Communist Party in the House of the People, said in Hoshiarpur at a public meeting that the CP did not believe in the ballot and that the Congress government could not be changed through the ballot box. His Party would organise countrywide strikes and paralyse Government and in that way change the Government.[4]

The implacable hostility of the CPI to the country's democratic Constitution was reiterated eighteen months later by P. Sundarayya, the communist leader in the Council of States when, on 4th September 1953, he declared that members of his Party were in Parliament to see that the Indian Constitution was wrecked and replaced by a new Constitution. The communist spokesman scouted statements made by non-communists that he and his colleagues had accepted the Constitution in seeking election to Parliament.[5]

Parliamentary Prestige

These frank pronouncements notwithstanding, there can be no question that membership of Parliament gave the communists considerable respectability and a first rate platform for agitation and propaganda purposes through which influence could be built up and pressure exerted. The communists fully utilised these opportunities. The shifting of the Party headquarters from Madras to Delhi in September 1952 was an indication.

As soon as Parliament assembled, the CP set up its own candidate, backed by the majority of the opposition members, for the Presidency of the Indian Union. The candidate originally suggested by *Cross Roads*, the Party organ, namely Dr S. Radhakrishnan, had already been nominated for the Vice-Presidency by the Congress Party itself. The communists also put up a candidate for the Speakership of the House of the People. Naturally, they could not carry either office.

The communists were able by skilful management to build up an importance for themselves in Parliament out of proportion to their numerical strength. This in turn strengthened the theory nurtured by them of the polarisation of forces in India between the Congress Party and themselves as the alternative. As soon as the Speaker was elected, the communist group requested that it should be recognised as the official opposition by virtue of its being the largest opposition group. While not accepting this contention, the Speaker allowed the seat reserved for the Leader of the Opposition on the front opposition bench to the Party spokesman, A. K. Gopalan. The Party had also managed to secure, in the allocation of time between different parties, a substantial proportion.

From the very opening of the debates, the communists took the initiative and drove the Government on the defensive. The first shot was fired by Gopalan who characterised the Presidential Address at the opening of the Session as 'a declaration of war against the Indian people'. He went on to add: 'It was impossible for this country to maintain friendly relations with both the people of Korea and the American aggressors who were exterminating them with germ warfare, or with the French imperialists and the people of Tunisia at one and the same time'.[6] This daring declaration of war brought forth a spirited rejoinder from Prime Minister Nehru, who in winding up the debate, accepted the challenge. It was obvious, however, from the speech of the Prime Minister, that, as he made it clear both at the beginning and at the end of his address, he would have much preferred to have friendly relations and the fullest co-operation with all groups in the opposition including the communists. Similarly, in later debates, when the boisterousness of the communists and the mendacity of their speeches provoked the House, the Prime Minister, even when he lashed at them, did not conceal his disappointment that the communist members had not been influenced by the parliamentary atmosphere in conforming to the decencies and conventions of parliamentary life.

Indeed, awareness in the public mind about the real aims and nature of the communists could hardly be expected to grow as a result of repeated statements by the Prime Minister to the effect that, although the ideals of communism were good and acceptable to him personally, the silly and irresponsible methods of violence and terrorism adopted, for a couple of years, by the Indian communists since February 1948 were objectionable and in fact did dis-service to their own cause.[7] The illusion thus persisted in the public mind that violence was not an inherent part of communist doctrine and that it was only the local Communist Party which was misbehaving.

This characterisation may, moreover, be considered to be unfair to the Indian communists, a determined and disciplined body of men who had made the best of a bad job with which they had been entrusted by their mentors abroad. It was not, after all, the Indian communists who were responsible for the Stalin-Hitler Pact or for the alliance between Russia and the British rulers of India during the second World War; nor did they on their own initiate the 'Zhdanov line'. Granted the disloyalty to their own country implicit in their allegiance to the Kremlin, they could hardly have served their own cause better. Quite apart from any question of fairness, such a formulation may also be considered unrealistic and therefore crippling in so far as counter measures were concerned. Police action, on which the Indian Government had so far largely relied, may be perfectly legitimate, but it may be argued that it is not the most effective way of resisting communist inroads. The sounder and more effective method may well be to combat them ideologically. But how can a disease be fought effectively if only the symptoms and not the source of the infection are attacked?

The crudeness and violence of communist speeches in the first Session of Parliament created in certain circles the impression that the Communist Party had failed to capitalise on its opportunities in that field. Dealing with this matter in a review of the Session, one of India's most experienced observers wrote:

'It would, however, be a fatal mistake to judge them by the poor figure the communists cut in Parliament and rush to the conclusion that they are losing ground in the country. The constituencies from which the communists were returned would only know that their members "fought the Government tooth and nail" and demanded a better deal for the poor. Nor would, from the communist viewpoint, their performance in Parliament be considered a failure – did they not make the best use of it to run down the Government and do propaganda for their own Party? What more did they expect?

'Apart therefore, from their alleged parliamentary failure, which would be so much water on a duck's back so far as their electorate is concerned, one can discover nothing that would indicate that the communists' influence in the country is now on the wane and that since the general elections, eight months ago, when they emerged the second most influential party in the country, the communists have lost ground.'[8]

Issues Raised

Among the various issues that were either raised by the CP in the course of parliamentary discussion, or in the discussion of which they participated, were the following:

'(1) A demand for the release of the remaining communist *détenus*.
'(2) The issue of passports valid for the Soviet Union, Communist China and Soviet satellite countries to those communist functionaries to whom they had been denied.
'(3) The demand for the withdrawal of the ban on the sale of Soviet literature at State Railway bookshops. This was described by Mr Harindranath Chattopadhyaya as 'thought control'.[9]
'(4) A drastic reduction in the salaries of Ministers and higher officials and the abolition of the Privy Purses being paid to the former ruling Princes.
'(5) The curtailing of the Defence budget by 50 per cent. This item on the programme was varied by one of the spokesmen demanding a 25 per cent reduction, while another demanded a cut of 66.6 per cent.

'(6) The severing of all ties with the Commonwealth and the development of closer economic and trade relations with the USSR, China and the East European countries.[10]

'(7) A protest against the flying of the Union Jack alongside the Indian National flag over the Houses of Parliament on the Birthday of Queen Elizabeth who had been accepted by India as the head of the Commonwealth. This protest against the flying of a "foreign flag" succeeded since it was later announced that this practice would be discontinued.

'(8) A demand for the stopping of the recruitment in the British Army of Nepalese Gurkha troops on the Indian side of the Indo-Nepalese frontier. This demand again was successful as the Prime Minister towards the end of the Session made an announcement that the Indian Government would withdraw the facilities hitherto given to the British Government for this purpose.

'(9) A demand for the withdrawal of the Indian Ambulance Unit assisting the United Nations forces in Korea.

'(10) Support for the Indian Government's attitude in regard to Kashmir, supplemented by a call for the withdrawal of the Kashmir question from the UN and the "ending of foreign interference".

'(11) The formation of linguistic States.

'(12) Opposition to the Preventive Detention Act, the renewal of which came up before Parliament in July/August 1952. The Communist Party opposed the very principle of the Bill. The Bill, however, went through both the Houses of Parliament with comfortable majorities.

By-elections that took place during 1952 and the first half of 1953 may be taken to indicate on balance a decline in the numerical strength of the Communist Party.

Splitting the Elite

To judge the extent of communist influence by election figures and parliamentary divisions would, however, be misleading. It has been a distinctive feature of the Communist Party that it functions through members of other political parties as well as its own. There can be no gainsaying that, among the intelligentsia generally, the communists made numerous recruits during these two years, and that there is no sign as yet of this trend being reversed. Part of the credit goes to the perseverance which is displayed in the effort with which the potential victims are pursued. Credit must also go to the skill with which issues are chosen on which to rally support.

While cultivating the Parliamentary front, the Communist Party did not by any means neglect the even more important task of advancing its ideas with the general public and of developing its organisation. The year 1952 was indeed marked by an even more intensive effort to win the minds of the intelligentsia, the country's ruling class, and to make inroads among those who occupied positions of influence and power. The operation can best be described as a move to split the Indian elite by creating a pro-Soviet and pro-Chinese section. Once a substantial part of the elite was thus mobilised, it would be possible to neutralise the rest, who would be rendered impotent to offer consistent and determined resistance to further infiltration and the undermining of the régime.

The real face of the Party was now masked to make it more appealing to the middle class. The unshaven tough, armed with acid bombs and pistols, was now replaced in the public eye by a handsome, clean shaven, well-dressed youth here and an artist there, a sympathetic social worker in yet another place. Culture mingled with peace and gave forth tender strains of music with Picasso's dove fluttering amiably above.

Response to this approach was forthcoming in liberal measure. Five years of independence, unaccompanied by startling gains in regard to material returns, education, medical relief or cleaner and clearer administration, provided a climate in which the communist charges and promises met with response. Communist China's 'example' and its 'achievements' were perhaps the biggest single factor in helping to achieve the gains that marked 1952.

Peace

'Peace' remained the main front which the communists operated in so far as the intelligentsia was concerned. Once the election campaign came to a close, the 'Peace' campaign was intensified. The All-India Peace Council held its session on 22nd and 23rd February 1952, with Dr. Saif-ud-din Kitchlew in the Chair. A conference of the Big Five for removing the threat of war was the slogan.

The All-India Peace Council and the Communist Party observed a 'Hands off Kashmir Day' on 15th March 1952. A.K. Ghosh issued a statement criticising the Indian delegates' support to the British proposal to extend Dr. Graham's efforts at mediation and exhorted the peoples of India and Kashmir to demand a withdrawal of the Kashmir issue from the United Nations.

Party units were instructed by the CP to hold meetings on 6th April to protest against the alleged use of germ warfare by the UN forces in Korea.

The All-India Cultural Conference for Peace, held in Calcutta from 2nd to 6th April 1952, was a major preoccupation. All Communist Party committees throughout India were called upon by the General Secretary in a circular to assist in these preparations. It was also arranged that a meeting of Party workers on the cultural front should be held on 30th and 31st April under cover of a bigger conference. At the same time, it was laid down that the Conference should be made to appear entirely autonomous from the Party.

The All-India Peace Council designated 25th June 1952, the second anniversary of the Korean War, as 'Korea Day'. The Peace Council called upon all Peace Committees throughout India 'to hold public meetings on that day to voice the Indian people's desire for an end to the Korean war; to increase their efforts in the campaign to ban germ warfare; to demand all governments, especially that of the United States, to observe the Geneva Convention prohibiting the use of germ weapons, and to propose the establishment of a court for the trial of germ warfare war criminals'. The All-India Peace Council also voiced its protest against the American crimes on Koje island.[11]

The next move on the 'Peace' front was the call for the convening of an 'Asian Peace Conference' in Peking some time in 1952. Among the names of the members of the Initiating Committee were to be found the usual names: Dr M.Atal, Mr Prithvi Raj Kapoor, Prof D.D.Kosambi, Mr Mulk Raj Anand, Sardar

Gurbax Singh and Mr Krishen Chander. The Preparatory Committee which met in Peking on 28th May 1952, with Prof D. D. Kosambi of India in the Chair, adopted the following agenda for the Conference:

'To safeguard the independence of Asia and the Pacific;
'To oppose war and expansion of rearmament;
'To oppose remilitarisation of Japan, the use of Japan as a base for aggression,
'To settle peacefully the problems of Korea and the problem of Viet-Nam, Laos, Cambodia, Malaya and other Asian countries;
'To oppose blockades and embargoes, and
'To develop normal economic and cultural exchanges.'

While the 'Peace' movement sponsored by the World Peace Council got off to a rather slow start in India, there can be no denying that, by the time the third session of the All-India Peace Congress met in Jullunder in the Punjab in September 1952, the communists had succeeded in bringing on that platform figures with much greater drawing power than such hard-ridden personalities as Dr Mulk Raj Anand who had till then dominated the scene. The communist success in securing the support of Dr Saif-ud-din Kitchlew and Dr J. C. Kumarappa, one time Gandhian economist, undoubtedly gave the movement a new look. The main resolution urged the Indian Prime Minister to invite the heads of the Big Five to meet in Delhi to conclude a Peace Pact, a call that still continued to be heard in the middle of 1953.

By October 1952, Dr Kitchlew was to be found at the Asian and Pacific Peace Conference in Peking where he presented the main report. Two months later the scene shifted to Vienna where on 19th December 1952, delegates to the Congress of the Peoples for Peace, again with Dr Kitchlew and Dr Kumarappa to the fore, adopted an appeal calling for a Big Five Pact for Peace.

From Vienna, Dr Kitchlew moved on to Moscow where he was awarded in the Kremlin on 5th January 1953 the International Stalin Prize 'for the promotion of peace among nations'. The even higher honour of a personal interview with Stalin was accorded to him, the diplomatic face of the Indian Ambassador being saved by

M

a formal interview being granted to him a few minutes before Dr Kitchlew was scheduled to call. Notwithstanding this undisguised support to the head of a movement which was then engaged in denouncing the Indian Government's policies as reactionary and subservient to Anglo-American imperialist war preparations, the Indian Ambassador held a diplomatic reception at the Embassy in honour of Dr Kitchlew.

On his return to Delhi from Moscow after fraternising with the Soviet dictators, Dr Kitchlew was received at the railway station by the President of the Delhi Provincial Congress Committee and other leading functionaries of the Congress Party in Delhi,[12] and was given a personal interview by the Indian Prime Minister at which he claimed he extended an invitation to Mr Nehru to join this communist front.[13] Thereafter, it was noted that Dr Kitchlew's visits to Bombay and other cities were marked by the presence, at functions in his honour, of certain well-known Congress Party leaders. On 27th March 1953, over 200 members of the Madras Legislature assembled in the offices of the Congress Parliamentary Party to hear Dr J. C. Kumarappa expound the tasks of the 'Peace' movement. The Deputy Leader of the Congress Party was among those present, and the meeting passed resolutions demanding an immediate cease-fire in Korea, the signing of a Peace Pact by the Five Great Powers, and support for the Vienna Peace Appeal.[14]

On his return to Delhi from this triumphant tour, Dr Kitchlew was presented with an address of welcome, allegedly on behalf of the citizens of Delhi, at a meeting presided over by Mrs Rameshwari Nehru and addressed by the President of the Provincial Congress Committee. It congratulated Dr Kitchlew on winning the Stalin Peace Prize and carrying the message of peace all over the world. Messages of goodwill were announced at the meeting from the President of the Indian Union, the Vice-President, the Prime Minister, the Speaker of the House of Parliament and the Commander-in-Chief of the Armed Forces.[15]

After this honour done to its head under the very nose of the Indian Government, there could be no question that the communist 'Peace' front had become a respectable institution. Its capacities as a platform of united front on which Congress Party members could stand alongside with communists became immense. The tone of disapproval of the Indian Government's foreign policy tended to be replaced by warm approval of everything that emanated from India's Ministry of External Affairs, and its devotees claimed to be the most loyal exponents of India's 'independent' foreign policy.

Perhaps an awareness of these dangers was responsible for a directive issued shortly after this by the Working Committee of the Indian National Congress as a result of a circular which was sent round to members of the Working Committee drawing attention to the Peace Committees 'which are invariably headed by communists' and which are 'designed to further certain political designs'. The directive read: 'Certain peace organisations, though ostensibly working for the promotion of peace, are designed to further certain political purposes. Congressmen should not, therefore, join these organisations or conferences or congresses that they organise from time to time. Nor should they go abroad to attend any such conferences or congresses'.[16]

This directive was no doubt the result of the fact that a large number of stalwarts of the Congress Party, who had hitherto not appeared on the communist platform, had in recent weeks been found to attend communist rallies organised by one or other communist front such as the 'Peace' Committees, the India-China Friendship Associations and the Indian People's Theatre Association.

Nothing was, however, said in the directive about the India-China Friendship Association with whose spokesmen, including communist members of Parliament, none other than the Parliamentary Secretary in the Ministry of External Affairs, had fraternised in Delhi only a few days earlier, and which had planned a bigger 'India-China Consultative Conference' later in the year.[17]

In any event, deprecatory gestures such as this could do little to stop the communists from utilising the tempting opportunities for intellectual infiltration provided by the main trend of the pronouncements of the Indian Government in so far as the main issues of world politics were concerned. These the communists distorted to make it appear that there was nothing to distinguish them from the Communist Party's own stand.

Perhaps nothing has been so adroitly exploited by the communists for their own ends as the persistent adulation and glorification of the Chinese Communist régime and its 'achievements'.[18] Thus, Mr K.M.Panikkar, India's Ambassador in Peking, had delivered an address in New Delhi in October 1951, in the course of which he is reported to have declared that the Peking régime 'is not a communist government' but 'a broad-based coalition' that has launched 'a dynamic social revolution'. Mr Panikkar had no doubt that ninety-five per cent of the Chinese people regarded the régime as their own, for they were associated with the formulation and execution of the government's policy at all stages and all levels. In June 1953, Major-General S.S.Sokhey, Member of Parliament, told the World Peace Council in Budapest: 'My country has developed an admiration for China and the greatest admirer of all is our Prime Minister, Mr Nehru'.[19]

So far did the inhibitions resulting from the obligations of friendship extend that in June 1952, Sir Chintaman Deshmukh, the Union Finance Minister, expressed in Parliament his difficulty in answering communist MPs who had persistently flaunted the 'achievements' of Russia and China. It was difficult, said the Finance Minister, to bring out into the open the facts which the Indian Government had in their possession and which went counter to these claims, because the Government had friendly feelings towards those countries.[20]

The tributes paid by Prime Minister Nehru and Vice-President Radhakrishnan to Stalin on the occasion of his death as a great factor for world peace beloved of the Soviet people set the tone for a campaign which ranged through the larger part of the Indian press and provided an opportunity for fraternising on the public platform between Communist and Congress Party members.

In March 1953, the official organ of the Communist Party professed to line up behind the Indian Prime Minister's denunciation of the North Atlantic Treaty Organisation with these words: 'All those who love peace and hate imperialism will welcome the denunciation by Prime Minister Nehru of the imperialist Powers who have banded together in what is called the "NATO". He said that this organisation, under the guise of a "defensive alliance", was "covering up", sheltering and defending the colonial domains of certain imperialist powers. He made it clear that "everybody who is interested in putting an end to colonialism will react strongly against NATO".[21']

The record in regard to Korea, with particular reference to the truce talks and the issue of repatriation – forced or voluntary – of Chinese and North Korean prisoners of war is also one that has added to popular confusion. The vital moral issue of Human Rights implicit in the clash between the UN and communist viewpoints in regard to the voluntary repatriation of prisoners of war received little recognition on the part of Indian spokesmen.[22]

It was not to be wondered at that there should be considerable adjustment in consequence in the Communist Party's original line of denunciation of Indian foreign policy.

On 17th May 1953, P. Sunderayya, leader of the Communist Party in Parliament, announced his Party's welcome of the Prime Minister's statement in Parliament on the Korea situation and the Chinese Communist proposals for the repatriation of prisoners of war.[23]

A few days later, A.K. Gopalan said that 'while his party could not agree with certain things in which Shri Nehru was supporting the Anglo-American bloc, they certainly welcomed his stand on the Korean question and such other things'.[24]

About the same time, a crypto-communist journal in an article entitled 'Bon Voyage, Nehru', observed: 'We had feared that the Commonwealth may bind Nehru to the American war machine. We now expect Nehru to lead the Commonwealth, or at least the saner elements thereof, to a break with that infernal machine'.[25]

It is not to be assumed, of course, that this attitude would continue permanently. The hot-and-cold treatment would no doubt call for a change when Moscow felt it was time to exert further pressure. Meanwhile, however, the communists could hardly be blamed if they believed that their present policy was paying excellent dividends and justifying itself by results. They could, for instance, draw attention to the fact that, in the course of a television broadcast in London in June 1953 Prime Minister Nehru made the following statements: 'Russia definitely desires peace, for whatever period it may be. I cannot say for what period ... I see absolutely no external danger in India from communism or any other source'. He did not think that China had any desire to expand. She had enough problems of her own, and so far as India was concerned, she had most friendly relations with China.[26] On the same day, he told another audience that the emergence of 'a strong, united, integrated State of China' was one of the most dominating factors of the present age. 'Forget communism – forget everything', he said.[27]

By the middle of the year 1953, the communists made no bones about drawing attention publicly to the possibilities opened up for their 'Peace' campaign by the attitude on the world affairs adopted by the ruling Congress Party.

In the course of an article, the official organ of the CPI commented thus on resolutions on Foreign Policy adopted by the All-India Congress Committee in July 1953:

'The resolutions adopted by the All-India Congress Committee on Foreign Policy when it met in Agra this week can be of help to the partisans of peace. For the AICC has now accepted some of the major slogans of the Peace movement: most important of all, it has accepted the position that "a Conference of representatives of the Great Powers should meet at an early date to discuss informally the various questions that have tended to produce conflict in the past" and should "consider the question of disarmament and the removal of political barriers to international trade and communications" ...

'The expression of these opinions by the highest organ of the ruling Party in India would be of great value to the Peace movement throughout the world ...

'Inside India itself, it will help the All-India Peace Council, when it meets next week at Patna, to develop a broad-based mass campaign for the popularisation of the Budapest slogan of Negotiation, and to draw into this campaign the large mass of Congressmen who have so far kept themselves out of the organised Peace movement.'[28]

This line was followed up a few days later when on 1st August 1953, the Indian Peace Council met in Delhi. Dr Kitchlew, its President, welcomed the Prime Minister's statement that Russia and China desired peace. The Prime Minister's recent statements were not, said Dr Kitchlew, very different from the views the Peace Council had held for a long time.[29]

E. M. S. Namboodiripad writing a week later in the CPI's weekly organ, clinched the matter when he wrote:

'The various points made by the Prime Minister at his Press Conference on 30th July, will help and strengthen the forces of peace in their struggle against those who are trying to sabotage the negotiations that are on the agenda on the various issues of international dispute . . .

'The Prime Minister's statement in favour of peace and against racialism should therefore be made the starting point for a powerful campaign for mobilising the people for peace, rather than for breeding complacency. It can and should be used to draw still broader sections into the campaign for peace.

'It is precisely such a campaign for peace that is visualised in the resolution of the All-India Peace Council adopted at the last Patna session.'[30]

The dangers of the situation thus created provoked the columnist "Vivek" to complain that : 'the communists have begun to work skilfully upon Mr Nehru. Their line of approach is to make him feel how fully they recognise his distinctness from those around him, the very special and fine quality that is his. Thus, on occasion after occasion, publicly and privately, they differentiate between the Congress Party and Mr Nehru, prominent members of his Cabinet and himself. From the Cabinet and the Party, they anticipate nothing but evil. But they make clear that from Mr Nehru their expectations are very different. They hark back continuously to the Nehru of old, Nehru the revolutionary, and lose no opportunity of contrasting him with the diehards, the Katjus and the Rajajis.

'Nor is this task of producing the proper impression confined to the declared communists, the open Party members. They have always found it extremely useful to work through ostensible independents, respectable names that impress through their emphasis on their separate identity. Such men, too, assisted in some instances by the memory of association in youth, lose no opportunity of stressing the incompatibility between the leader and his followers, the implication being all the time how much happier and more effective, the leader would be if he shed a large number of his followers, replacing them by the real progressives to be found in the communist and independent ranks.

'Another potent and obvious way of acquiring influence has been the taking of a line in complete consonance with Mr Nehru's own views when it is clear that there is a cleavage often not declared but still real, between Mr Nehru and many of his followers. There can scarcely be greater gratification than when former opponents become vociferous supporters, while the followers give at best a grudging acquiescence. The discussion about the Government of India's recent agreement with the Kashmir Government gave ample scope for this manoeuvre. There can be no doubt that a large number of the Congress Party resented the one-sided nature of the agreement. In deference to Mr Nehru's strong inclination, they expressed no opposition but there was scarcely any enthusiasm. The communists, on the other hand, hailed it with acclamation as a great piece of statesmanship, not that they were not shrewd enough to be able to see the real objective, but that it seemed to them a worthwhile opportunity to move towards the winning over of Mr Nehru.

'Another aspect of the communist appeal emphasised for the purpose of making an impression on Mr Nehru is the continuous reiteration of the efficacy of the method of the short-cut as exemplified by achievements in Russia and China. The communists in effect imply: "All this constitutionalism and respect for law that your people regard as necessary, how it holds things up! But if you put yourself at our head and take the line we urge, what is there not possible? Our achievements can then really be spectacular and the credit of course will all be yours as our leader."[31]

Without a doubt, the 'Peace' campaign had yielded its architects, in India and abroad, golden dividends.

The Ganhdian Heritage

Closely linked with the Peace Front was the attempt to infiltrate into the ranks of Gandhi's followers and to 'capture' Gandhi,

Public Enemy No. 1 throughout his life. An attempt was now to commence to claim that the communists were Gandhi's real heirs. This move commenced with a request from the All-India Peace Council to the World Peace Council asking for permission to observe the death anniversary of Mahatma Gandhi in October 1951. The Secretariat of the International Cultural Commission of the World Peace Council appears, however, to have cold shouldered the suggestion. Nonetheless, the move was pushed forward with considerable cynicism and conspicuous success during the next two years, at the end of which the Politbureau's Review Report presented to the Third Congress of the Party covering the period was to include Gandhian ideology as one of the 'reserves of the ruling class'. 'Far more serious than the direct organisational hold of the Congress or Nehru, however, is the hold of the Gandhian ideology, which is still powerful among the mass of the people ... It should be particularly borne in mind that more than three decades of Gandhian leadership in the national democratic movement has created a tradition of particular forms of struggle which has affected large masses of workers, peasants and middle classes'. The key point of contact was Mr J. C. Kumparappa, one of the functionaries of the All-India Village Industries' Association sponsored by Gandhi. His repeated visits to Peking and Moscow, which were sponsored by the communists, led Mr Kumarappa to adopt the position that the nearest thing to Gandhism in practice that Mr Kumarappa could find was the Chinese communist dictatorship. He defined Gandhism as communism stripped of violence, though more eminent Gandhians like Acharya Vinobha Bhave, the late Mr K. G. Mashruvala, the Editor of the *Harijan*, and Mr S. N. Agarwal, General Secretary of the Indian National Congress, took pains to refute this kind of amalgam by insisting on the irreconcilable nature of the two ideologies. There can be no doubt that a certain amount of confusion of thought has been successfully caused by some of Gandhi's former disciples using Gandhi's name to further the communist efforts with which they are now associated.

Culture

Not far removed from the Peace front was the cultural. The sale of communist literature was intensified with the beginning of 1952. Already from 4th to 10th November 1951, a conference of the workers of the People's Publishing House and its outstation representatives had been held and it had been decided that theoretical Marxism should be propagated in different Indian languages, along with books on the Party's activities on the cultural front, as well as translations of well-known Russian novels. As soon as the elections were over, efforts to step up the circulation of Russian periodicals were set in train. Four zonal centres were established in Delhi, Bombay, Madras and Calcutta. Distributors of Soviet literature were not only to be exempt from postage and freight, but were also to be given a discount ranging from thirty-three and one-third per cent to fifty-five per cent. Enrolling of five subscribers for any Soviet periodical would entitle one to be listed as a free recipient for one year. *Vishal Andhra,* a Telugu daily, was started by the communists in June 1952 with a brand new rotary equipment costing several hundreds of thousands of rupees. This was to function alongside of *Prajashakti,* the existing Communist Party weekly in that language.

On 14th March 1952, the Indo-Soviet Cultural Festival and Convention were held in Bombay and out of this emerged the Indo-Soviet Cultural Society to replace the Friends of the Soviet Union which, over a period of a decade, had become too exposed as a Party front and had been designated as such by the Government of India. Dr A. V. Baliga, a surgeon, was nominated President of the Indo-Soviet Cultural Society, while Prof V. K. R. V. Rao of Delhi University, Prof P. C. Mahalanobis, Statistical Adviser of the Government of India, Dr Meghnad Saha, scientist and MP and Mr Harindranath Chattopadhyaya, poet and MP, were nominated Vice-Presidents. Names of a number of well-known writers, painters, musicians, dancers, educationists and lawyers are to be found in the list of members of the National Council of the Society.

Intense activity marked the holding of an International Industries Fair in Bombay in the opening months of 1952, followed by an International Film Festival. In both cases, exhibits and films from the Iron Curtain countries predominated and won the admiration of large numbers of credulous visitors, working a veritable psychological revolution among sections of the middle class.

The Cultural Festival organised by the Indian People's Theatre Association in Bombay in April 1953 was an undoubted success.

The constant coming and going of so-called cultural, literary, film and artistic delegations from the Soviet Union and Communist China was another feature. Each of these visits was utilised by the local communists for purposes of political demonstration, the making of contacts and the winning of adherents. Some of these delegations were official ones. Others were non-official ones sponsored by fellow-travelling fronts. Thus, Bombay was visited in December 1951 by an official Chinese Cultural Mission; from January to March 1952, it had the International Industries Fair; in March/April 1952 the International Film Festival. In the same month it was also visited by a Russian delegation at the invitation of the Indo-Soviet Friendship Society and later there was a visit by a Soviet Artists' Delegation accompanying an exhibition of Soviet art. Conversely, the holding of international conferences abroad and the sending of delegations from India was very marked.

Students

An obvious focal point of attack were the universities where both teachers and students offered an attractive target. The communist student front, the All-India Students' Federation, is affiliated to the International Students' Union in Prague. Apart from providing directives, this Comintern front also helps in 'softening up' students by making appropriate donations and gifts for the 'relief' of Indian students.

Activity on the youth and student fronts was intensified with the beginning of 1952. Already in August 1951, the AISF had restarted its fortnightly organ called the *Student*.

The AISF now decided to work on two fronts – an open front

and an underground front. On the open front, the communist students were to adopt United Front tactics and influence students towards their point of view. On the other hand, the underground front was to try and recruit more members and further the Communist Party policy without exposing them in the process. Pamphlets in support of the latter front were to be issued anonymously so that the printers and publishers might not be traced. A senior Party member was designated to take charge of the student funds. These were among the decisions understood to be reportedly taken at a secret meeting held in Madras from 5th to 10th October 1951. Among other decisions understood to be reportedly taken was one that it should be disclosed cynically after the meeting that the AISF was not to take part in politics or support any party in the coming elections. Another decision was that an attempt should be made to capture college unions and high school 'Parliaments'. Students were to be informed that the CPI had decided that party members among the students should not be deputed to foreign countries unless they had something new to learn. Student functionaries already abroad were directed to complete their studies and return home to India as soon as possible.

Perhaps in response to the overt decision not to participate in politics or the election campaign, the Government of Assam lifted the ban on the Assam Students' Federation in November 1951 with the result that that organisation was actively mobilised as part of the communist election front operating through student squads.

Aligarh Muslim University has been marked by communist activity. In December 1951 the Aligarh Students' Federation held its meeting and passed the usual resolutions about Nepal and other issues. A rally organised on that occasion was presided over by Dr Saif-ud-din Kitchlew, President of the All-India Peace Council. Nepal Day was observed by the students on 2nd December.

In the beginning of 1952, the International Union of Students directed the AISF to observe an 'International Day of Solidarity of Youth and Students against Colonialism' on 21st February. With the office now shifted to Calcutta and its affairs run by a local group, it was decided at a meeting of the AISF secretariat towards the end of February that the existing office-bearers should function for the Communist Party on other fronts and should be replaced by new students.

Despite visa restrictions, the International Union of Students tried to send emissaries to India. It asked the Calcutta Federation of Democratic Youth to intervene actively with the Government of India for the issue of necessary visas and explained that on its part it was renewing its efforts through the Indian Embassy in Prague. These efforts were evidently successful since Nixon, Secretary of the World Federation of Democratic Youth, managed to get into India and toured the country creating communist cells among young folk.

The annual conference of the Delhi communist student front was held in February 1952 and it had the honour of having Dr S. K. Sen, Vice-Chancellor of Delhi University, in the Chair.

In January 1953 it was reported that 'in response to the request of the Andhra Provincial Students' Federation, the International Students' Union, Prague, sent a free gift of medicines worth over Rs 25,000, including some very rare drugs, for distribution among the victims of Rayalseems famine'.[32]

About the same time, as a 'symbol of friendship between the Soviet and the Indian people', the Soviet Embassy in Delhi presented and the Delhi University received 450 books and eighty English and Russian journals which were designed to help teachers and students of that University 'to understand better Soviet culture, economy and science and the peaceful intentions of the Soviet people, and purge the lies spread about our country by war-mongers'. This purpose was blandly explained by a Soviet spokesman at a ceremony attended by the Soviet Ambassador and the Vice-Chancellor, Dr S. K. Sen.[33]

Though the character of the All-India Students' Federation is by now pretty well established, it was noted that, when the annual session of the Federation met in Hyderabad in January 1953, not only did the authorities provide accommodation at the Nizam's College for the holding of the session and other facilities, but they actually closed the colleges for half a day in order to enable the session to attract a large number of students.

Infiltration has similarly advanced in Delhi University. Prof V.K.R.V.Rao, who constantly appeared on communist front platforms such as that of the Indo-China Friendship Association, was the leading signatory to a manifesto signed by a hundred lecturers of Delhi University denouncing the UN General Assembly for branding the Chinese communists as aggressors in Korea. It was possible for the auspices of the University Union in Delhi to be secured for a meeting to mourn the death of Stalin, with Prof V.K.R.V.Rao in the Chair, on 6th March 1953.[34]

In April 1953, communist strength among the lecturers and students in Khatmandu, the capital of Nepal, was so considerable that they were able to call a joint strike of professors and the communist-dominated student organisation. This strike was to protest against the 'colonial status' of Nepalese teachers who were being paid in Nepalese currency, while Indian lecturers were paid in Indian currency. From this the agitators concluded that the present Nepal Government was anti-national and servile to India.[35]

By and large, it would perhaps be possible to say that greater success appeared to reward communist efforts in the case of lecturers than of students. The student body, as was shown by elections to the National Union of Students, was still predominantly non-communist, and anti-communist elements were fairly active and strong. Among teachers, however, there was little resistance to infiltration. Thus, the 28th session of the West Bengal College and University Teachers' Conference, which met on 3rd and 4th April, was inaugurated by one of the delegates to the Moscow Economic Conference and proceeded, without opposition, to pass resolutions expressing profound sorrow at the death of Stalin and adopting the Soviet line on 'peace'.[36] Hardly any Vice-Chancellor of a University or Head of a Department had yet spoken out against communist intervention in the field of education and called for a halt to be put to it.

The Government of the State of Bombay, however, showed commendable awareness of the dangers of this development by announcing in the State Assembly that action was being taken to stop members and adherents of the Communist Party from serving in government establishments including schools. This action followed on the misuse by certain communist teachers of their positions in State schools to indoctrinate the young pupils under their control.

Youth

Besides students, other sections of youth are not altogether overlooked. Under constant prodding from the World Federation of Democratic Youth, efforts were made in one part of India after another to foment youth conferences and fronts. These efforts did not meet with much success, but they provided a cover for contact to be established with the younger sections of white-collared workers who were then activised for the purpose of capturing and dominating trade unions serving this class of employees.

An editorial in the Cominform journal of 28th March 1952, stressed the importance of youth organisations in regions such as India, the Near East, the Middle East and Africa, where the national liberation movement was on a lower stage of development than elsewhere and where the need to enlist youth in the struggle against colonial oppression and national independence was all the greater.

Lawyers and Doctors

Other sections of the intelligentsia were by no means neglected. While the International Association of Democratic Lawyers was at work and had so far succeeded in forming a branch in Bombay, an opening meeting of which was held in March 1953, the preparations for a 'World Medical Congress', originally scheduled to be held in Rome in 1952, provided an opportunity to infiltrate among medical men.

Writers and Artists

Writers were catered for by the 'Progressive Writers' Association', a longstanding front which had gone out of circulation but had recently been revived in view of the more propitious atmosphere. The 'Indian People's Theatre Association' was similarly 're-organised', with new names adorning the letter heading in place of those which had by now been thoroughly exposed. A very successful conference was held in Bombay in March 1953 attended by many artistes, including script writers, screen stars and producers. It would not be inaccurate to say that in Bombay, which is the home of the Indian film industry – in bulk the second largest in the world – communist influence was dominant.

Scientists

Perhaps in no other section of the intelligentsia was there quite as dangerous an inroad made as among scientists. Major-General Sir Sahib Singh Sokhey, one-time head of the Haffkine Institute, later a member of the WHO Secretariat in Geneva, and recently nominated by the Indian Government to the Council of States as a distinguished scientist, was a leading scientific figure whose support had been secured. General Sokhey constantly appeared on such platforms as the Indo-China Friendship Association and the Peace Council and was a leading light in the Indian Association of Scientific Workers which is affiliated to the well-known comintern front, the World Federation of Scientist Workers.[37] In the middle of 1953, Gen Sokhey led the Indian delegation to the communist Peace Congress in Budapest, and was later awarded a Stalin Peace Prize.

Businessmen

Even businessmen, who would have been thought to be beyond approach, were receiving appropriate attention. The groundwork was laid by a resolution of the World Peace Council meeting in East Berlin in February 1951 when the call was given for a World Economic Conference. This met in Moscow in August 1952. While the front ranks of Indian industry refused to be attracted, some patriotic and fairly influential businessmen were inveigled into attending the conference in the company of communist functionaries and fellow-travellers. Some of those who returned from the Moscow Conference set about trying to form an organisation in their respective countries which would co-operate with the

'International Committee for the Promotion of International Trade' which was set up at the Moscow Conference as an agency through which the communists could carry on their campaign to break down the blockade on the supply of strategic and war materials to the Soviet bloc and Communist China, and which would create misunderstanding and tension between different national sections of the business world. A British Council for the Promotion of International Trade sprang into existence soon after the conference and an Indian Council for the Promotion of International Trade was inaugurated in Bombay by none else than the President of the Indian Merchants' Chamber on 8th January 1953. It was claimed by the officials of the organisation that their Council was not affiliated to the international organisation bearing the same name. Later, in order to emphasise the dissociation, the businessmen concerned changed the name of the organisation, which is now know as the Indian Council of Foreign Trade and is certainly not controlled by communist elements.

What made these moves dangerous was the international communist policy of playing up 'national capitalism' against 'Anglo-American imperialism'. This thesis originated from Communist China, where it undoubtedly succeeded in confusing and dividing the industrial and commercial class prior to the seizure of power by Mao Tse-tung, and was now being applied in India and the other underdeveloped countries of Asia and Latin America. The existence of a considerable amount of economic nationalism among the Indian industrial and business community, and the feeling that in many fields of enterprise they were being elbowed out by larger and better financed corporations based on the UK or USA, undoubtedly provided a basis for communist groups to use and divert to their own purpose. Meeting in Calcutta in January 1953, the enlarged plenum of the Central Committee of the Communist Party of India included among its decisions one which declared that 'national industry must be protected against the competition of foreign goods' and concerns.[38]

In August 1953, E. M. S. Namboodiripad signalised this shifting of the line in the Party journal in answer to a question:

'*Q.* So far, the CP I had been advocating nationalisation of all key industries. But now its programme states that only the industries owned by Britishers will be nationalised. Why this change in the programme?

'*A*. That the CP I advocated for some time the nationalisation of all key industries does not mean that it was a correct slogan. As a matter of fact, it was an incorrect slogan from the very beginning.

'It should be mentioned in this connection that Marxism-Leninism does not countenance the idea of the edge of the revolution in colonial and semi-colonial countries being directed against native capitalism . . .

'It was in keeping with these fundamental principles of Leninism that the programme of the Communist International, when outlining the "most important of the special tasks of the Communist Parties of the colonial and semi-colonial countries' speaks of 'nationalisation of large-scale enterprises (industrial, transport, banking and others) owned by the imperialists' and not the large-scale enterprises owned by the native capitalists".

'That the Communist Party of India departed from these specific injunctions of the Communist International shows that the Party was committing the very same mistake against which the International headed by Lenin had warned them – "painting the bourgeois-democratic liberation trends in the backward countries in communist colours".

'The correction of this mistake, the restoration of the original basis laid down by the International, the concretisation of the word "Imperialists" by making it clear that, so far as India is concerned, imperialism means British imperialism – that is all that the new programme of the Party has done.' [39]

Women

Women were being increasingly affected. The Women's International Democratic Federation had been active in the last two or three years and its efforts culminated in the attempt to obtain support in this country for the 'World Congress of Women' in Denmark in June 1953. A National Preparatory Conference was convened in the first week of May and an appeal in this connection was issued in March by leading women fellow-travellers including Miss Anne Mascarene, MP, Mrs Renu Chakravarty, MP, Ismat Chugtai, Mrs Aruna Asaf Ali, Hajra Begum, Mrs Gyanchand and Mrs R. K. Karanjia.[40] A large group of Indian women later attended the meeting in Copenhagen.

Labour

In the Trade Union field, the international contacts of the communist-controlled unions were maintained and the AITUC was represented at meetings of the General Council of the World Federation of Trade Unions. Trade Union contacts with the Chinese communists were also fostered.

It may be mentioned here that parallel invitations to visit Peking on May Day were issued to the Socialist-controlled Hind Mazdoor Sabha and the Congress-controlled Indian National Trade Union Congress. The first organisation accepted the invitation and some of its delegates on return joined in the chorus of approval of the Mao Tse-tung régime and its achievements, while others were critical. The INTUC on the other hand, rejected the invitation as also did the major trade union federation in Pakistan.

While, for the first five or six years after the war, the communists failed to regain the ground they lost among organised workers in the early post-war years since both the Indian National Trade Union Congress and the Hind Mazdoor Sabha (controlled by the Congress and the Socialists respectively) refused to have anything to do with the communist-controlled All-India Trade Union Congress, by the middle of 1952 a definite trend was visible indicating some revival of response to communist activity on the Trade Union front. The response the communists secured was most noticeable among what may be described as white-collar workers, such as employees of banks, insurance companies and government offices. The combination of literacy in English and consequent susceptibility to propaganda coupled with low income and unsatisfactory working conditions provided an appropriate field. Another sector where success was registered was in regard to aviation employees where the Air-India Employees' Union and the leadership of the Aero Workers' Federation passed into communist hands. Yet another field dominated by the communists was that of the petroleum industry. By April 1953, it was possible for the communists to form a Federation of Indian Petroleum

Workers claiming to represent 15,000 petroleum workers distributed over fifteen centres all over the country.[41]

The May Day rallies organised in 1953 by the communists and the AITUC were certainly more impressive than the efforts of their democratic rivals. That in Calcutta was certainly the biggest demonstration the city had ever seen on 1st May. In some places, dissident Socialists were to be found on the communist platform.[42]

One of the factors making for this success was, paradoxically enough, the superior legal advocacy that the communists were able to provide in a situation where recourse to Industrial Courts and Tribunals was part of the daily routine of Union functioning. Trade Union workers of the nationalist and socialist persuasion bitterly complained that, while lawyers of the democratic persuasion treated industrial disputes in the same manner as any commercial cause, the Communist Party maintained in the field full-time members of the Party who belonged to the legal profession and who were available without cost to Unions affiliated to, or under the influence of, the All-India Trade Union Congress.

These limited successes encouraged, in the autumn of 1952, a revival of the slogan of 'trade union unity'. This demand, pressed vigorously through the units of the AITUC, was also buttressed by a manifesto issued in October 1952 by Mr N.M.Joshi and Mr Mrinal Kanti Bose who had, for over a decade now, rotated on the periphery of the communist movement. The suggestion put forward by them was that the INTUC, the Hind Mazdoor Sabha, the United TUC (a non-Stalinist but Marxist grouping in Bengal) and the AITUC should merge in one federation, with one affiliated union in each industry.

By this manoeuvre, the communists once again sought to put in the wrong the non-communist Trade Union workers who were forced to oppose this ostensibly reasonable move for unification. While the INTUC and the HMS resisted the pressure, the United TUC led by Mr M.K.Bose expressed agreement in principle to merger with the AITUC.

By the beginning of 1953 it was evident that at least certain elements in the socialist-controlled HMS were prepared to associate with communist unions for certain limited purposes. Thus, on

7th January, a joint demonstration was held before the Delhi Assembly to present a charter of seventeen demands to the Labour Minister. This charter was signed by 36 trade unions in the State of Delhi which included those affiliated to the HMS and the UTUC as well as the AITUC. As a result of this move, the communists moved on to take steps to set up a permanent Joint Trade Union Committee in Delhi representing the AITUC and the HMS, the UTUC and unaffiliated unions. These steps were taken despite the threat of disciplinary action against local HMS leaders who were threatened with expulsion by the national socialist leadership.[43]

An indication of the reviving influence of the communists in the Bombay working class was given on the occasion of Stalin's death in response to a call for stoppage of work on 9th March given by the Secretary of the Bombay Committee of the Communist Party of India as a mark of respect to the memory of their dead chief. Ten textile mills and thirty silk mills remained completely closed, while a score of others worked with depleted complements.[44]

At an annual conference of the UTUC held in Calcutta from 7th to 9th March, Mr M.K. Bose reported on the progress made towards trade union unity. He informed the delegates that both the AITUC and the Hind Mazdoor Sabha were prepared for merger of the UTUC with their organisation. The difficulty was that, while the AITUC was for the merger of all trade union federations, the HMS created difficulty by insisting on the exclusion of the AITUC. A committee was appointed with Mr Bose as convener to go further into this problem.[45] On 18th March, a spokesman of the AITUC assured a workers' rally in Calcutta that once the AITUC and UTUC joined hands, the Hind Mazdoor Sabha would not be able to keep away from them for long.[46] By May, it was announced that a joint session of the AITUC and UTUC was being planned for July.[47] Simultaneously, a decision to open twelve 'trade union schools' at centres in different regions for training over four months 300 young organisers was made public.

The one big set-back the communists suffered was in the sphere of the railways. There, as a result of negotiations between the All-India Railwaymen's Federation, the most representative body of railway workers with Mr Jayaprakash Narayan, the socialist leader, as President and the late Mr Hariharnath Shastri, President of the Indian National Railways Workers' Federation affiliated to the INTUC, a decision to merge the two unions was taken in April 1953. A significant part of this development was that the efforts of the communists to participate in this process of unification were firmly turned down by both sides.[48]

By and large, the outlook in the Trade Union field was that of a persistence of communist activity over the next few years which might reap increasing returns if the democratic unions affiliated to the INTUC and the Hind Mazdoor Sabha continued their internecine quarrels. Even otherwise, efforts to maintain a grip on workers engaged in industries of strategic importance such as the docks, petroleum and aviation could be expected to continue.

The Peasantry

The peasant front did not show as much activity as that of the trade unions. Perhaps the States where the communists made most advance on this front were the Punjab and Pepsu. There the Lal (Red) Communist Party pursued during the opening months of 1952 its campaign for taking forcible possession of land from Biswedars (landlords).

In the beginning of 1952, faint efforts at reorganising the peasant front became noticeable. A document prepared by E.M.S. Namboodiripad on the agrarian question was circulated. This document dealt with agrarian problems in different parts of the country, recommended the reorientation of the Party's outlook on the Kisan front to carry on a merciless struggle against the right opportunist and left sectarian mistakes in its understanding and practice and to consolidate the gains and achievements of the last five years so that the party could be in a position to lead millions of peasants in their revolutionary struggle in the months ahead. In order to achieve this end, he suggested that the party should formulate the immediate demands of the peasantry in the light of the working of the Land Reforms Bill, the Acts and Rules connected with the procurement and prices of food grains, rationing and supply of essential consumer goods and seeds, the plans and work-ing of irrigation, and organise systematic study of rural economy and the application of Marxist-Leninist theory on agrarian ques-tions to the concrete conditions obtaining in the country. He also recommended the study of the history of the peasant movements in the various States, the organisation of agitation amongst the peasants and the systematic recruitment and education of Kisan militants, particularly those drawn from landless and poor classes.

Bankim Mukherji, General Secretary of the All-India Kisan Sabha, in a circular letter to organisations in the States, pointed out the necessity of holding negotiations for a merger of the two chief organisations – the All-India Kisan Sabha and the United Kisan Sabha.

The end of the Telengana struggle had found the communists at a low water-mark of their influence in the countryside. Within two years, however, it was obvious that their losses were more than made good. In Telengana itself, a recrudescence of terrorist acti-vity, which took the form of threatening peasants in Nalgonda District and collecting grain at the point of the gun, was reported by the beginning of 1953. Bands of communist strong-arm men, locally described as 'rathri doralu' (bosses of the night), were reported to be rampant again.[49]

Reports of peasant discontent fostered by communists began to appear from various corners of India, including Assam and Nepal. By far the worst situation, however, developed in the State of PEPSU, where Indian Government spokesmen admitted that the communists had been able to set up zones of parallel government. Self-constituted 'Panchayats', which owed no allegiance to the law of the land, were dispossessing farmers of their lands and 'distri-buting' them to landless labourers. Neither the farmers nor the police were, over a period of months, able to counter the mass intimidation practised by the Communist 'Panchayats'. Finally in March 1953, the Government of India, faced with a situation where the province was rapidly sinking into chaos, had to suspend the operation of the Constitution and take administrative power in their own hands. The hope was expressed that the President's rule over a period of several months might be able to 'clean up' this unhealthy situation on one of India's most significant frontiers.

In April 1953, the communists felt strong enough to revive their old front, 'the All-India Kisan (Peasants') Federation'. They were further emboldened to moot the idea, through the President of their Conference, of an Asian Peasant Convention to be held in New Delhi by the end of 1953 in order to help cement 'fraternal bonds and mutual understanding between peasants of all Asiatic countries and strengthen the forces of peace and dissipate the clouds of imperialist war from our fair continent.[50]

It was obvious that communist efforts would continue during the next phase along the lines of seeking to establish a 'Yenan' at some suitable point in India. Defeated for the moment in Telengana in Hyderabad State, the concentration of forces shifted to Punjab and PEPSU in the north west. There, the merger of the Lal (Red) CP–a relic of the old Ghadhr Party–in the middle of 1952 brought new strength to the Communist Party of India. Simultaneously with this, similar efforts were under way in the northeastern frontier tracts of Manipur, Tripura and Assam. Kashmir was perhaps the region where communist penetration proceeded farthest.

Kashmir

In September 1952, the leader of the communists in Kashmir, Dhanwantri, addressed what was described as the 'first public meeting of the Communist Party of India in the State'. That did not mean that the Communist Party did not exist in the State in the preceding years. Indeed, communist penetration in Kashmir was already well ahead of the advance made by the Party in almost any other part of India. What the announcement signified was that the Communist Party had decided that the time had come to move forward by dropping the veil behind which it had functioned during the five years since independence. That veil was none other than the Kashmir National Conference led by Sheikh Abdulla, Prime Minister of the State. It was alleged that out of seventy-five members of the Kashmir Constituent Assembly, not less than fifteen were secret communists, that in the Cabinet no less than three were communist adherents.[51] It was common knowledge that the President of the Kashmir Constituent Assembly was a communist adherent. Among the positions that he held was that of Vice-President of the All-India Peace Council. Lower down the administrative scale the communists planted their men in key positions such as district magistrates. One of these was reported to have attended the Srinagar District Peace Conference held at Zinapur.[52]

The policy followed during the past few years of successful communist infiltration of the ruling party in Kashmir was that of giving limited support, not unaccompanied by attempts to build up a 'united front from below' against the Kashmir leadership.

The results of these policies were so successful that an observer reported that 'the Indian communists are gleefully proclaiming in every nook and corner of the Punjab and Pepsu that it is only a matter of a year or two when the Indian Red revolution would be initiated in Kashmir, the Indian Yenan. The Red Army rising from that hilly state would, they claim, by backed by the armed might of New China and Soviet Russia.[53]

It was against this background of success that the decision of the communists in Kashmir to fly their own banner and distinguish themselves from the ruling party needed to be understood.[54]

The cleavage between the Union and Kashmir Governments on the one hand and the Praja Parishad, an organisation of the Hindus of Jammu State pressing for the unconditional accession of Kashmir to the Indian Union, provided an excellent opportunity to the communists to come forward as the champions of the Kashmir Government against a 'communal' opposition.

The united front between the communists and a section of the leadership of the Kashmir Government was symbolised by the first Democratic Youth League Conference held in Jammu from 1st to 3rd May 1953. Alongside of 'official' communists like Dhanwantri, who presided, were to be found at that conference, Mr Ghulam Mohammed Sadiq, President of the Kashmir Constituent Assembly, and Mr Krishan Dev Sethi, a member of the Constituent Assembly, who functioned as Chairman of the Reception Committee.

Donations made by Sheikh Abdullah and other ministers of the Kashmir Government were announced. It was noticed that the convention received the co-operation of officials as well as professors of the local Government College. Free board, lodging and transport were provided to peasants. Just a few days previously, the local socialists had been refused permission to hold even a May Day meeting by the District Magistrate of Jammu, but this three-day session found no difficulty in getting official licence.[55]

CHAPTER TEN

The Third Congress

27th December 1953 to 3rd January 1954

The First Congress of the Communist Party of India had met in Bombay in 1944; the Second Congress met in Calcutta from 28th February to 6th March 1948; the Third Congress convened in Madurai in the State of Madras on 27th December 1953. It was attended by about 300 delegates claiming to represent 50,000 members throughout the country.

The proceedings of the Congress continued from 27th December to 3rd January, covering most of the day and on three occasions lasting through the night into the early hours of the morning. All the sessions were closed to the Press and the public and these were allowed to get only a glimpse of what happened by means of hand-outs, doled out and statements made by Party spokesmen after the conclusion of each session. As it happens, however, a report of the proceedings in the closed sessions along with the full text of several of the documents circulated to the delegates was made available by the Democratic Research Service, Bombay, in a publication entitled *Communist Conspiracy at Madurai*.[1]

Having elected a Presidium of five, the Congress settled down to its business. The delegates were informed that greetings from Communist Parties in twenty-six countries of the world had been received. Only one of these was, however, read out, and that was— significantly enough—from the Communist Party of the Soviet Union. This message ran as follows:

'The Central Committee of the Communist Party of the Soviet Union is sending its ardent, fraternal greetings to the Third Congress of the Communist Party of India.

'The Communist Party of India, being the mouthpiece of hopes and aspirations of working masses of the Indian people for many years, has been leading and directing the struggle of the working class, peasantry, and all toilers of India for their fundamental rights, for their vital interests, for national independence of their motherland.

'The Communist Party of India, together with all progressive-minded people of the country, has been consistently fighting for preserving peace in the countries of Asia and in the whole world.

'We heartily wish the Communist Party of India every success in the further strengthening of the Party, in education of the Party members in the spirit of loyalty to the Banner of Communism, to the cause of proletarian Internationalism, in uniting the broad masses of the Indian people for accomplishing the tasks undertaken by the Communist Party of India in its new Programme.

'The Central Committee of the Communist Party of the Soviet Union'.[2]

Among fraternal delegates who addressed the Congress were Mr Harry Pollitt of the Communist Party of Great Britain, and Dr Wickremsinghe and Mr Kennemann of the CP of Ceylon.

The first major item of business was the consideration of the Review Report of the Politbureau covering the period since the All India Party Conference of October 1951. This Report was supposed to do duty in place of the much fuller political organisational report customary on such an occasion. It was explained to the delegates that the failure of Provincial Committees to submit their own reports in time had led to this unfortunate default. Nonetheless, there was considerable criticism on the point and a draft resolution of censure was actually given notice of by none other than fourteen members of the Party Headquarters Staff. That resolution ran as follows:

'The Third Congress of the Communist Party of India takes serious note of the fact that the Central Committee has failed to submit its Report to the Congress as specifically enjoined by the Party Constitution.

'Despite the fact that Provincial Committees have not submitted their Reports in time for the CC to prepare its own Report, the Congress feels that a Report of its own functioning, both political and organisational, by the CC would have helped the Congress to assess the problems and the tasks before the Party.

'The Congress urges upon the Central Committee to draw lessons from this failure on its part, and calls upon the Party as a whole to improve and strengthen Party functioning, so that such a situation may not be repeated in future.'[3]

Politbureau Report

The Review Report of the Politbureau[4] commenced with the dis-. cussions of the All India Party Conference held in Calcutta in October 1951 and the unanimous election of a new Central Committee. Then the Report went on to refer to the important advance registered by the Party during the general elections at the end of 1951.

The Party had also been able to register big advances after the elections. Of great significance in this connection were the results of the municipal elections in 1953 in Utter Pradesh, till then a stronghold of the Congress.

The role that the Party had played 'in several important struggles including some of the biggest like the struggle for the Andhra Province, the Saurashtra struggle and the anti-Tram fare increase struggle in Calcutta has once again shown that the Party is increasingly becoming the leader of popular struggles'. The Report sought to generalise the experience of the entire activities of the Party during the period under review. According to the Report, some of the most important features of 'the new wave of mass struggles' were as follows:

'*Firstly:* It is greater in sweep and momentum than at any time since the transfer of power in August 1947.

'*Secondly:* The majority of struggles are on concrete issues facing the lives of people . . . taxes, food subsidy, levies, wages and bonus, evictions, etc, but there have also been immense mass actions of such political issues as civil liberties, linguistic provinces.

'*Thirdly:* While there is still great unevenness of the movement, areas which in the past seldom saw struggles against the Congress Government now became scenes of big actions. This includes politically backward areas like Rajasthan, Saurashtra, Vindhya Pradesh etc, on one hand and strongholds of Congress like UP on the other.

'*Fourthly:* The new wave of mass struggles embraces new classes and sections also . . . teachers, patwaris and other Government employees.

Even sections of the big bourgeoisie voice opposition against certain policies of the Government . . . like refusal to protect Indian industries against foreign competition.

'*Fifthly:* An immensely important role is played by the working class. In repelling the attack of the bourgeoisie, the working class displayed a high degree of unity . . . forged in action, class solidarity, militancy and initiative which some time makes even INTUC Unions participate in struggles. Working class struggles encourage all classes and sections to wage struggles for their own demands. Also on several occasions the working class has come out in action on issues affecting the entire people, although this is far from being the general feature yet.

'*Sixthly:* Struggles of one section or class evoke spontaneous popular sympathy and sometimes especially when the Government launches severe repression, the entire people of the area go into action, as happened at Lucknow recently. Followers of all parties, including masses following the Congress, take part in the struggle. Especially when an issue affecting all classes and sections is taken up, when mass campaign on its basis is conducted, even though the issue itself is an immediate economic issue, the struggle rapidly assumes the form of a mass political struggle against the Government and broadest popular unity gets forged . . . Saurashtra, Rajasthan, above all, Calcutta where the struggle against the increase in tram fare imposed by the British-owned company is the biggest mass struggle since August 1947.

'*Seventhly:* The presence of Communist and other democratic parties and elements in the Legislatures helps to strengthen the struggles and focus attention on the demands.

'*Eighthly:* Due to the unity and militancy of the people and the weakening position of the monopolists, landlords and Government, many of the struggles succeed in winning concessions . . . which, though not big by themselves, heighten confidence of the masses in their own strength and further weakens the Government.

'*Ninthly:* The struggle increasingly assumes a political content because of the intervention of the Government on the side of the exploiters and because of the growing realisation on the part of the people that the solution of their immediate problems is linked with the general problem of replacement of the present Government by a democratic Government.

'*Tenthly:* The Communist Party plays an increasingly important role in the struggles, which increases the prestige and influence of the Party and draws the masses towards it.

'*Eleventhly:* and finally: As the result of all this, as the result of the growing fiasco of the Government policies, as the result of increasing strength of the mass movement, contradictions sharpen in the Congress, Congress organisations get increasingly split into warring factions, conflict develops between Congress Committees and Ministries each blaming the other for the growing isolation of the Congress ... conflict develops inside the Congress Legislative Party, conflict develops between the Congress and its allies leading, in provinces where the Congress is especially weak, to Governmental instability and ministerial crisis.'

The Report then proceeded to give the other side of the picture: 'Though very much weakened and disintegrating, the ruling classes have still at their command vast reserves with which they can temporarily at least arrest the tempo of people's struggles.' These were catalogued as the 'traditional hold of the Congress ... the personality of the Prime Minister ... the hold of the Gandhian ideology ... the manoeuvres of certain parties of the opposition, particularly those of the leadership of the PSP on the one hand and of the Jan Sangh and other communal organisations on the other'.

A long discussion then followed on the organisational form of the 'Democratic Front', in the course of which the independent role of the Party was stressed and particular reference was made to the dispute between the Central Committee of the Party and the People's Democratic Front of Hyderabad led by Dr Jaisoorya and Mr G. M. Shroff.[5]

The Report then went on to stress that the key slogan should be that of a 'Government of Democratic Unity'. Efforts at forming such a Government 'can be made only under certain circumstances, chief of which is that the Communist Party and other genuinely democratic elements should be in a dominant position within the opposition'. It was also stressed that 'the question of the formation of a Government of Democratic Unity' was a question arising from the struggles of the common people for the realisation of their immediate demands.

The Report then reviewed what was described as the miraculous recovery made by the Party during the period under review, and elaborated on the position on the Trade Union, peasant and other fronts. It proceeded to draw attention to the organisational weakness of the Party in performing its major tasks and stressed the importance of setting up a 'collectively functioning' Central Committee and Politbureau.

The Report registered notable progress made by 'our comrades in the Peace movement and in the movement for Indo-Soviet and India China Friendship'.

'The Party Congress', declared the Report, 'has a twofold task. It is to evolve the correct policy by pursuing which alone the people's movement can advance. It is also to create organisational guarantees to ensure the effective carrying out of that policy'.

The Report concluded, significantly enough, by referring to the 'position that our country occupies today in world policies as the biggest semi-colonial country yet to win freedom'.

The next item of business was the adoption of the Party's Programme. This was introduced in the form in which it had been approved by the All India Party Conference of October 1951 prior to the General Elections, and was re-endorsed with only one amendment, which was in regard to the subject of language.

Political Resolution

The draft of a Political Resolution, the main business of the Congress, produced a marathon debate which spread over three days and the Resolution was finally adopted at a midnight session as the New Year came in. No less than 455 amendments were tabled to this Resolution, which revealed a cleavage between the Party bosses led by A. K. Ghosh and S. A. Dange on the one hand, and the 'Left of centre' opposition led by Rajeshwar Rao, consisting of the delegates from Andhra, Bengal, Punjab and the supporters of Ranadive on the other. To the 'right' of the platform were to be found the former General Secretary, P. C. Joshi, and his supporters.

Commencing with the statement that 'the signing of the Armistice in Korea on 27th July 1953 was a mighty victory for the heroic Korean and Chinese people, 'the draft Resolution[6] referred to the 'tremendous strength' gathered by the world Peace Movement, and the ever-sharpening conflicts and contradictions 'inside the imperialist camp and in the relations between the imperialist powers and dependent countries'.

'Significant in these respects', proceeded the Resolution, 'is also the role played by the Indian Government on a number of important international issues in the recent period – a role appreciated by the peaceloving masses and States. The Indian Government's denunciation of the atom bomb, its help in ending the hostilities in Korea, its condemnation of the tactics of Syngman Rhee, its opposition to the American move to transform Pakistan into a war base are factors helping the cause of peace.

'The cause of peace has been further strengthened by the growing bond of friendship and of cultural relation between the people of India on the one hand and the USSR and Chinese People's Republic on the other. The conclusion of the recent trade agreement between India and the USSR on mutually advantageous terms carried forward this process and can also help to reduce India's dependence on imperialist Powers'.

The alleged 'Pact' between the US and Pakistan is then referred to as having 'brought the war danger to the very threshold of India'.

The need is then expressed 'to intensify the fight against British imperialism, for quitting the Commonwealth and for the confiscation of British capital'.

The Resolution then went on to refer to the 'catastrophic crises in our agrarian economy ... The agrarian crises has grown into a national crises'. The failure of the Five Year Plan was alleged and the 'Nehru Government, dominated by monopolists and landlords' was accused of refusing to undertake those 'basic economic and political changes' which alone could resolve the crisis. 'In every sphere the Government continues the reactionary policies of the past ... Against these policies of the Government, against the growing offensive of the landlords and the monopolists, mass resistance has grown rapidly during the last two years ... What we are witnessing today is not merely the maturing of an economic crises, but along with it the initial stages of the development of a political crisis. Already in States like Travancore-Cochin, and in

O

Andhra, it is possible for us to raise ... the replacement of the present Government by a Government of Democratic Unity ... as a practical slogan ... The slogan of a Government of Democratic Unity is a slogan which demands organisation and unleashing of mass struggles on the widest scale ...

'The three inseparable tasks on the carrying out of which will depend the success of the democratic movement are the building of the Party, the building of the mass organisations and the building of the Democratic Front'.

The thesis posed by the 'Left' opposition against this proposal was one that had been produced on the eve of the Congress by the Andhra group led by Rajeshwar Rao. This Andhra Thesis (Appendix B) conceded that 'America is the spearhead of world reaction and the main enemy of Peace and Freedom for all people', but rejected concentration of fire on America at this stage. 'The chief enemy of our national freedom today', it urged, 'is British imperialism'. The current pattern of referring to 'Anglo-American imperialism' was criticised as defective for the following reasons:

'(1) It is unreal and factually incorrect to talk of American imperialism as American capital does not form more than 3-4 per cent of foreign capital investments in India.

'(2) It is so because it is British imperialism that has directly ruled over us for the last 200 years and is still keeping us in its grip (ie economically direct and politically indirect even today); more than eighty per cent of the foreign capital in India belongs to the British.

'(3) It is so since that when we are demanding complete national independence, we are demanding secession from the British Commonwealth of which our country has been forced to be a member and not from the United States of America.

'(4) It is also wrong to talk of general anti-imperialist fight without specifying the particular imperialism that is dominating over our country as this outlook, if logically extended, leads us on the verge of erroneous conclusions of the Trotskyite school of thought which advocate world revolution against world imperialism, ie the theory of permanent revolution.

'(5) It is totally wrong to talk of general anti-imperialism because this view point refuses to take note of the advancement of the revolution.'

All this, it was argued, brought one to the conclusion that 'British imperialism is the chief enemy of our national progress and therefore of our national independence. It is British imperialism that has allied itself with the native tendal interests and is defending the feudal order, barring all roads to prosperity and advancement; it is British imperialism that has allied itself with a section of the national bourgeoisie and defending the rotten colonial order; it is British capital that grips our national economy and impedes our national industries and bar national progress; it is British imperialism that has drawn to its side a section of the national big bourgeoisie and with their help tied us to the chariot of the British Commonwealth. So when we talk of anti-imperialist revolution it specifically means, in the present set-up a fight against British imperialism for national independence and freedom, but not against Anglo-American imperialism or world imperialism in general'.

Between these two points of view, one backed by Moscow in the person of Harry Pollitt and the other by 'nationalist' nuances, the battle raged long and indecisively.

When at last the Resolution was put to the vote, it was found that no more than half of those present endorsed it. As many as eighty-seven delegates from Andhra and Bengal formally declared their abstention by means of a statement made on their behalf by Basava Punniah.

With the Political Resolution out of the way, the Congress proceeded with the beginning of the New Year to a discussion of the draft Resolution on Organisation. It was not found possible, however, for either this or the draft amendments to the Party Constitution to be adopted, and both matters were shelved by being relegated to the Central Committee.

US-Pakistan Pact

Another resolution that evoked a fierce debate and acute division of opinion was that on the 'US-Pakistan Pact' of military assistance.

Describing the 'Pact' as a 'continuation of the policy of the

American warmongers . . . for launching a Third World War', the Resolution[7] called upon the people of India to unite against 'the attempts of the U S imperialists' to blackmail India to line up behind their war policy'. Hesitating to give a call for an alliance with Soviet Russia and Communist China in the face of the 'warmongers', the Resolution nonetheless denounced those 'powerful reactionary and communal forces, backed by landowning and financial circles, who are egging on the Government of India not to have friendly relations with the Soviet Union and China'.

Once again, the Congress found itself divided sharply and evenly between those who regarded 'American imperialism as the main enemy of the Indian communists and those who regarded the main opponent to be 'British imperialism' and its 'Indian stooges' represented by the present Indian Government. The opposition to the resolution inveighed against the tendency to overestimate the war danger. They warned that the immediate task of 'National Liberation' was in danger of being sidetracked by a false emphasis on the 'American menace'. On a crucial vote, the Congress was found to be split 105 against 105.

Other resolutions adopted at the tail end of the Congress referred to the impending elections in the State of Travancore-Cochin and to the denial of *visas* to alien communists for the purpose of attending the Congress.

Faced with the fact that the discussion on the Political Resolution and 'U S-Pakistan Pact' had shown that the Party was split wide open both on internal and external issues, those conducting the Congress were driven to the conclusion that the only way of enforcing any kind of authority or discipline was to placate the opposition by proposing contrary to the usual Communist practice a composite list for election to the Central Committee and the Politbureau containing names from the major groups in the Party, excluding only P. C. Joshi at one extreme and B. T. Ranadive at the other. Since a small Central Committee such as had preceded the Congress would be too small to accommodate such a motley crowd, it was decided to double the strength of the Central Committee and increase that of the Politbureau. In the result, no less than thirty-nine names were proposed from the platform for the

Central Committee. Even so, the detailed results of the voting (Appendix C) show that the 'Leftwing' opposition succeeded in defeating one nominee, namely, Hazrah Begum, in the official list and electing Dr G. G. Adhikari instead.

Even the doors of the Politbureau had to be thrown open to the rebels. An expanded Politbureau of nine persons was nominated, consisting of Messrs Ajoy Ghosh, E. M. S. Namboodiripad, S. A. Dange, P. Ramamurthi, Z. A. Ahmad, C. Rajeshwara Rao, P. Sundarayya, Ranen Sen and Hari Kishnan Singh Surjeet. Of these nine, four could be described as 'undependable' from the point of view of the policy adopted by the majority of the Congress.

One more setback for the platform remained before the business of the session concluded. When the Steering Committee proposed that the next Congress should meet after three years, the rank and file of the delegates forced it to accept an amendment moved by Vishvanath Mukerjee that the Congress should meet after two years, on the ground that the composition of the Politbureau and the Central Committee was not such as would enable them to be entrusted with the affairs of the Party for a longer period.

Two policy addresses were delivered before the secret sessions of the Congress concluded. One was by A. K. Ghosh, who had been renominated as General Secretary of the Party. The other was by Harry Pollitt. Pollitt's concluding address which, unlike his opening one, was carefully suppressed from the public as well as from rank and file members of the Party, was revealing. He frankly confessed to the delegates that he was depressed at the proceedings of the Congress and that he did not know what to tell people if they asked him about it. He was also angry, and he scolded the delegates and leaders like a schoolmaster.

Their 'secret' confabulations ended, the communists emerged on the evening of 3rd January to face a large rally of about 200,000 people, where they elaborated on selected items from among their decisions.

Conclusions

Certain conclusions emerge from the story of the Third Congress which has been pieced together here from the reports put out by the CPI, as well as the disclosures made by the Democratic Research Service.

The first broad conclusion that follows is that the Party has not been converted to the path of peaceful change and has the intention of reverting at the earliest opportunity to the course of armed insurrection and civil war. The professions of constitutional functioning are only a facade behind which the preparation for the ultimate seizure of power can be carried out.

The Politbureau Review Report as well as subsequent statements made by Party spokesmen make it abundantly clear that the course adopted at the Congress follows the general line laid down in May 1951. S. A. Dange is reported in fact to have said in the course of discussion on the political resolution that no change was necessary because the relationships between the classes remained the same today as they were in 1951. With our present knowledge that the Programme and Policy Statement of May 1951 were only the visible part of the iceberg, the larger part of which remained submerged below the surface in the form of the Tactical Line prescribed by Moscow, it follows clearly that the key document that inspired the policy and programme of 1951 continues to inspire the policy and programme of 1954.

This conclusion is confirmed by none other than the Cominform journal, *For a Lasting Peace, For a People's Democracy* of 5th February 1954, which, in a report on the Congress, wrote: 'On the basis of a correct analysis of the present situation, it has armed the Party with a clear perspective and laid down firm foundations for the detailed working out of the tactical line in every sphere and every area'.

Indeed, this could not be otherwise, since that document is of basic theoretical significance, and provides the theory of revolution, in the Indian context, for the entire period. The basis of the Tactical Line, namely, that India is a semi-colonial country yet to be liberated is found reflected in the concluding paragraph of the Review Report which refers to India as 'the biggest semi-colonial country yet to win freedom'.

When, during the discussion on the Political Resolution, a delegate objected that a 'Government of Democratic Unity' such as was now advocated was not the same as a Government of People's Democracy, A. K. Ghosh is reported to have replied that there was no fundamental difference between the two, and that a Government of Democratic Unity was conceived only as a first stage of the People's Democratic Government, which remained the ultimate ideal. 'We raise this as an agitational slogan', he explained, and stressed that such a government would be an organ of struggle which would allow them to exert pressure within the legislatures and to carry on mass mobilisation outside. In one of his many interventions, the General Secretary remarked that the fact that the Government of Democratic Unity would resist opposition should not be stated at this time.

The conclusion is obvious that the Tactical Line, which conjures up the vision of 'hundreds of streams of partisan struggles merging with general strikes and uprisings of workers in the cities', remains fully operative.

Certain conclusions also follow in regard to the 'Peace' movement and the United Front. About the former, the Tactical Line is brutally frank. 'The Peace Movement', it states, 'is not a pacific movement, not a movement mainly for recording abstract support for peace. It is a fighting movement for concrete action in defence of peace and, against the imperialistic warmongers, including those waging colonial wars'.

In so far as the United Front is concerned, the charges made by Dr N. M. Jaisoorya and G. M. Shroff of the People's Democratic Front in Hyderabad State showed that these fellow-travellers of the CPI during and since the General Elections of 1951 had learnt some bitter truths. In their letter[8] they said 'The working class leadership in practice means CPI leadership and in our experience they (the communists) have always attempted to equate leadership with CPI leadership since the CPI does not recognise any other party than itself as the working class party. We may be mistaken, but this is the impression we have gained from the actions and behaviour of their lesser lights with the petty-Commissar mentality. But, all things considered, the CPI has failed to establish itself in national leadership in the past. It is also admitted that it has passed through sectarian periods. In such a background the slogan takes a shape in practice to somehow impose this leadership on every front at all strategic levels. The "somehow" includes even un-democratic methods and intrigues. That leads to undemocratic functioning and a gulf between the CPI and the other constituents of the Front. It must be also pointed out that this call is not merely local but from the centre and probably forms a basic principle.'

In their letter, Dr Jaisoorya and Mr Shroff also charged the Communist Party with 'extra-territorial loyalties' and alleged that their policies were being determined by Moscow or the Comintern or the Cominform. They also accused the Communist Party of believing in violence or armed struggle and demanded that they eschew it unreservedly.

Instead of providing any satisfaction or assurance of better behaviour, P.Ramamurthi on behalf of the Central Committee of the CPI, in a letter to these two gentlemen dated Delhi, 16th November 1953[9] accused them of repeating the 'usual anti-Communist slanders' and likened them to the 'imperialists and feudal landlords and monopolists' who had been hitherto guilty of such 'slanders'.

Inner Party Crises

The other major fact that stands out of the proceedings of the Third Congress is that of continuing inner-party crisis and of in-ability to resolve the internal contradictions and to come to definite decision in regard to the basic political line. Even Mr Harry Pollitt with all the weight of Moscow behind him was unable to fulfil his assignment of healing the breach. Internal differences appear to have crystalised to such an extent and the viewpoints represented by the various groups to have become so irreconcilable that the leadership was unable to enforce the iron discipline for which it is famous. In the result, the rank and file members of the Party would appear to have enjoyed a spell of free discussion normally unknown in the Communist fold. The utter lack of confidence in the integrity of almost all important party leaders on the part of the rank and file, which was thus revealed, was remarkable. The fact that, apart from B. T. Ranadive at one end and P. C. Joshi at the other, the functionaries like A. K. Ghosh, S. A. Dange, E. M. S. Namboodiripad and P. Ramamurthy had no policy of their own and were therefore driven continually to manoeuvre between different factions was now widely understood.

Concretely, the issues on which the Third Congress revealed sharp differences of opinion were in regard to the assessment of the political situation, the tactics to be adopted in regard to the forms of the struggle and a United Front with other parties, the attitude to be adopted towards American and British 'imperialism' and the present Indian Government and, last but not the least, the control of the Politbureau and the Central Committee of the Party.

The results of the elections to the Central Committee showed that a very unstable equilibrium existed in the Party. There was a hard core of extremists at both ends. The former General Secretary, P. C. Joshi, polled 107 votes at one end, while B. T. Ranadive got 145 at the other. In between was a shifting body of moderates who control the party apparatus. While an open cleavage was averted, the Party was likely to be plagued in the coming two years by the fact that the composition of both the Politbureau and the Central Committee was heterogenous. The dissensions in the Party would now be reflected in its highest organs.

Lastly, there was little sign throughout the Congress of the influence of Mao Tse-tung and the Chinese Communist Party. It would appear that even their message of greetings was not read to the delegates. On the other hand, Moscow was omnipresent in the person of Harry Pollitt who spoke with authority on behalf of the international communist movement. His task was evidently twofold. First, to heal the breach in the Party. Secondly, to get the Congress to accept the anti-American and pro-British line which the current ends of Soviet diplomacy dictated.

Was the Congress a Success?

Was the Congress a success? Perhaps the best answer was that provided by none other than Harry Pollitt in the course of his final

address at the secret closing session of the Congress when he casti-
gated the delegates for their shortcomings. Pollitt listed the weakness that had been disclosed at the Conference:

(1) Lack of political preparation and the absence of the usual
political organisational report. 'I warn you', Pollitt threatened,
'this must not happen again'.

(2) Divided leadership and undue emphasis on differences and not
on points of agreement.

(3) The whole proceedings were bogged in a discussion on the role
of British and American imperialisms. 'Listening to the discussion', commented Pollitt acidly, 'I feel it was a conference of
lawyers discussing who gets the highest vote'.

(4) The discussion was as if India and the CPI were in complete
isolation from the rest of the world. There was gross underesti-
mation of the war danger and the importance of the fight for
'peace'.

(5) Pollitt's greatest grievance was about the lack of importance
given to the American 'menace'. 'After seven days', he complained,
'you discuss the US-Pakistan Pact which is the most serious
thing in the external situation concerning India. Any other party
would have discussed it at once'. Continuing, he said: 'It is the
USA which is the chief aggressor preparing a third world war.
This is a challenge to your Party and mine. Both Britain and India
hold the key to world peace. I am pleading for both our countries
because we are vulnerable'.

CHAPTER ELEVEN

The Outlook

The ten chapters that have gone before have told the story of the Communist Party in India and the reader can evaluate for himself or herself its real nature and rôle. A few generalisations may be attempted as a footnote to the story of the Indian Communist Party before proceeding to consider the outlook.

First, it is clear that the CPI was conceived in Moscow; that the larger part of the pioneering work was done by men from Britain and elsewhere; that, as the Premier of Madras State, Mr C. Rajagopalachari, has charged, the Indian communists receive help from abroad 'in the shape of directions and instructions';[1] and that the Party's whole career shows that no major change in policy has been or can be carried out without a directive from the international communist movement.[2]

Secondly, in the course of their career, the Indian communists have had to undertake many a left and right-about-turn and perform many a somersault at the behest of Moscow; yet there is hardly a figure of any importance, since M. N. Roy broke with the Comintern as far back as 1929, who has come out in the open to break with the Party and denounce the subservient rôle imposed on it.

Thirdly, within the framework of their loyalty to a foreign Power and their indifference to the interests of the Indian people, the Indian communists have been shown by the record to be a disciplined and devoted body of men and women who have made the best of a difficult task. Perhaps no other party could have survived the accumulation of blunders and betrayals which have been prescribed to them by their mentors. While their pathetic intellectual sycophancy may be condemned, their capacity for hard work and devotion to the cause cannot and should not in fairness be underestimated.

Fourth, the activities and fortunes of the Indian Communist Party are not directly inspired or affected by the condition of the Indian people, their poverty or their prosperity, but by the fortunes of the Soviet dictatorship of which they are an appendage. The Indian communists in practice, though not always in their professions, recognise and accept this dependence.

Organic Link

This organic link was re-emphasised in statements made in the course of the Congress of the Communist Party of Soviet Russia in Moscow in October 1952. These were denounced as a clear case of intervention in the internal affairs of India by the Parliamentary Secretary to the Prime Minister in the Council of States.

Malenkov's reference to India is thus reported: 'The peoples of the Colonial and dependent countries are putting up an increasingly determined resistance to the imperialist enslavers. The growing scope of the national liberation movement is shown by the struggle of the people of Viet-Nam, Burma, Malaya, the Philippines, and Indonesia, as well as by the growth of resistance in India, Iran, Egypt and other countries.'[3]

Stalin himself supplemented this with an expression of gratitude to fraternal parties and groups and an expression of support to them: 'Naturally, our Party cannot remain indebted to the fraternal parties, and it must in its turn render support to them and also to their peoples in their struggle for emancipation.'[4]

A. K. Gopalan, communist spokesman in the House of the People, then in Moscow undergoing prolonged 'medical treatment', who was the only fraternal delegate to the Congress from India, responded to this (according to a Moscow message dated 15th October) by conveying to the Congress 'the revolutionary greetings of the peace-loving Indian people'. The Indian people, according to Gopalan, saw in the Soviet Union 'a great, loyal and disinterested friend'.[5]

Two months later, the General Secretary of the Communist Party of India, Ajoy Ghosh, added in his message to Stalin on his seventy-third birthday:

'We, the Indian communists feel strong and confident of the future in that you are helping us, as the result of the communists and democrats the world over, with your wise guidance on the major problems of our struggle against imperialism and feudalism . . .

'Particularly do we feel grateful to you for the wise words of advice which you gave all the communists and democrats of the world, during the course of your speech at the Nineteenth Congress . . .

'We are confident that, with you to guide us, we will be able to rapidly overcome the several weaknesses that exist in the democratic movement of our country and in our own Party, so that India will be able to take her proper place in the world-wide movement of the common people for lasting Peace and People's Democracy.'[6]

In the light of these considerations, a solution to the communist problem in India cannot be looked for altogether within the frontiers of India but is as much part of the global issue between freedom and totalitarianism as the war in Korea or in Indo-China or the struggle over the divided city of Berlin.

The Communist Party of India claimed, as of December 1953, to possess 50,000 members and 25,000 candidates. Considering that, at the Party Congress held in February 1948, only half that number had been claimed, and taking into account all that has happened since, it is possible that this figure was pitched somewhat on the high side. Mr M. N. Roy had estimated membership to be anywhere between 15,000 and 50,000.[8] Even so, taking stock of the position, Ajoy Ghosh, the General Secretary of the Party, had referred in the Cominform journal of 7th November 1952, to the need to extend Party membership of the right type as 'the biggest single problem facing the Party'. He deplored the fact that 'even in Madras State where we polled 2.6 million votes, our Party membership is far less than 1 per cent of the votes polled by us' and that 'even this membership is not properly organised and only a fraction of it ideologically-politically developed'. The Party's position, according to Ghosh, among the agricultural workers and poor peasants, 'which constitute the granite foundation of the proletariat' was still extremely weak. A little later, the Party Secretary was to lament, in an issue of *New Age*, a political monthly edited by him, that 'practically all articles that appear in the *New Age* have to be written by comrades working in the Party office'.

Whatever the size and state of the membership the fact remains that even the formality of a Party Congress through which they could be consulted was not gone through for nearly six years, the second Congress having taken place in Calcutta in February 1948 and the first Congress in Bombay in 1944. Despite repeated promises to hold such a Congress, this gathering was put off from time to time. Meanwhile, membership of the Central Committee was arbitrarily reshuffled by the Party 'bosses' more than once. A sitting of the enlarged Plenum of the Central Committee which took place in Calcutta from 31st December 1952 to 10th January 1953, decided that a Party Congress should take place in September 1953 and provincial conferences by June. This date was later postponed to October and the Congress at last assembled at Madurai in the State of Madras on 28th December 1953, the birthday of Mao Tse-tung.

New Directions

In what direction may one expect the Communist Party to be oriented in the coming months and years? What line is likely to be followed? Perhaps the only thing that can be said with any assurance is that there will not be one definite line to be followed for any length of time and that the traditional zig-zag which has so far characterised the line of international communism and therefore of its constituent elements, including the Indian section, will be pursued. Even apart from the general line of the international movement, it is inevitable that, placed as India is in relation to the cold war, the hot-and-cold treatment which Moscow is accustomed to accord to all except its own satellites on the one hand and its main global adversaries on the other hand will be applied with particular intensity to a country like India. Logically, the oscillations in the Party line should extend from the extreme of a united front expressing itself in the slogan of rallying 'national capitalism' against 'Anglo-American imperialism' and of supporting, and participating in, an all-Party government, to the other extreme of sabotage, guerrilla warfare and civil war. It is unlikely, however, that, except in the event of a global clash, either alternative will be pursued to its logical conclusion. What is much more likely to materialise is a combination of both policies mixed in varying proportions, with one or the other standing out for the time being as the dominant motif. Elements of both policies are indeed to be found incipient in the Party's present position.

The dominant stress in the two years that have elapsed since the last General Elections and the relative success it brought to the Communist Party has been on parliamentary opposition and the fighting of elections. Even that opposition is, in the case of the Federal Government, diluted and tempered with limited support in so far as certain aspects of external relations such as the Far East, the Middle Eastern Defence Organisation and other collective security measures are concerned. It does not by any means follow, however, that the other task of keeping the cadres intact and steeling them for direct action and of preparing the ground for creating a 'Yenan' in India is being overlooked.

A strike of policemen in Madras City in the beginning of 1953 revealed that the Secretary of the Constabulary Association, who had only six years of service to his credit, was under communist influence[9] and, according to a high police official, the volume of records seized, following a raid on the Association's premises and the arrest of its leaders, showed that there was 'evidence of communist influence' in the activities of the Association.[10]

Despite assurances that arms illegally secured would be surrendered to the police in Hyderabad State, authoritative sources in the State revealed at the beginning of 1953 that only fifty or sixty weapons had been surrendered and that nearly 2,000 weapons of all descriptions including rifles continued to be in the possession of the communists.[11] Answering a question in the House of the People, the Home Minister stated on 4th March that, according to information received by the Government, 'orders were issued from high quarters not to surrender any more and that this had resulted in a failure to carry out the intention professed by the Communist Party'.[12] On 21st April, the Minister for States declared on the floor of Parliament: 'Leaders of the Party said very grandiloquently that they would surrender arms, but they actually surrendered only 124 arms and some ammunition. This was thought to be absolutely inadequate and the pursuit continues'.[13]

It is not so much in the South as in the North-East and North-Western regions adjoining the Chinese communist frontier that the centre of gravity of future 'direct action' would appear to be located. By the beginning of 1953, it was obvious that the communists had established a sort of parallel government in numerous villages in the Patiala and East Punjab States Union where a likely field for the renewal of their experiment in mass violence was offered by unimaginative and wooden-headed landlords, the unsatisfied land hunger of the rural masses and helpful friends and allies across the border. The mechanism devised was to set up self-appointed *panchayats* (village councils) which started dictating to farmers and to State officials and in many cases illegally incited the seizure of lands from farmers and their 'distribution among the landless'. By March, the situation had deteriorated so far that the President of the Republic found it necessary to suspend the operation of the Constitution in that State and to take power into his own hands until normal conditions could be restored and fresh elections held. Presenting the President's Proclamation to the House of the People on 5th March 1953, the Home Minister remarked that 'in many areas parallel administrative authority has been established and is said to override the State itself'.[14] Addressing Parliament in the course of a debate approving the establishment of the President's rule, the Home Minister revealed that seventy to eighty such *panchayats* had been set up in three out of eight districts of the State. 'They collect Government revenues', he declared, 'try cases, not ordinary cases but murder cases and cases involving serious offences. They compel obedience and they do not allow anybody to go to law courts, magistrates or judges. The sentence passed by them in a murder case was a fine and blackening of the accused's face'.[15] When P. Sunderayya, the leader of the Communist Party in Parliament, denied these facts, the Home Minister quoted from Sunderayya's own statement made in the course of a speech in Pepsu in August 1952, when he said: 'I have brought a model before you – that of Telengana'.[16] Almost a month later, on 6th April, the Adviser to the Rajpramukh appointed by the Union Government, in the course of his first report to the Government of India, while claiming an all-round improvement in the law and order situation, conceded that communist groups still ran their parallel government through *panchayats* in some seventy to eighty villages.[17]

A major weakness from which the communists have hitherto suffered in their effort to create an autonomous territory where the writ of the Indian Government may no longer run has been their lack of adequate supplies of arms.[18] It may be expected, however, that the common frontier which the country now has with communist China in Tibet will serve to create conditions in which the drawing of parallels with Yenan in communist China will cease to be altogether academic.[19]

From the middle of 1952, only six months after the General Elections, indications were forthcoming that the failure to obtain quick results from electoral successes, particularly through the formation of communist-dominated coalition cabinets in the States of Madras, Travancore-Cochin and Hyderabad, was leading many communist minds to turn elsewhere. Even the electoral successes were claimed by those who had so recently been denounced as 'ultra-leftists' to be the reward of their own violent activities and the slogan went round that 'Telengana had been vindicated'. There was talk of Ranadive coming back to high office within the Party.

While this understanding undoubtedly reflected an oversimplification of the position, evidence for the suggestion was not lacking since A.K. Gopalan, the leader of the communist group in the House of the People, had himself blandly declared in a speech in the Punjab that nothing had happened to disprove the communist belief that revolutions did not take place through the ballot box.[20] Similarly, in November 1952, S.A. Dange, at a trade union meeting in Hyderabad was reported to have declared: 'Since the Telengana communists started surrendering their arms, the violent activities of the Government as well as the Congress have increased. If this state of affairs continues and the Party thinks there is no other way, they will not hesitate to take up arms again in order to defend themselves and the people'.[21]

P

In May 1953, the communist-controlled Andhra Kisan Sabha (Peasant Union) was reported to have expressed itself in favour of a change of policy as a result of the failure of the communist legislators to fulfil promises made to the electorate and reverses in municipal elections resulting from the leadership of the Party concentrating on legislative work. These views were reported also to have been expressed at a meeting of the Executive of the Andhra Communist Party in May, which was reported to have addressed itself to alternate methods of making advance.[22]

The Madras Premier, Mr C. Rajagopalachari, evidently considered the portents of a reversion to violent and extraconstitutional methods serious enough to sound a severe note of warning in the course of his address inaugurating the Malabar Pradesh Political Conference at Palghat on 23rd May 1953. Describing the trend of thought in communist circles, Mr Rajagopalachari said: 'Many of them doubt whether it was wise to win in the elections and take part in open parliamentary work. They feel they were better off underground. They feel parliamentary activities have resulted in jealousy, ambition, supine satisfaction and rifts. They are, therefore, desperately looking out again for something that may confuse the issue. So they look out for some unauthorised procession and a lathi charge, some unnecessary strike and marches of unemployed workmen or sit-down demonstrations. These may make their men forget their doubts and differences and also confuse the public mind. Desperate remedies disclose the existence of a desperate disease . . . If Communists give up parliamentary work they will be doing a foolish thing. If they go underground or do acts of economic or other sabotage, they will have to be dealt with severely and it will be done. If they are wise, they will stick to parliamentary and open work. That is the straightforward way when the law allows it. They will get everything just from me. Of course, they cannot commit murder or other grave offences and hope to get away with it. That is the only condition that I lay down. I shall deal with everything else sympathetically and justly and with no Party bias'.[23]

A New Shadow

A trend that may not be without its implications for the direction of future communist policy is that marked by the emergence of Peking as one of the directing centres of international communism in so far as the region of South and South-East Asia is concerned. Moscow's rebuke to Ranadive and the latter's apology to Mao Tse-tung (recorded in an earlier chapter) were the first indications of the fact that the Communist Party of India was being asked to keep an eye on Peking. Thenceforth, R. Palme Dutt's monopoly in directing the communist apparatus from London on behalf of Moscow was broken.

Peking is believed to be the home of the Far Eastern equivalent of the Cominform named the 'Peace Liaison Committee of the Asian and Pacific Regions'. There is also located in Peking an 'Asia-Australasian Liaison Bureau of the World Federation of Trade Unions'. Liu Ning-i, a member of the Central Committee of the Chinese Communist Party, is reported to be the Secretary-General of both organisations.

Peking is, however, a long way away, and there are advance bases of international communism nearer the Indian frontiers. One of these centres is believed to be in Kunming, where are located the headquarters of the 'volunteers for the Liberation of India, Burma and Thailand'. These volunteers could, 'if an emergency arose', be assisted by the 13th, 14th and 15th Chinese communist army units totalling 100,000 men.

Another centre is reported to be at Monglen, in Eastern Burma, at a point where the Burmese, Thai, Indo-Chinese and Chinese borders meet. This is the headquarters of the 'Central Committee of the People's Liberation Armies' in South East Asia.

Direct liaison is also in existence between neighbouring national units. On 22nd January 1953, the Defence Ministry of the Burmese Government released the text of a letter dated 7th June 1952, from the Riverine Regional Committee of the Communist Party of India to Burmese insurgents. This letter proposed the establishment of a joint office in one liberated area . . . to facilitate our future relationship'. That this was no platonic plea is revealed by the letter which records that 'on the arrival of Comrade Ishwor Singh and the group sent by the Communist Party of India, Manipur District, to our Party, we find that we can maintain regular relationship with you through them. We are of the opinion that this contact is best and safest'.[24]

A few days later it was announced that Irabat Singh, formerly Secretary of the Manipur Communist Party, who had entered Burma illegally and was operating with the Burmese communist rebels, had died in rebel-held territory in Upper Burma. A score of other Indian communists from Manipur were, however, still with the Burmese rebels 'studying the pattern of the Burmese communist revolution'.[25]

There can be no question, from the evidence available, but that Peking has joined London as a transmission channel between Moscow and India. It is much too early yet to say whether India is being slowly transferred from the sphere of influence of the British Communist Party to that of the Chinese Communist Party. All that can be said is that while communist China is held up as the model and Mao Tse-tung's assumption of the rôle of leader of the communist parties in all Asian countries not under communist rule appears to have been accepted by the Communist Party of India,[26] Moscow unquestionably remains the fountain head.

Dictator's Death

As soon as Stalin died and speculation started throughout the world on the effects this would have on international communist policy and strategy, there was to be found a hope expressed in certain circles about the beneficial effects on Indian communist policy and the loosening of the link with Moscow.

The Communist Party of India lost no time, however, in sending a cable to Malenkov in the following terms: 'The Central Committee of the Communist Party of India greets Comrade Georgi Maximilianovich Malenkov, loyal disciple and colleague of the Great Stalin, and the Stalinist leadership of the Communist Party of the Soviet Union, under whose guidance the USSR continues to lead humanity in the struggle for peace, and friendship between nations.

'We declare our solidarity and pledge the support of the Indian working people and the Indian Communist Party in the common struggle for common objectives.'[27]

Any wishful thinking about a change in communist policy in India was put an end to by no less authoritative a source than A. K. Gopalan, leader of the Communist Party in the House of the People, on his return to India from Moscow in May 1953. According to a statement he made in Delhi, there had been no fundamental change in the Soviet Union's basic policies since Stalin's death. 'So far as the basic policies are concerned, there can be no change and there is no change', he said.[28] The communist spokesman drew the correct conclusions in regard to the application in India of the changes in the Kremlin when he declared two days later in Madras that there was no change in the policy of the Communist Party of India.[29]

As far as can be seen, the policy of the Party will continue to present two faces. The first face will be presented to the Government and the ruling intelligentsia, both of which will continue to be targets for propaganda, pressure and infiltration. The attempt to split the elite and to place adherents in key positions will continue in the hope that the will to resist of the ruling classes may thus be pulverised. Alongside of this will continue the building up of the Party's cadres and action squads, indulgence in language and action which will serve to keep up the morale and the fighting spirit of the rank and file, and the building up of local and regional bases of operations for use when the hour strikes.[30]

In any attempt at estimating the outlook for communism in India, an evaluation of the factors and influences – economic, social, spiritual, emotional, psychological and organisational – which help or hinder the spread of communist ideas and organisation in India must play a part.

The Opposition

It must be conceded that consistent ideological opposition to communism has hitherto been negligible. Confirmed anti-totalitarian groupings are as yet confined to small sections of the intelligentsia. The Indian Committee for Cultural Freedom came into existence in March 1951 when an Indian Congress for Cultural Freedom, attended by over a hundred Indian writers and intellectuals, met in Bombay and adopted a Declaration which concluded as follows: 'The new tyranny founded on the theory and practice of totalitarianism is the gravest challenge man has faced in civilised history. The defence of cultural freedom is, in the main, the defence of free society against this challenge. Indifference or neutrality towards this totalitarian tyranny amounts to a renunciation of the Indian tradition and our human heritage, and a betrayal of all spiritual values'. The Committee which is an intellectual United Front of democrats, including Congressmen, Socialists and non-Party intellectuals, publishes a monthly bulletin entitled *Freedom First* and is making slow but steady headway against the tide of neutralism which is predominant in academic, professional, journalistic and literary circles.[31]

The Democratic Research Service, Bombay, which is somewhat more polemical, has as its aim 'the study of political and economic philosophies and organisations throughout the world. It seeks to disseminate information on these subjects and in particular to bring within the reach of the general reader material on the values of Democracy, the successful working of the democratic process in various parts of the world and the dangers which Democracy has to face. The objective of the Democratic Research Service is to contribute towards the education and enlightenment of public opinion in India to a fuller realisation of the need to defend India's national independence, her democratic way of life and the freedom of the individual, and of the possibilities of social and economic advance through democratic processes'.

These organisations have yet to evolve an effective nationwide membership and influence. In Calcutta, there is a Society for the Defence of Freedom in Asia, which functions independently, while in Travancore-Cochin an Anti-Communist Front has emerged. What is significant about these groups is that they are all, in varying degrees, united fronts of lovers of freedom joining hands in resistance to totalitarian infiltration. Between them, however, they have as yet but touched the fringe of the problem.

The press of India, which might have been expected to play an educative rôle, remains by and large either complaisant or apathetic in the face of communist propaganda. Leading 'capitalist' newspapers have communist cells or correspondents who give a pro-Soviet and anti-Western Democracies slant to editorial comment and presentation of news. The President of the All-India Conference of Working Journalists is a fellow-traveller. Where such infiltration does not exist, neutralist sentiment on the part of the staff provides the necessary opportunities. The number of daily newspapers which take a consistently anti-communist line is very limited, while only half a dozen weekly journals in the English language stand out for their unswerving advocacy of democratic policies.

Religion

Much more significant in the long run than purely intellectual anti-totalitarianism in a country such as India is likely to be opposition based on religion. Nothing else is more obviously menaced by the possibility of communist success in India than the Hindu way of life with its age-old traditions, its firm hold on the family and its all pervasive influence. A similar fate will undoubtedly face other religions such as the Muslim and the Christian. The absence of any attempt to arouse the mass of the people to the threat held out by communism to the religions they cherish is a noticeable feature of the Indian scene. To a certain extent, the vogue of 'secular democracy' and the denunciation of 'communalism' and 'religious revivalism' have undoubtedly contributed to inhibit an appeal to religious sentiment.

Even parties based on religion such as the Hindu Mahasabha and the Jan Sangh, which constantly warn against the menace that Pakistan offers to Hinduism, are remarkably silent on this threat.[32] By and large, the Hindu mind does not yet appear to have awakened to the seriousness of the challenge which it now encounters, but it is unlikely that, given the leadership, it will in time fail to do so.

Perhaps the only organised religious opposition that has so far been forthcoming has been that of the Catholics, which shows a high degree of awareness and sophistication.

The Socialists

Of the existing political elements, perhaps only the socialists can claim to be consistent opponents of communism, whether in the sphere of trade unions or of student or peasant organisations. So, too, in the long run, the world view of the socialists is getting more and more consistently anti-totalitarian. Thus, asked in Calcutta on 16th January 1953, which he considered the greater danger to Asia, colonialism or communism, Mr Jayaprakash Narayan, the Praja Socialist leader, said that 'colonialism was dying out and soon it would be a memory. On the other hand, Russian expansionism was a new menace'.[33]

Can the opposition of the Socialists be depended on to continue? Till recently, the only dents that the communists were able to make in the socialist armour were minor ones which took the form of acts of indiscipline on the part of local functionaries of the Party who were inveigled into united fronts on specific issues without reference to the central organisation of the Party. There was a tendency, however, for these instances to be more numerous in 1953. Occasional resignations of members who went over to the communists or expulsions for disruptive activity were reported. The most noteworthy revolt of this nature came from the State leadership of the Praja Socialist Party in Bengal which entered into an understanding with the communists for the purposes of a by-election to the State Assembly and with communist support succeeded in winning a by-election against the Congress in May 1953.

In November 1953, however, when the National Executive of the Praja Socialist Party endorsed an electoral pact of a limited nature in the State of Travancore-Cochin with the United Left Front, consisting of the Communist Party and two Marxist splinter groups, the Revolutionary Socialist Party and the Kerala Socialist Party, directed against the Congress Party, a step was taken which after an interval of fourteen years opened the door to the possibilities of a United Front.

The Five-Year Plan

Among other factors which must be considered as being ranged against the success of the communists is the Five-Year Plan of Economic Development of the Indian Government. Because of the hope that it holds out of an improvement, democratically achieved, in the people's living conditions, and because in securing its consummation American Technical Co-operation Aid and the Colombo Plan have an important part to play, the Plan has been recognised by the communists as a threat to their hopes of success. While protesting that it would be 'slandering the Communist Party to say that it will sabotage the Plan', the communist leaders seldom spare an occasion to do precisely what is denied by them. Thus, a statement issued from the central headquarters of the Party in January 1953 declared that the Plan 'would only lead to further dependence of India on British and US imperialism and further impoverishment of the people because the financing of the Plan would go on, not from the profits of the monopolists, but by increased burdens on the people, and thus intensify the crisis'.[34]

Four months later, answering a question about the Party's attitude to the Plan, *Cross Roads*, after refuting the claim that it was a plan of national reconstruction, pronounced it to be 'a plan which will keep intact India's semi-colonial economy, intensifying the agrarian and industrial crisis and impose greater burdens on different sections of the people including the industrialists, merchants, middle classes and artisans. But the plan does benefit one section of the people and that is a narrow clique of landlords and monopolists . . . The plan does not at all solve the food shortage, rather it intensifies it . . .

'That is why the political resolution of the Central Committee of the Communist Party in India passed last March declares: "The Plan refuses to make democratic transformations in land relations, which alone will smash the fetters on agricultural production and release the creative energies of India's millions of peasants . . ."

'Any plan of national reconstruction should have been concentrated on the industrial development of the country'.[35]

Gandhi

The influence of Gandhi and his teachings is undoubtedly a major obstacle in the path of communist advance in India. While the Communist Party of India has attracted a section of the English-speaking intelligentsia and is to-day more entrenched among its ranks than it is among classes less privileged, the Indian masses on the other hand have shown, by their unique response over three decades to Mahatma Gandhi, that the man who evokes a response in their hearts is the one who talks to them of non-material values like God, Love, Truth, Human Brotherhood, and the Equality of the untouchable Harijan and the proud Brahmin.

Gandhi represents the complete antithesis to the communist and has been recognised as such in the Moscow press and radio for over three decades. The communist swears by dialectical materialism – matter is essence, the mind a by-product; Gandhi preached the supremacy of spirit and mind over matter. To the communist, the end justifies the means; to Gandhi, the means were everything – means and ends were like the seed and the tree; and so Gandhi pronounced Soviet Communism to be 'repugnant to India'. Stalin, Malenkov and Mao preach the need to hate the class and national enemy; Gandhi the need to love all. Communism seeks to centralise and collectivise everything; Gandhi preached the need to decentralise and to distribute power both politically and economically. The communist glorifies the State; Gandhi, conscious of the distinction drawn by Reinhold Niebuhr between *Moral Man and Immoral Society*, stressed the individual as an end in himself. Identifying himself with the lowliest in the scale of caste – the Harijan or untouchable – Gandhi recalled the words of Him who said: 'Inasmuch as ye have done it unto one of the least of these, my brethren, ye have done it unto me'.

'Bhoodan Yagna'

Since the spirit of Gandhi still haunts the communists, it is natural that Acharya Vinobha Bhave's movement for the voluntary distribution of land should also attract communist wrath. Answering a question put in the communist organ, P. Ramamurthy gives this reply: '*Bhoodan Yagna*', as its very name signifies is no movement of the people. It is charity – charity in land . . . The communists are realists . . . *Bhoodan Yagna* by Acharya Vinobha Bhave and tributes paid to it by Nehru and other Congress leaders are a recognition on their part of the acuteness and urgency of the land problem – not in the sense that it must be solved immediately . . . but in the sense that, if illusions are not sewn, the peasants all over India will follow the heroic example of Telengana and take to the path of organisation and struggle . . . Therein lies the sinister aim of the *Yagna*'.[36]

It is not only in the illusions *Bhoodan Yagna* may spread that the communist senses danger. Its actual performance is perhaps equally worrying. Jayaprakash Narayan, in the course of a tour of Hyderabad State in furtherance of this campaign, has drawn attention to its revolutionary superiority over communistic methods and its greater capacity to deliver the goods. The socialist leader, who himself collected sizeable donations of land, referred to the events in Telengana and said that 'within two and a half years, the communists had only distributed 32,000 acres of land, after destroying crores of rupees worth of property'. By contrast, through *Bhoodan Yagna*, 'within two years over 50,000 acres of land had been collected in the State without any bloodshed. Over twelve lakh acres had been collected throughout the country. The *Bhoodan Yagna* movement was creating a new atmosphere of fraternity and brotherhood. That was a revolution indeed'.[37]

Jayaprakash pointed out that, with the solitary exception of the communists, all political parties had supported Acharya Bhave's movement. Explaining why the communists did not co-operate with the movement, Mr Narayan said that 'they knew full well that if the movement succeeded they would have to wind up their show'.[38]

Finally, in the way of the Communist Party lie the democratic Constitution of the Republic, an independent judiciary, an efficient system of administration and armed forces disciplined and loyal to the country.

Assets

When we turn from the impediments in the way of the advance of communism to the assets it possesses, perhaps the first of those that come to mind are the possibilities offered by the vast illiterate and economically depressed population of India, divided by religion, caste and language into an infinity of groups. Such a population naturally provides suitable soil in which to plant the communist seed.

The basic problem is that the population is large and growing, yet production is low and stagnant. The average annual *per capita* income is Rs 256 (£19 4s. od. or $54.00) but the population is increasing at the rate of about 4,000,000 a year. Obviously there can be little margin for the saving and investment needed to modernise techniques and tools and increase production – in other words, to raise the terribly low living standards that prevail. The need for external capital investment and technical know-how is obvious, but the scarcity of such available capital from overseas and the ambivalent attitude towards the acceptance of foreign economic aid common among influential and vocal sectors of public opinion in India rule out any quick and easy solution.

If the 'objective situation' is favourable to the growth of a doctrine such as Moscow and Peking provide, the psychological and emotional climate is hardly less congenial. A variety of factors go into the making of this complex. Outstanding amongst these is the weakness of democratic tradition. 'We have in India', writes M.N.Roy, 'a formally democratic government, but it is neither good, nor efficient nor stable ... The establishment of political democracy and a free society is, in the last analysis, conditional upon the popular mentality, which is determined by cultural traditions ... Judged by that standard, the future of democracy in India is not bright.'[39]

At the same time, note has to be taken of two emotions widespread among the literate classes. The first is the resentment and envy that come naturally to an impoverished people when viewing the almost unattainable prosperity of the United States and which are in no way diminished by the necessity of having to accept favours from it. The second is the racial consciousness and antagonism which is created as a natural reaction to the claims to 'White' superiority made in Africa, America and elsewhere, not unaccompanied by a recollection of 'White' imperialism in India itself.

The empty mind and soul provide as good a breeding ground for communism as an empty stomach. This is particularly true of a country where there is new literacy and new education. Thousands of young men and women in India have acquired the art of reading, the capacity to learn; they look around the world and try to understand what is happening. They want an answer to the problems – economic, social and political – that puzzle them. Why then don't they get a job which they think they deserve? – and so on. Who gives them the answers? To-day the only people who think it worth their while to provide answers are the communists.

The fact that communist propaganda is making much more headway among the bourgeoisie and prosperous groups, such as administrators, educators and scientists, than among the peasantry and the working class lends support to the thesis that it is not poverty or even starvation that primarily predisposes men to the attraction of communism. While economic factors undoubtedly play a part, the basic motivations are psychological and emotional. It is the psychological and emotional void created by the loosening of the hold of the traditional religions of India that provides room for what is essentially a new religion of materialism. It is the literate middle-class man so affected who utilises and exploits the economic conditions of the rural and urban toilers.[40]

Northern Neighbours

To these basic emotional pulls has been added, in recent years, yet another – that of security and survival. History only rarely records cases of nations which do not orient their attitudes in the light of 'realistic' considerations of being on the winning side or, at the least, of not provoking the strong. There can be no doubt that a large section of the Indian intelligentsia has been given the impression, probably mistakenly, that time and history are on the side of the Soviet-Chinese bloc – that not only do they in the long run represent the wave of history, but that even in the short-term military balance of forces they are in a position to overrun the whole of the Eurasian land mass. Thus, after building up a picture of the inevitable triumph of the Soviet-Chinese bloc, a crypto-communist journal wrote regarding a press interview given by a woman who had suggested that India's foreign policy should be reoriented so as to align the country with the Democracies: 'She may not perhaps realise that shrewd observers consider this unsolicited *démenti* as evidence of her playing into the hands of the American propagandists. God forbid, she may not live to regret these words'.[41] More recently, P. Sunderayya, communist floor leader in the Council of States, told a Congress legislator who had crossed him in debate: 'You are a dying force; we are a growing force'.

Such attempts at intimidating the waverers have not been weakened by the communist success in creating a stalemate in Korea unsatisfactory to the United Nations; by the conquest, without resistance, of India's peaceful neighbours in Tibet; or the unresisted advance by the communists in April 1953 into Laos, which was abandoned for the time being.

The significance of the massing of Chinese communist troops along India's Northern and North-Eastern frontiers cannot in this context be overestimated. The Community Party of India certainly is not unaware of its import for, immediately after the occupation of Tibet, a statement of policy issued by its Politbureau in November 1951 had this to say: 'We cannot fail to note the fact that the Chinese Red Army was surrounded and threatened with annihilation again and again until it reached Manchuria. There, with the industrial base in hand, the great friendly Soviet Union in the rear, the Chinese Liberation Army, free from the possibility of any attack in the rear, rebuilt itself and launched the final offensive which led it to victory'.[42] Perhaps it is as a result of drawing the right moral from this text that the Indian communists have ceased concentrating on Telengana in the south and have shifted their efforts to build an Indian 'Yenan' in Kashmir, Pepsu or Himachal Pradesh on the north.

A decisive asset the communists possess is their link with Soviet Russia and communist China. This has reference not only to material aid in the way of directives, personnel and funds that they receive, but also the tremendous prestige the organisation derives from having two powerful governments at its back. The value of this support is further enhanced by reason of the widespread belief in the 'achievements' of these 'progressive' régimes which communist propaganda, aided by confused thinking on the part of well-meaning people,[43] has been able to spread in India over the past few years.

This reflected glory in which the Indian communists shine was best illustrated on the occasion of Stalin's death when Ajoy Ghosh, General Secretary of the Party, delivered himself of the sentiment that mankind had lost its 'noblest representative', the movement for 'human liberation' (*ie* the Communist Party) its greatest leader, and the cause of peace its most indefatigable champion.[44] This identification would not have perhaps amounted to very much if it had not been for the fact that leaders of the Indian Government and, with a few exceptions, the entire press[45] of the country joined in paying somewhat similar tributes to Stalin. It would be safe to say that this situation was the equivalent of the gain of several thousand adherents to the Party. Recognising this, the Politbureau of the Communist Party decided to cash in further on the situation by calling for the observation of a 'Stalin Week' from 30th March to 5th April.[46]

Perhaps more effective in its morale-providing capacities than the Soviet Union is the Chinese communist régime. Many who by now find it impossible to maintain their illusions about the nature of the Soviet Russian State are able without strain to transfer their illusions to the great Chinese 'experiment'. For one thing, it is not yet easy, by concrete evidence, to challenge the claims made on its behalf. For another, the fact that the Chinese are

Asians is a factor on which racial sentiment is brought to bear. The remark that the Chineseness of Mao Tse-tung's régime is stronger than its communism is illustrative of this sentiment.

Dangerous Polarisation

A factor which, since the last General Elections, is telling on people's minds is the apparent polarisation of forces in India between the Congress Party in power on the one hand and the Communist Party in opposition on the other. The fact that the Communist Party secured, of all opposition groups, the largest number of seats in the Union Parliament and that in several States it emerged as the second biggest party on the threshold of power has made a deep and lasting impression. The other fact that the total communist vote, which was in the neighbourhood of 4.5 per cent, is less than half of the total vote polled by the Socialist Party, and that the Praja Party (which has now merged with the Socialist Party) also polled over five per cent of the votes is, by and large, overlooked. Another factor that makes for this apparent polarisation is the fact that the dividing line between the Congress and Praja Socialist Parties, both of whom are based firmly on parliamentary democracy, is a somewhat thin one and resolves itself mainly into a question of the tempo of advance towards a classless society. Similarly, on foreign policy, the stand of the two Parties is, for the common man, difficult to distinguish.

To add to these considerations came the negotiations in March 1953 between Mr Nehru and Mr Jayaprakash Narayan, the Praja socialist leader, for an understanding between the two Parties which might make possible a coalition both in the Federal Government and in the States. Though the move did not fructify, it provided precisely that argument in favour of the thesis of polarisation which the Communist Party is so keen on advancing – that there is nothing to choose or distinguish between the Congress and the Praja Socialist leadership.[47]

The situation is not improved by the fact that many adherents of the Congress Party, for their own purposes, chime in with the communist thesis of polarisation. Their idea undoubtedly is that, if the communists are held out as the only alternative to the present Congress régime, the latter's position becomes unassailable. In actual fact, however, this can only have the effect of canalising all possible discontent against the Congress government into Red channels, thus helping to create somewhat of the same situation as that in China, where the middle groups were pulverised in the polarisation between the Kuo Ming-tang and the Communist Party.

Balkanisation

The Communist Party's line in regard to the limits and boundaries of the States that make up the Indian Union is based on the Soviet theory, as opposed to the Soviet practice, of the right of each 'nationality' to have its own 'sovereign' State involving the right of secession. Such a stand has the double merit of helping in the Balkanisation of the country, which would facilitate its being taken over by the communists and, at the same time, playing on one of the basic emotions of the people, namely, linguistic nationalism.

Support of linguistic States has been common ground between all political parties in India, including the Congress and the Socialist Parties. Communist propaganda has, however, sought to ignore this and claimed as its own success the advance made by the linguistic principle through the formation of the State of Andhra based on the Telugu language. The *Daily Worker*, London, thus carried a despatch from New Delhi: 'The Communist Party and the Indian people won a historic victory to-day when the Government was forced to announce that it would set up an Andhra State. The announcement follows years of struggle led by the Communist Party culminating in a united movement which paralysed all government in the area'.[48]

In the agitation for the formation of a Karnatak State based on the unity of the Kannada speaking peoples, the communists are taking a leading part. Violent rioting designed to put pressure on a meeting in the Spring of 1953 of the Karnatak Pradesh Congress Committee led to arrests of communist agitators. In May 1953 came into existence the Akhand Karnatak Rajya Nirwana Parishat

Q

(Association for the establishment of an Independent Karnatak State), with the support *inter alia* of the communists.[49]

Previous chapters have shown how the communists have never scrupled to join hands with sectarian and obscurantist groups like the Akalis in the Punjab and the Dravida Kazagham in Madras. In the beginning of 1953, however, they saw the opportunities provided for them by the unceasing campaign against what is called 'communalism' (meaning the fostering of consciousness based on religion) and advocacy of 'secular democracy'. Thus, at the end of a meeting of the Central Committee of the Communist Party held in Bombay in April 1953, it was announced that a decision had been taken to carry on 'a ceaseless campaign against the policies of communal organisations allied to feudal reaction which are trying to impose on the Government policies which are still more reactionary than at present'.[50]

This stand is undoubtedly an astute one. For one thing, it helps in creating that weakening of religion and the consequent spiritual vacuum in which the false religion of materialism can enter most effectively. Apart from this long term advantage which, in a country like India, might well prove decisive, there is the short term advantage of using this alleged common opposition to 'communalism' to infiltrate the minds, if not the ranks, of the adherents of the ruling Congress Party. The very noise that is made about the menace of 'communalism' automatically obscures, whether it is so intended or not, the other danger of communism whose adherents meanwhile bask in the sunshine as exponents of 'secular democracy'.

Which Way The Tide

Speaking in the State of Travancore-Cochin on 23rd May 1953, Mr C. Rajagopalachari, the Premier of Madras, to whom, above all, credit goes for having protected southern India from communist rule after the last General Elections, made certain far-reaching observations: 'The disillusionment has come – communism has lost its glamour all over India wherever it had found some footing . . . The Communist Party in India is not very happy now. They are, it may be said, in the doldrums . . . Communism is down and out in India . . . Communism has crossed over the peak of its success in India and it is now on the decline – a precipitous decline . . . The truth is there is no future for communism in India. There is too much reverence and true religion and proper respect for moral value in India for communism to make headway'.[51]

A prompt rejoinder to this analysis came from P. Ramamurthi, Leader of the Opposition in the Madras State Assembly: 'The Chief Minister might delude himself with the idea that the Communist Party's influence had waned, but the very fact that the Congress was afraid of an election and was entering into an unprincipled alliance with those people who contested the last general elections with specific pledges to fight the Congress in Andhra, spoke volumes for the influence of the Congress. In the recent village *panchayat* elections, which are still continuing throughout the State, the Congress has been suffering tremendous reverses even in those areas where the Communist Party did not contest during the last general elections'.[52]

While this comment may be dismissed as a case of special pleading, against the sentence of death passed by Mr Rajagopalachari may be placed the opinion of another weighty expert on the subject, Mr M.N. Roy. Though this view was advanced several months earlier than Mr Rajagopalachari's judgment, the factors on which it is based are long term and cannot be said to have altered in the intervening period.

'The Communist Party still remains', wrote Mr Roy, 'the dark horse of the Indian political situation . . . The Communist Party in India is not a negligible force. Barring the Congress, it alone has an effective organised machinery which, according to Lenin's description, can combine legal and illegal activities. The numerical strength of the Communist Party may be anywhere between 15,000 and 50,000, but it is a cadre party whose strength is not to be measured by the number of its members only. The decisive factor is the capacity for mass mobilisation, either directly or through ancillary or peripheral organisations . . . The latter (communists) have the advantage of a sanction behind their promises. It is the example of China and the power of Russia . . . The

Communist Party also counts upon the sympathy and support of anonymous high-placed individuals ... The spectacular emergence of the Communist Party is mainly due to the fact that it represents a clear and persistent opposition to the party in power – politically, socially and ideologically ... The Communist Party offers the point of crystallisation for the disillusioned and the discontented ... In this atmosphere of despair and disillusionment, a programme promising a clean sweep of the established order has a strong appeal ...

'The sanction of the communist appeal is not its ostensible social idealism but the formidable power of the Russo-Chinese bloc ...

'A doubtful passion and a nebulous social idealism combine in widespread sympathy for communism among the educated middle-class. Admiration for Soviet Russia is the third factor which makes communism popular. It is rather an admiration for the powerful and the successful than an intelligent understanding and appreciation of communism ... It is not so much the ideal of social justice as the promising of dictatorial power that attracts the more ambitious members of a class which occupies the most hopeless and helpless stand in the established order. As a rule they man the leadership of the Communist Parties in Asia. Dictatorship of the Politbureau, therefore, would be their dictatorship ...

'In Asia the decisive moral resistance to communism is bound to be weak because there is no democratic tradition to defend ... The Asian mentality, being still largely mediaeval, is authoritarian and naturally attracted by the idea of dictatorship. Therefore communism can easily infiltrate the nationalist movement.'[53]

Whom is one to believe – Mr Rajagopalachari or Mr Roy? At a first glance, there may appear to be, particularly in the south of India where Mr Rajagopalachari spoke, some evidences of a communist decline reflected in comparative lack of success in local elections and the temporary breaking up of the united fronts so laboriously erected earlier. That the communists themselves for the moment accepted defeat in the South was evident from the shifting of their central office from Madras to Delhi and the diversion of their paid cadres to the States on the North-West and North-East borders of India.

Taking the country by and large, however, the tide among the intelligentsia still definitely flows in favour of the communists and the long term prospects for the Party can, by no means, be considered bleak.[54] The basic reason for this view is set out with considerable force by Mr M.N.Roy in his article. This is that what is decisive is not the economic factor, nor the poverty, nor even the illiteracy of the people. What are decisive are the psychological and emotional factors and these largely conspire to help the communists. These could undoubtedly be counteracted by inspiring and dynamic leadership. Unfortunately, this is not yet forthcoming. Under cover of a confused and confusing neutralism which fogs all issues, communism meanwhile steadily advances.

The mixture of satisfaction and impatience with which this situation is viewed by the communists was well spelt out by none other than R.Palme Dutt, one of the high priests of international communism:

'This development of Indian popular feeling has not only manifested itself in the growth of the peace movement but, in conjunction with the new developments of the situation, has also found a certain measure of reflection in new indications in India's diplomatic position.

'The moving tribute paid by Premier Nehru to the memory of J.V. Stalin; the significant interview of the Indian Ambassador with Stalin shortly before his death, as well as the interview of Dr Kitchlew with Stalin, the firm condemnation by Nehru of the new moves of General Eisenhower in relation to China and Formosa, and the threat of extended war in the Far East; the rebuff to the Bevanite proposals for India to build a 'Third Force' bloc, *ie*, equally in oppoitison to People's China and the Soviet Union as to the imperialist Powers; and the sympathy shown to the struggle of the people of Kenya against oppression – all these indications have attracted widespread attention.

'There is no doubt that in the present world situation, in any country which is directly tied to the imperialist war camp, as through membership of the Atlantic Pact, the conception of 'neutralism' represents a very important tendency expressing the desire of considerable sections of middle-of-the-road opinion to achieve disentanglement from the American war bloc and from American domination.

' "Neutralism", however, cannot be a solution to the problem of peace. The achievement of peace requires a positive policy for peace. If the plans for a third world war, and especially the plans for unleashing war on a major scale in Asia, were to reach fruition, those plans would inevitably involve India in the very heart of the conflict, and could bring on India all the horrors and devastation which have befallen the peaceful people of Korea.

' "Neutralism" is in itself no answer to such a menace. What is essential is to act now in association with all peoples striving for peace in order to ensure the defeat of such policies for war, and the victory of the aim of peace.'[55]

One's estimate of the outlook for communism in India must to a certain extent be determined by one's understanding as to whether the threat of communism is primarily internal or external. On this issue Lenin's view that the sources of the growth of communism are partly internal and party external, and that in different countries the proportion of these two factors varies, would appear to be unexceptionable.

To the extent that in the case of India the threat is external – and the previous chapters show that this is not a negligible factor – a lot depends on what happens in the rest of the world and what others, both communists and democrats, do beyond Indian frontiers, as well as within them.

A Matter of Priorities

A realistic assessment of priorities is often rendered difficult by the state of mind, so often to be found in India and elsewhere, which discounts the need for specific measures to combat communist inroads and urges that all that is necessary is to investigate the blemishes and inadequacies of the working of democracy, in particular those on the economic plane, and to set them right. Dealing with this view, Mr A. D. Gorwala, a distinguished former Civil Servant and one of India's best informed commentators, wrote recently:

'It is certainly desirable that the causes that led to the house catching fire should be inquired into and, to the greatest extent possible, removed. But a man whose house is on fire has to observe certain priorities. He must rush to put out the fire. He must deal promptly with the arson that is still going on. It is also for him, no doubt, to consider the causes of the unfortunate inflammability and the remedies for it. His anxiety to do this should not, however, lead him to prevent the fire brigade and the police from getting on with their first task by appealing to them to turn themselves into a committee to report on the inadequacies of this structure in particular, and on the methods of fireproof construction in general. All the three phases, the putting out of the fire, the preventing of further incendiary acts and the immunisation of the house from fire, can of course be borne in mind, but the respective urgencies must be observed in action, if results are to be obtained. The third phase can in no circumstances be a substitute for the first or the second. What is in the minds of those who insist that attention should be confined to it alone ? Do they, by any chance, desire to minimise the gravity of the deed and the culpability of the doers in an effort to divert attention away from both ?'[56]

Reference has been made earlier to the part played by the instinct of national security in helping the sentiment of neutralism. People seldom rally to a cause, however just, if they feel it is doomed to fail. It is Justice holding the flaming sword that rouses masses of people to live, and if need be die, for a cause. There is in India considerable doubt about Western strength and sagacity. Confidence in the capacity of the Democracies to win a global conflict that may be forced by the communists has still to be carried to the Indian people.

The aphorism that 'an idea cannot be stopped by force' is, in this context, somewhat overworked. It is based, in present circumstances, on the misconception that international communism is a potent idea; in reality it is now primarily a plot and a conspiracy. Neither abstract justice, nor abstract ideas, nor prosperity is sufficient to defeat a conspiracy that is based on the use of force and fraud, and possesses the instruments to apply them. It is not enough that the democratic cause be understood to be fair and just; there must be no less a conviction that the Democracies have the power to uphold justice – particularly in Asia. Since 1945 the tide has moved the other way. Ten countries of Eastern Europe, plus North Korea, China and now Tibet, have successively been engulfed. The acceptance by the UN of a divided Korea is the latest of communist triumphs. The communists in India are taking full advantage of these facts to cajole and intimidate. Five years from now, they say, India will be what China is to-day: if you want to get on the band-wagon, now is the time. Those who watch the names that appear on communist 'peace' appeals and 'Indo-Chinese Friendship' fronts know that the communist threats are not without their effect.

Even given the confidence in democratic strength, however, one final doubt would remain in many Indian minds. Have the Democracies the capacity to win a peace? Have they the wisdom, the maturity, to lay the foundations of a world community based on the equality of all peoples and races? The basic policies of the Democracies have savoured too much of a mere bolstering of the territorial and political *status quo*. Defences seem constantly improvised – a hole plugged here, a leak stopped there. With recent experience before us, perhaps it would not be unfair to suggest a parallel going far back in history – the reproach that Demosthenes addressed to the Athenians in 351 BC:

'Shame on you, Athenians ... for not wishing to understand that in war one must now allow oneself to be at the command of events, but to forestall them ... You make war against Philip like a barbarian when he wrestles ... If you hear that Philip has attacked in the Chersonese, you send help there; if he is at Thermopylae, you run there; and if he turns aside you follow him to right and left, as if you were acting on his orders. Never a fixed plan, never any precautions; you wait for bad news before you act'.

Clearly, mere containment is no longer enough. Something more dynamic is needed if a responsive chord is to be struck in Asian hearts.[57]

The overall strategy of the communists appears to remain that which was laid down by Lenin many years earlier: 'In the last analysis, the upshot of the struggle will be determined by the fact that Russia, India, China, etc, account for the overwhelming majority of the population of the globe'.[58]

If ever India 'goes communist', it will neither be as a result of an election nor even of a violent mass revolution of a conventional nature. It will rather be by means of a *coup d'etat* or seizure of power effected by establishing a base of operations somewhere in the country and gaining possession, through internal and external pressure, of the levers which control power – the State, the armed forces, the radio and the press. Such an attempt has indeed been made not far from India's own borders.

It was in March 1951 that the Prime Minister and Defence Minister of Pakistan, Mr Liaquat Ali Khan, made certain startling disclosures on the floor of Parliament in regard to a communist conspiracy to overthrow the Government that had been unearthed a few days earlier: 'The conspirators seemed convinced that there was no possibility of achieving their objective through popular support or by the use of democratic or constitutional means. They planned, therefore, to resort to force with the support of the armed forces. The plan envisaged the removal of high military officers and civilians, and the seizure of effective power. The country was to be brought under a military dictatorship, when existing authorities, both civil and military, had been eliminated. The Government was thereafter to be patterned on the communist model but under military domination. For this purpose economic and constitution-making missions were to be invited from a certain foreign country'.[59] Nearly two years later, on 5th January 1953, after a protracted and thorough trial, fourteen of the fifteen accused in the Rawalpindi Conspiracy Case were convicted and sentenced.

The attempt in Pakistan no doubt failed but the rather similar attempt made in Czechoslovakia, on the other hand, succeeded in February 1948. It succeeded because President Benes and his Foreign Minister, Mr Jan Masaryk, believed that they could be the bridge between the Democratic and Soviet worlds. Their great mistake was that, being democrats themselves, they could not envisage the real nature of the Soviet Politbureau and the workings of its mind. They refused, despite all the evidence, to accept the fact that for the Soviet dictatorship the question of friendship with other governments simply does not arise, that the choice presented to all other States is that between hostility and subservience.[60]

While the Communist Party in India can, in purely domestic

terms, hope, at best, to possess only a nuisance value, there can be no question that against the background of the international situation, this is nothing more than a short-term and partial evaluation. Encouraging signs of a growing awareness of this were discernible in the unequivocal attacks on the Indian communists made by Prime Minister Nehru in the course of his speeches in Travancore-Cochin during the electoral campaign in that State in the beginning of 1954. 'The Communist Party,' he charged, 'leans or depends on, or looks to, foreign countries'. He accused the communists of 'going about posing as if they are Russians . . . Their body was in India but their mind was somewhere else . . . The communists have no roots in our soil. Their slogans are born in some other country[61] . . . The communist policy changes a great deal, but one thing remains constant, and that is their entire thinking is based on something outside India[62] . . . The capacity of the Communist Party to condemn anything done in India and acclaim only those done in Russia or certain other countries was something un-understandable'.[63] The Prime Minister instanced the use of the Soviet flag as a symbol of this extra-territorial nature of the Party. 'Look at their flag', he observed, 'they have copied the Russian flag'.[64] Moving on from this, the Prime Minister drew the only possible conclusion when he said: 'Their policy indicated a lack of allegiance not only to the national flag but to the conception of India itself'.[65] He warned his listeners: 'If you follow the communist policy, I am sure the unity of India will be shattered'.[66]

India is still at a stage in which the process of softening up through a policy of blowing hot and cold can be followed without causing undue alarm. The heat need only be turned on after the countries of South-east Asia have been disposed of. In such a situation, the Communist Party in India is a dagger pointed at the heart of democracy in the most populous country of the world outside the Iron Curtain. Its role is to disrupt the national economy create intellectual confusion, infiltrate into key positions and prepare for the day when, in the face of national emergency or international crisis, it may be in a position to paralyse the will to resist. Only purposeful democratic leadership that arouses the country to the internal and external dangers with which it is faced can immunise India from this threat. In the final analysis, it is in the hands of non-communists that the destiny of India rests.

Tactical Line

Not Peaceful but Revolutionary Path

(1) The immediate main objectives set forth in the Draft Programme of the Communist Party of India are the complete liquidation of feudalism, the distribution of all land held by feudal owners among the peasants and agricultural workers, and achievement of full national independence and freedom. These objectives cannot be realised by a peaceful, parliamentary way. These objectives can be realised only through a revolution, through the overthrow of the present Indian state and its replacement by a People's Democratic State. For this the Communist Party shall strive to rouse the entire peasantry and the working class against the feudal exploiters, strengthen the alliance between the working class and the peasantry, a broad nationwide United Front of all anti-imperialist classes (including the national bourgeoisie) sections, groups, parties and elements willing to fight for democracy and for freedom and independence of India.

(2) While resorting to all forms of struggle, including the most elementary forms and while utilising all legal possibilities for mobilising the masses and taking them forward in the struggle for freedom and democracy, the Communist Party has always held that in the present colonial set-up in India and in view of the absence of genuine democratic liberties, legal and parliamentary possibilities are restricted and that therefore the replacement of the present state uphelding the imperialist feudal order by a People's Democratic State is possible through an armed revolution of the people. The concrete experience of the last three years in India, after the so-called transfer of power, has only confirmed this thesis.

Combinations of Partisan War in the Countryside and Workers Rising in the Cities

(3) Nevertheless, wrong and distorted ideas have prevailed in our Party ranks about the exact character of this armed struggle and the exact form it will have to take in order to ensure victory. For a period after the 2nd Party Congress the dominant tendency inside the Party leadership

was to forget the colonial nature of India's economy, to refuse to draw lessons from the experience of the revolutionary movement in China and other colonial countries, to minimise the immense importance of peasant struggles and to put forward the thesis that political general strike in the cities and in industrial areas is the main weapon of our revolution, that such a strike will itself unleash countrywide insurrection and lead to overthrow of the present state.

Afterwards, on the basis of wrong understanding of the experience of the Chinese Revolution, the thesis was put forward that the Indian revolution would develop exactly in the same way as the revolution in China and that partisan war would be the main or almost the only weapon to ensure its victory.

While the former thesis minimised the importance of the peasant masses and their struggles, the latter thesis minimised the importance of the working class and its action. Both tactical lines were the result of ignoring the specific situation in India and of the tendency to draw mechanical parallels with other countries.

In theory, as well as in the practice, both tactical lines amounted to repudiation of the key task of building the alliance of the working class and the peasantry, repudiation, therefore, of the task of building the united national front of which this alliance alone could be the firm basis, repudiation of the leadership of the working class in the anti-feudal and anti-imperialist revolution.

(4) In order to evolve a correct tactical line it is necessary to discard both the erroneous theses given above and to take into account all the factors of the Indian situation. India is a vast country, with a backward and basically colonial economy and with 80 per cent of its people dependent on agriculture. In such a country partisan warfare, as the experience of China has shown, is one of the most powerful weapons in the armoury of the revolutionary movement and the weapon will have to be wielded by the Communist Party in their fight for national liberation. At the same time it must be realised that there are other specific factors of the Indian situation which are such that this weapon alone cannot lead to victory. In China, the split in the united national front in 1927 simultaneously split the armed forces also and the Communist Party had an army of 30,000 to start with. Moreover, because of the sparse development of Railways and other means of transport, the enemy found it difficult to rapidly concentrate his forces against the areas held by the communists. Despite these advantages enjoyed by the revolutionary forces, they were repeatedly encircled by the enemy. Time and again

they had to break away from this encirclement and threat of anihilation and migrate to new areas to rebuild again. It was only when they made their way into Manchuria and found the firm rear of the Soviet Union that the threat of encirclement and threat of anihilation had come to an end and they were able to launch that great offensive which finally led to the liberation of China. It was thus the support given by the existence of a mighty and firm Soviet rear that was of decisive importance in ensuring victory to the tactic of peasant partisan warfare in the countryside in China.

(5) In these respects the situation in India is different. We have no army to start with, it has to be created. The transport system in India is far more developed than in China, enabling the Government to swiftly concentrate big forces against partisan areas. And above all, geographical position of India is such that we cannot expect to have a friendly neighbouring state which can serve as a firm and powerful rear. All these do not mean that partisan warfare has no place in India. On the contrary because of the factors given earlier, partisan war must be one of the major weapons in our armoury as in the case of all colonial countries. But this weapon alone cannot ensure victory. It has to be combined with the other major weapons that of strikes of the working class, general strike and uprising in the cities led by armed detachment of the working class. Therefore in order to win victory of the popular democratic revolution, it is absolutely essential to combine two basic factors—the partisan war of the peasants and workers uprising in the cities.

(6) Partisan areas will inevitably arise in various parts of the country as crisis deepens and as the mass peasant movement rises to the level of revolutionary seizure of land and food grains, paralysing and wiping off local forces of the enemy. These areas and the revolutionary forces operating in them however continually face the danger of encirclement and anihilation at the hands of the enemy. Even becoming into existence of liberated territories with their own armed forces in several parts of the country will not eliminate this danger because these areas will themselves be surrounded by hostile forces from all sides. Therefore partisan war alone, no matter how widely extended, cannot ensure victory over the enemy in the concrete situation prevailing in India. When the maturing crisis gives rise to partisan struggles on a wide scale, when the partisan forces in several areas are battering against the enemy, the workers in the cities, in vital industries and especially in transport system will have to play a decisive role. The onslaught of the enemy against the partisan forces, against liberated areas will have to be hampered and paralysed

by mass strike actions. With hundreds of streams of partisan struggles merging with the general strikes and uprising of the workers in the cities, the enemy will find it impossible to concentrate his forces anywhere and defeat the revolutionary forces but will himself face defeat and anihilation. Even inside the armed forces of the Government the crisis will grow and big sections will join the forces of revolution.

Alliance of Workers and Peasants as Condition of Victory

(7) Such a perspective demands the closest alliance between the working class and the peasantry and the realisation of the working class leadership in this alliance. This alliance will be built in action, by the bold championship by the working class of the demands of the peasantry, by the direct support given by the working class in the form of demonstrations and strikes to the struggles waged by the peasantry. Leadership of the working class will be realised not merely through the leadership of the Communist Party but above all through the direct mass action of the working class itself in support of the demands and struggles of the peasantry. Of all classes, the working class is looked upon by the peasants as their most closest friend and ally. Many workers come from the rural areas and are connected with the peasants by a thousand and one ties. Actions by the working class not merely the existing struggles but also, as the history of our national movement shows inspires the peasants in the neighbouring areas, radicalised them in developing new peasant struggles. In the present situation in India when all classes, all sections, except the exploiting are facing starvation and when hatred against the present government is growing and strike actions of the working class on such issues as food, ration cuts can be most powerful weapons to inspire the entire people, to give concrete forms to their discontent, to build their unity in action and to raise the popular movement to higher level. By fighting not merely for its own demands but the demands of all discontented sections and classes especially the peasantry, by acting as the foremost champion of the interests of the general democratic movement, the working class will come forward as the leader of the revolutionary people and build their revolutionary unity. (8) It is of the utmost importance therefore that the party creates political consciousness in the working class, makes it conscious of its role of hegemony, overcomes the present disunity of the working class, wins over the majority of the workers in the vital industries and builds a powerful underground movement with factory and workshop committees as its nucleus. The best and most advanced elements must be

recruited in the Party. All this demands intensive political agitation in the working class, patient day to day work, leadership of immediate struggles for the winning of the concrete demands and the building up of a strong trade union movement. Only a united working class and a working class conscious of its role of hegemony can build national unity.

Partisan War of Peasants

(9) In the rural areas the party has to rouse all sections of the peasants, including the rich peasants against feudal exploitation and build their unity basing itself firmly on the agricultural workers and poor peasantry who together form the overwhelming majority of the population. While the liquidation of feudalism and the distribution of land to the peasants must remain the key slogans of the agrarian revolution for the entire period, it is necessary to formulate immediate specific demands for each province and each area, like reduction of rent, fair prices for agricultural products, abolition of feudal levies and forced labour, living wage for agricultural workers, etc., and lead actions for the realisation of these demands. The agrarian crisis is maturing rapidly and the peasant masses are seething with discontent against the present Government which rose to power on the basis of their support and afterwards betrayed them. Despite however this widespread discontent and despite the numerous peasant actions that have taken place in many parts of the country the peasant movement in the country as a whole remains weak and large sections of peasants have not yet been drawn in active struggles because of absence of organisation and firm leadership. It is our task to overcome this weakness by intensive popularisation of our agrarian programme, by formulation of such concrete and easily understood demands as can become the basis of the broadest mass action, by patient day to day work and correct leadership of struggles to realise these demands, and by building in the course of these struggles a network of peasant and agricultural workers organisation with underground units in villages as their leading and guiding centres. Volunteer squads of the most militant and conscious sections of the peasant have to be formed to defend the peasant movements against the attack of the enemy squads that will form nucleus of the partisan squads as the movement will develop and reaches the stage of seige of land and partisan warfare.

(10) As the crisis matures, as the unity consciousness and organisation of the masses grows, as strength and influence of the party develops and as the enemy resorts to more and more ruthless measures to crush the agrarian movement, the question of when, where and how to resort to

arms, will be more and more forced on the agenda. As the question is of immense practical importance it is absolutely necessary that the party will be able to give all clear and unambiguous answer to it.

It must be realised that because of the vast area of India, because of uneven level of mass consciousness and mass movement in different parts of the country, uneven actueness of the agrarian crisis and uneven strength and influence of the party itself, the peasant movement cannot develop at the same tempo everywhere. Premature uprising and adventurist actions of every type must be undoubtedly eschewed at the same time it will be wrong to lay down that the armed actions in the form of partisan warfare should be resorted to in every specific area only when the movement in all parts of the country rises to the level of uprisings. On the contrary in the course of development of the movement a situation will arise in several areas which would demand armed struggle in the form of partisan warfare. For example, in a big and topographically suitable area where the peasant movement has risen to the level of seizure of land to the question of how to effect that seziure and how to defend the land will become a burning and live question. The Party is of opinion that partisan warfare in such a situation, undertaken on the basis of genuine mass peasant movement and the firm unity, under the leadership of the peasant masses, especially the most oppressed and exploited strata, combined with other forms of struggle, such as social boycott of landlords, mass no-rent struggles, agricultural workers' strikes can, if correctly constructed and led, have a rousing and galvanising effect on the peasant masses in all areas and raise their own struggle to a higher level.

Wherever such partisan struggles develop they must also be combined with mass actions of the working class, especially in the neighbouring areas, in the form of strikes and demonstrations. Undertaken on the basis of most careful participation and assessment of all factors the partisan struggles must be conducted with the utmost boldness and tenacity defending the gains of the movement by every means at our disposal. At the same time the party has to act with the utmost flexibility when overwhelming forces of the enemy are concentrated against the partisan areas and partisan forces run into the danger of defeat and total annihilation.

Partisan Struggle and Individual Terrorism

(11) In spite of the offensive nature of the partisan struggle it is necessary to emphasise in our agitation and propaganda in the initial nature

the defensive nature of partisan struggle, saying that the objective of partisan struggle is above all to defend the peasants from the attack of the government and its punitive organs. In doing so, special attention should be paid to the demands for which the peasants are fighting and the atrocities of the government which force the peasants to take arms. It is necessary at the same time, to point out that it is the government that is responsible for violence and bloodshed. Partisan struggles are frequently confused with individual terrorism, it is asserted that individual terrorism is part of partisan struggle and not only a part, but even a basis of partisan struggle. This is absolutely wrong. What is more, individual terrorism, contradicts the spirit and objective of partisan struggle and it is absolutely incompatible with partisan struggle. In the first place the objective of individual terrorism is to destroy particular individuals while not pursuing the aims of not destroying the regime of feudal exploitation and subjugation of the people, whereas the objective of the partisan struggle is not to destroy particular individuals, but to destroy the hated regime in a prolonged struggle of the popular masses. In the second place, individual terrorism is carried out by individuals— terrorists—or by small squads of terrorists acting apart from the masses, and without any link with the struggle of the masses, whereas the partisan struggle is carried out by popular masses and not by individuals, is carried in close contact with the struggle of the masses against the existing regime.

Since individual terrorism is carried out not by the masses but by individual terrorists acting apart from the masses, individual terrorism leads to the undue minimisation of the role of the mass movement and to equally undue exaggeration of the role of the terrorists who are alleged to be capable of securing the liberation of the people by their own forces independent of the growth of the mass partisan movement. It is clear that such a feeling created by individual terrorism can only cultivate passivity among the popular masses and thereby undermine the development of partisan struggles. Therein lies the second main harm done by individual terrorism to the revolutionary movement.

To sum up: Individual terrorism undermines the possibility of unleashing partisan struggle of the masses and should be rejected as harmful and dangerous.

It is Necessary to Strengthen the Party

Despite the tremendous radicalisation that has taken place among the masses during the last three years and despite the many mass actions that have taken place and are taking place, it would be gross exaggeration to assert that India is already on the verge of armed insurrection or revolution, that a civil war is already raging in the country, that the Government, its leaders and agents are already completely isolated and so on and so forth. Such exaggeration leads to the ignoring of the concrete tasks facing the party, the organising and advocacy of adventuristic actions, and the issuing of futile calls for action and pompous slogans which bear no relation either to the existing level of mass consciousness or to the actual maturity of the situation. In practice, it results in the self isolation of the party, making it easy for the enemy to destroy it. It results in handing over the masses to the Socialists and other disruptors.

Equally wrong are they who through their reformism see only the weakness and disunity of the popular movement, the offensive of the enemy and advocate a policy of retreat and 'lying low'; a policy of regrouping of forces, eschewing all militant actions in the cities and countryside for the present. Tactics based on such an understanding of the situation will result in the worst type of reformism and make the, Party trail behind the masses instead of leading them.

(13) Reality of the situation is that the crisis is maturing fast. Under its impact the masses are getting fast radicalised and a period of big battles lies ahead. The Governments failure to carry out a single pledge that it gave to the people, its failure to tackle a single problem, especially the problem of agrarian reform and food for the people, all these are fast shattering the illusions. Already the majority of the people look upon, the present government as a government of exploiting cases, as a government of landlords and capitalists. Most of them still believe that this government can be changed and a real popular government take its place without resort to armed revolution and by means of general elections; nevertheless in their struggle for their day to day demands—adequate wages, fair price for agricultural products, restoration of ration cuts, etc., hundreds and thousands are coming out in action in all parts of the country. The growth of the popular movement still lags behind the growth of popular discontent, only a small fraction of the people have as yet been drawn into the actual struggle against the government. This leg is due not merely to the repressive measures of the government but primarily and, above all, to the weakness of the party and the existing disunity of the progressive forces. It is one of the key tasks of the party to forge the unity of the working class to unite the popular forces on the basis of the concrete programme and to grow into a mass party so as

to be able to supply the leadership which alone can unify and extend the mass movement to raise it to a higher level.

The Party has to give the slogan that the present government has to go and be replaced by a popular government, representing the unity of the democratic forces, a government that will break with the British empire and carry out the programme of the agrarian reforms and democracy. It has to utilise the coming general elections for the most extensive popularisation of its programme, for mobilising and unifying the democratic forces, for exposing the policies and methods of present government. It has to lead themselves in their day to day struggle and take them forward step by step so that the people through their own experience, come to realise the necessity and inevitability of armed revolution.

The Party must not preach the inevitability of fascism but utilise the enormous volume of the democratic opinion in the country to unite the people to halt the growing drive towards fascism on the part of the present government. Through patient and systemtic day to day work, through the bold championship of the demands of the people, through correct leadership of the concrete struggle of all sections of the people, the Party will grow and be able to fulfil its role as organiser and leader of the people's democratic movement.

(14) It is necessary therefore to put an end to the interminable discussion that has been going on in our party on the question of Chinese path, on the question on how armed struggle is to be conducted. Such discussion disorganise the party, dissipates its strength, and leaves the mass leaderless, precisely when they need the leadership of the Party most urgently. Discussion of such matters, carried out almost openly as they have been till now, reveal all our plans and make it difficult to carry them out in practice.

The fact is that if the crisis bursts out in the near future, the party in its present and disorganised and weak state will not be able to fully utilise it to lead the people to revolution. It is not yet prepared to shoulder the gigantic responsibilities that such a situation will place on it. It is necessary therefore that the present weaknesses are overcome with the utmost rapidity, the ranks of the party are unified and steps are taken to extend the mass bases of the party and strengthen it. While recruiting the best elements from the working class and other fighting classes into the party and developing into a mass party, it is necessary at the same time to exercise the utmost vigilance against the swamping of the party with elements that cannot yet be considered fully tested and trustworthy. The system of candidate membership must be introduced for this purpose. It is also necessary that while utilising all legal possibilities, the existing illegal apparatus of the party is strengthened enormously.

The Struggle for the Preservation of Peace

(15) One of the most important tasks facing our Party in our country is the task of mobilising the Indian people in the struggle for the defence of peace. Being one of the most largest and populous countries of the world, and occupying a key position in South-East Asia, India has a tremendous role to play in the battle against the Anglo-American warmongers and for the preservation of peace. It is the job of the Communist Party to ensure that India plays that role.

The forces of peace in our country are potentially growing. Love and admiration for the Soviet Union widespread in all sections, including the middle class intelligentsia. The liberation of China and her emergence as a great power, the manner in which the People's Government in China is successfully tackling the problems of food, famine, floods and diseases have profoundly influenced our people. Especially powerful is the sentiment against American aggression in Korea, so widespread the sympathy for the Korean people that even the most reactionary newspapers have had to criticise the American aggressors. This powerful mass sentiment as well as the other factors have compelled even the Nehru Government to take a stand against the most blatant acts of the American imperialists (the threat to use the atom bombs, the branding of People's China as an aggressor, etc.).

The Party however, has yet not succeeded in transforming the widespread peace sentiment into a powerful peace movement, because as on other issues, our approach to the issue of peace was extreme by sectarian. The peace movement, in the main, remained the movement confined to the existing mass following of the Party and the trade unions and peasants' organisations under our influence. The peace platform was utilised for abstract denunciation of the Government on all conceivable issues and to popularise struggles that only the Party waged. It inevitably was the result of restriction of sweep of the mass movement and a failure to win over as peace partisans all the genuine lovers of peace. It is only recently that these harmful methods are abandoned.

Another manifestation of sectarianism is the failure to link the issues of peace with the live issues of the people, the failure to show the connection between the drive towards war and mounting war budget of the Nehru Government with the rise in prices of the necessities of life, the reduction of government expenses on education, the neglecting of housing accommodation, growing attack on civil liberties, etc.

It is of the utmost importance to abandon all sectarianism to develop a real broad based peace movement. The growing and the strengthening of the national movement helps the cause of peace. The strengthening of the peace movement also facilitates the growth of the national liberation movement. These two movements therefore must develop in close relation with each other, each strengthening the other. Nevertheless, they are not identical. The platform of the peace is a broader platform. It can and must include all supporters of peace, all elements who for various reasons are opposed to war and are prepared to take their stand against all measures calculated to extend and unleash war.

(17) It is necessary for the peace movement to correctly appraise the foreign policy of the Nehru Government in relation to peace and to adopt a correct attitude towards all specific manifestation of that policy.

While the peace movement must support all these specific acts of the Government which hampers the plans of the warmongers, *eg* Nehru's declaration against atom bomb add the vote against the American proposal to denounce People's China in the UNO, must also simultaneously point out the half-hearted and vacilating nature of the Government's policy and wage a determined battle to mobilise a mass opinion in favour of a consistent peace policy.

As a matter of fact the Nehru Government's policy cannot be called a policy of peace. It is essentially a policy of manoeuvring between the main enemy of peace, the United States of America, and its junior partner, Britain, on the one hand and the peace loving countries on the other. Nehru fears the consequence of world war and therefore advocates a policy of 'moderation' of not going 'too far'. At the same time the Indian government continues to be an active member of the British commonwealth which is a partner of the American imperialists in aggressive wars. The Indian Government has not condemned the American war of aggression in Korea nor repudiated its support to the illegal resolution of the UNO sanctioning that aggression. It has not condemned the British imperialists who are waging war in Malaya—but on the contrary permitted them to recruit Gurkha soldiers against the Malayan people. It has not denounced the French aggression in Viet Nam and continues to give facilities to the French imperialists for the transport of troops and war materials.

Therefore, in addition to mobilising the people against the threat of the atom bomb, for support of Stockholm and Warsaw appeals one of the specific tasks of the peace movement in India is to rally the people against these policies of the present Government which abet and aid the colonial wars waged by the American, British and French imperialists against the peoples of south-east Asia. The peace movement is not a pacific movement, not a movement merely for recording abstract support to peace. It is fighting movement for concrete action in defence for peace and against the imperialists war-mongers including those waging colonial wars.

(18) The peace movement must fight against all attempts to sow hostility against the Chinese People's Republic. It must explain to our people how the liberation of Tibet is not a threat to peace but a decisive blow against the instigators of war. It must uphold the heroic actions of the Chinese volunteers who by smashing the plans of American warmongers who enslaved the Korean and Chinese Peoples strengthened the cause of world peace.

(19) We must also fight all warmongering propaganda against Pakistan, pointing out how the growing tension between Pakistan and India is the rest of imperialist manoeuvres and how it helps the enemies of the peoples of both states. We must demand a drastic reduction in the military budget and a policy of friendship and close alliance between India, Pakistan and Ceylon.

(20) The peace movement must wage a determined battle against slanders of the Soviet Union against all those who strive to depict the consistent peace policy of the Soviet Union as a policy of war and aggression. Basing ourselves on the lucid and clear cut statement of Comrade Stalin in reply to *Pravda* correspondent, we must concretely expose the real instigators of war and uphold the shining example of the Soviet Union which is devoting its energies and resources to further improving the condition of the people and leading the entire progressive humanity in the struggle for the preservation of peace. Firm friendship between the peace loving people of all countries must save the world from the menace of war and the people of India have to play a big role in establishing this friendship–this fact must be made a part of the consciousness of the entire people.

Andhra Thesis

What is the precise nature of our revolution ? Regarding this there were a number of arguments and different viewpoints that has appeared in the course of our discussions. Some comrades had contended that the nature of our revolution is anti-feudal and anti-imperialist. Some others argued that it is not only anti-feudal and anti-imperialist, but also anti-capitalist. Now it has been made clear that it is totally wrong to characterise it as 'anti-capitalist' also, but it is only anti-feudal and anti-imperialist. In this connection we have to admit that those who argued that it is only anti-feudal and anti-imperialist revolution also had not been able to draw the full conclusions on it, and many erroneous conceptions prevailed as a result of which many wrong and ultra-leftist slogans and programmes of action have come out. What are these erroneous conceptions and how to correct them ? Let us first see what we mean by anti-imperialist revolution.

In the programme it has been stated that we have to fight against British Imperialism for our complete national independence. I hear that some comrades who have not fully grasped this point have run into some amazing conclusions and have gone to the extent of saying that the present programme must have been written by Dulles because American Imperialism, *the chief enemy of the world proletariat* is not brought out in the programme as *the Chief Enemy of our national Independence*. It is quite natural to get such wild reactions in the background of run-riot inter-Party discussion and the wrong education and erroneous political understanding so far prevailed on this issue.

Some time after the Second Party Congress we altogether forgot about the role of imperialism as a force that is gripping our national economy and enslaving it, barring all our national progress. In our agitation and propaganda the fire against Imperialism was almost absent. When it was brought by some comrades to the notice of the then existing PB, instead of correcting it, had advanced another totally wrong formula that 'freedom means not from this or that imperialism only but imperialism in general, that is world imperialism, etc.', thereby submerging the specific in the general, blurring the vision and direction of the entire force of attack. After the LPPD editorial and subsequent discussions, when imperialism has again been brought into the picture as the enemy of our national independence, the pattern has become to talk of Anglo-American Imperialism, that is both imperialisms clubbed together as the enemies of our national independence and enslavers of our people.

The present discussions reveal that this view is also defective and wrong. You will naturally ask me why it is so. It is so because (1) it is unreal and factually incorrect to talk of American-imperialism as the American capital does not form more than three to four per cent of foreign capital investments in India; (2) it is so because it is British imperialism that has directly ruled over us for the last 200 years and is still keeping us in its grip (*ie* economically direct and politically indirect even today); more than eighty per cent of the foreign capital in India belongs to the British. (3) It is so since that when we are demanding complete national independence, we are demanding secession from the British Commonwealth of which our country has been forced to be a member and not from the United States of America. (4) It is also wrong to talk of general anti-imperialist fight without specifying the particular imperialism that is dominating over our country as this outlook, if logically extended, leads us on the verge of erroneous conclusions of the Trotskyite school of thought which advocate world revolution against world imperialism, *ie* the theory of permanent revolution. (5) It is totally wrong to talk of general anti-imperialism because this viewpoint refuses to take note of the advancement of the revolution.

We know that the present Anglo-American contradictions are the chief inner imperialist contradictions of the day. This contradiction manifests itself not only in the international arena in general but has also its specific expression in our own country. America is trying to elbow out British from its dominant position in the market. Britain and the native interests that are closely allied with her are vitally interested in opposing all such attempts in their own way. That is how Anglo-American contradiction is expressing itself in our country. Instead of utilising this contradiction for the benefit of the advancement of the revolutionary movement, if we club both imperialists together and declare both of them simultaneously, and equally our national enemies to be fought out and liquidated, it not only becomes moral but also lands us in the stand of 'fight all the enemies of the Proletariat at one stroke' instead of fighting them one after another in its own turn. It also conjectively amounts at this stage, to fighting the battles of English imperialists against America.

All this brings before us one salient point, namely that British imperialism is the chief enemy of our national progress and therefore of our national independence; it is British imperialism that has allied itself with the native tendal interests and is defending the feudal order, barring all roads to prosperity and advancement; it is British imperialism that has allied itself with a section of the national bourgeoisie and defending the rotten colonial order; it is British capital that grips our national economy and impedes our national industries and bars national progress; it is British imperialism that has drawn to its side a section of the national big bourgeoisie and with their help tied us to the chariot of the British Commonwealth. So when we talk of anti-imperialist revolution it specifically means, in the present set-up a fight against British imperialism for national independence and freedom, but not against Anglo-American imperialism or world imperialism in general.

Now comrades raise the questions: Is not American imperialism the spearhead of reaction and the chief enemy of the Soviet Union, People's China and other People's Democratic State ? Is not American imperialism hatching conspiracies against communist parties throughout the world, our party being no exception ? Is not American imperialism trying to penetrate into our country and exploit and enslave us ? When such are the facts are we not to fight American imperialism as well ? These are all very pertinent questions and we have to answer them correctly. Our party, as the Vanguard Detachment of the Indian working class which is a party of the world working class has to fight against American imperialism. This is our inviolable international obligation or rather a revolutionary duty on our part. We, as a party of the working class, as a party, of the world working class have our national and international duties to discharge. Internationally speaking America is the spearhead of world reaction as the main enemy of Peace and Freedom for all the people. We, situated as we are in a country under a particular state, have some concrete tasks to perform. The chief enemy of our national freedom today is British imperialism. When we have to fight for the complete freedom of our own territory the fight will be against British imperialism. It is our national enemy. America figures as our international enemy. We should neither forget our task of fighting British imperialism nor absolve of our international responsibilities of exposing and isolating American imperialism. It will be also wrong to deduce syllogisms of formal logic, asserting that:

> our international enemy is also our national enemy,
> the chief international enemy is American imperialism,
> therefore our fight for freedom is against American imperialism.

This does not take us anywhere near the truth or the success of our fight for freedom.

American imperialism has to be thoroughly exposed and all its reactionary ideological propaganda has to be constantly laid before the people and rouse them to the consciousness of fighting these conspiracies, the war manoeuvres of American imperialism and thus prevent our country from being drawn into the whirlpool of war on behalf of the American imperialism against the world peoples' camp.

If we forget the concrete question of British imperialism and the concrete task of fighting it for our national freedom and only indulge in general talk of fighting Anglo-American imperialism we reduce ourselves to the position of tall-talkers and fail to mobilise the people for the struggle for complete national independence from British imperialism.

If we ignore the task of exposing and isolating American imperialism as the chief enemy of the world people and world peace and confine ourselves to the narrow shell of our fight against British Imperialism, we again reduce ourselves to the position of bourgeois nationalists.

We have one national enemy and a separate international enemy. The struggle against one particular national enemy for our national freedom is not in contradiction with the fight against another international enemy though the nature of the fight varies. Bourgeois nationalism and bourgeois internationalism are two irreconcilable conceptions because of the very inherent contradictory nature of the bourgeois class and their interests. The bourgeois class, in the final analysis, never considers either nationalism or internationalism as sacrosanct. For them everything is subserving to their class domination and class exploitation.

For the proletariat it is not so. The proletariat can afford to be the real defender of itself, that is of its national interest, as well as of the international interest of the people because it stands against all exploitation.

Earlier when we had to face a similar situation, *ie* of facing one international enemy in the form of German Fascists and another separate national enemy in the form of British Imperialism, we could not co-ordinate the struggle against both correctly. For some time we argued that the main question for us was our national freedom and therefore we could not bother about the international enemy. Later when we realised and woke up to the danger of the international enemy we had almost neglected, ignored and sidetracked our fight against the national enemy. I am referring here to the period of the anti-fascist war. The present correction not only restores us the clear perspective of the nature of our anti-imperialist struggle at the present state, but also goes along in correcting our very erroneous outlook on the problem which has been persisting since a very long time. Lastly, before I conclude, let me remind you of the inner imperialist contradiction and how they were utilised by the CPSU (B) and the CPC. Take for instance the Treaty of Brest-Litovsk and the non-aggression pact of the USSR (1939), etc. Similarly our Chinese comrades had also applied the Marxist theory of inner imperialist contradictions to their struggle for freedom and national independence. They concentrated against the chief imperialist enemy of their freedom which was for sometime the Anglo-French bloc, later Japanese imperialism and subsequently now American imperialism. As a matter of fact, even though Britain has the territory of Hongkong under its control, they (China) now do not talk of liquidating British imperialism along with American imperialism, etc. If today British imperialism feels that Chinese Republic is soft towards them and therefore it is time to make use of the Chinese difficulties for its own ends and slackens its attack on Chinese Republic. It is all for the good because in the long run it is not British imperialism that is going to gain by present Chinese attitude towards it, but on the contrary; after eliminating the present menace of American imperialism the Chinese Republic will eventually direct its attention against British imperialist positions. In our case also, if American imperialism thinks that our Party and our class is not so much hostile to their penetration into India and we are not concentrating fire on American plans swallowing British interests, let them think so and our revolution is not at all going to suffer thereby. At present it remains as an Anglo-American conflict. It is none of our business to take sides. It is also none of our business to encourage either. If in the course of these Anglo-American conflicts and contradictions America elbows out British from India and becomes dominant and if in the meanwhile we would not be able to achieve full independence and if America then remains our chief national enemy, it will be our task to concentrate our main fight against American Imperialism. This understanding is nothing new to Marxism-Leninism though we are learning it for the first time in all its implications. As a matter of fact, Lenin's thesis on imperialism is the basic document where this point of view has been dealt with at length. It is basing on this thesis that the revolutionary movements have been working out their tactics and strategy. *Let us imbibe this and never again derail and deviate from this.* Now it will be clear for you all why in our programme we concentrate fire on British imperialism and figure it as the chief and immediate enemy, of our national freedom and stop talking of Anglo-American Imperialism in a general way, as we have been doing till now.

Third Congress of
The Communist Party of India

Results of Election to the Central Committee

1	Ajay Ghosh	293
2	E. M. S. Namboodripad	293
3	A. K. Gopalan	291
4	P. Sundaraya	288
5	Jyoti Basu	286
6	Achutha Menon	286
7	Renen Sen	285
8	Hari Kishen Singh Surjeet	283
9	M. N. Govindan Nair	282
10	Dasarth Deb Burman	280
11	P. Ramamurthi	278
12	Sohan Singh Josh	278
13	C. Rajeshwar Rao	278
14	S. S. Yusuf	277
15	Yogendranath Sharma	277
16	S. G. Sardesai	277
17	S. A. Dange	275
18	Gurucharan Patnaik	273
19	D. Venkatasa Rao	273
20	Ravi Narayan Reddi	272
21	Z. A. Ahmed	268
22	Phani Bora	266
23	M. R. Venkatraman	266
24	Romesh Chandra	261
25	N. Prasad Rao	260
26	S. S. Mirakjar	255
27	Aruna Asaf Ali	254
28	Basava Punniah	252
29	H. K. Vyas	247
30	N. L. Upadhyaya	245
31	Dinkar Mehta	241

32	Muzafar Ahmed	239
33	Sudam Deshmukh	238
34	M. Hanumantha Rao	230
35	S. G. Patkar	219
36	L. R. Khandkar	212
37	Bhupesh Gupta	205
38	G. Adhikari	194
	(elected, defeating the official candidate Hajra Begum)	
39	Y. D. Sharma	192

List of Defeated Candidates

1	Hajra Begum	188
2	Vishwanath Mukherjee	173
3	B. Srinivas Rao	164
4	B. T. Randive	145
5	Yela Reddi	122
6	Bhavani Sen	120
7	P. C. Joshi	107
8	N. C. Shekher	69
9	Bhalchandra	62
10	Kamadar	53
11	Kalyan Sunder	49

NOTES

CHAPTER ONE

1 Report on Indian Constitutional Reforms, 1918, page 14.
2 *Ibid*, page 1.
3 *Ibid*, page 86.

CHAPTER TWO

1 *India and Communism.* This confidential and hitherto unpublished report compiled in the Home Department of the Government of India for the information and use of ranking officials and revised up to 1st January 1935, came into the hands of the present writer a couple of years later when he was Joint Secretary of the All-India Congress Socialist Party. The author has checked its veracity at various points with Mr Philip Spratt, one of the founders of the CPI, who figures prominently in it, and who is now one of the Secretaries of the Indian Committee for Cultural Freedom. The report is a remarkably able and accurate presentation and analysis of the first stages in the life of the CPI and has provided authoritative material for inclusion in Chapters 2 and 3 of this monograph.
2 *India and Communism.*
3 *Ibid.*
4 V. I. Lenin: Thesis on Report on the Tactics of the Russian Communist Party to the Third Congress of the Comintern. *Selected Works*, Lawrence & Wishart, London, volume X, page 731.
5 *India and Communism.*
6 *Ghadr Party:* Moscow was not content merely with sending her agents direct to India, but also established contact with the Ghadr Party with headquarters in San Francisco, working for the emancipation of India from outside. This was a movement originally started in the United States of America on the eve of the World War 1 by Lala Har Dayal, an Indian patriot, who died in exile. Communism has, however, a way of using nationalism, particularly in colonial countries. Some of the members belonging to the Ghadr Party joined Moscow, in the first instance for ideological reasons;

later on, they became converted into obedient instruments of Soviet policy. Very early in 1922, one Rattan Singh and Santokh Singh attended the Fourth Congress of the Communist International as delegates from India on behalf of the Ghadr Party in San Francisco. Rattan Singh went to several places including China on behalf of Moscow. Later on, he was reinforced by one Teja Singh Swatantar, another Communist worker. Concerted action by these two persons led to an arrangement by which an annually increasing number of the Ghadr Party's recruits were despatched to Moscow for a year's training in espionage and sabotage. In 1934, according to the intelligence of the British Government in India, there were about sixty Sikh students in the Oriental University in Moscow, besides those who had already been despatched as finished products. See also an article by Professor Tilak Raj Chadda in *Thought*, Delhi, 14th June 1952.

7 *India and Communism.*

8 *Ibid.*

9 *Ibid.*

10 *Ibid.*

11 *Ibid.*

12 *India and Communism.* Spratt's attitude then is, perhaps, best summed up in his own words, taken from his statement before the Court of Sessions at Meerut: 'I did what I could to carry out the policy of the Communist International in the name of the British working class and of the Communist Party, by co-operation with what I thought was the only body actively and effectively working for the National Revolution in India, that is, the Workers' and Peasants' Parties.' Incidentally, because of his later defection from communism, Spratt's name no longer appears in the communist account and chronicles of the Meerut Conspiracy Case.

13 *India and Communism.*

14 *Ibid.*

15 *Ibid.*

16 *Ibid.*

17 *Ibid.*

18 *Ibid.*

19 This was the finding of the Sessions Court at Meerut. (*India and Communism.*)

S

20 *League against Imperialism.* The League against Imperialism, a Comintern outfit, had already had a successful conference in Brussels which was attended by Jawaharlal Nehru and other militant nationalist leaders of Asian countries.

'Let us note this fact,' says Mr. C. K. Narayanaswami in the *Bharat Jyoti* (Bombay) of 22nd June 1952. 'It was the resolution introduced by Shri Jawaharlal at the Madras Session of the National Congress (1927) which gave deliberate and definite shape to the ideological content of our foreign policy. That resolution was conditioned by the Congress against Imperialism which met in Brussels and at which Shri Nehru represented India.'

21 *India and Communism.*

22 The following quotation from *Kranti* of 13th October 1928, edited by Dange, gives an inkling of the inflammatory nature of the appeal made to the workers: 'Remember that the strike is not ended but only suspended. Although we go to the mills, we do so boiling with rage. There will be no peace *until capitalism is overthrown.* For capitalism is hatching dangerous plots to cut down wages, reduce the number of men and increase the hours of work. News of all these plots can be obtained every week through *Kranti.'*

23 *India and Communism.*

24 For a full list of the accused, see R. Palme Dutt: *India To-day,* page 341.

25 *India and Communism.* With regard to finding (xv), Mr Philip Spratt has recorded his dissent. According to him, almost half the accused were nationalists or trade unionists who were largely ignorant of the real nature of the conspiracy and of its underhand methods. When those were revealed during the trial, they were taken aback. The demoralisation and quarrels among the prisoners during the later stages of the trial could partly be attributed to this factor.

26 *India and Communism.*

27 *Ibid.*

CHAPTER THREE

1 *India and Communism.*

See also Madhu Limaye's *Communist Party, Facts and Fiction,* pages 18–19.

2 *India and Communism.*

3 *Ibid.*

4 *Ibid.*

5 *Ibid.*

6 *Ibid.*

7 *Ibid.*

8 *Ibid.*

CHAPTER FOUR

1 *The Communist* (organ of the Central Committee of the Communist Party of India), volume I, no. 12, September 1936, page 2.

2 *The Congress Socialist*, Organ of the All-India Congress Socialist Party, March 1936.

3 *The Communist*, volume I, no. 12. September 1936, pages 10–11.

4 *Ibid*, pages 3–4.

5 Circular no. 4 issued on 25th July 1936 by the Politbureau to the Central Committee of the CPI.

6 *Ibid.*

7 See an undated leaflet entitled 'Appeal to the Congress Rank and File' issued by the CPI (Section of the Communist International)

8 *The Communist*, volume I, no. 12, September 1936, page 16.

9 *Ibid*, page 8.

10 Jayaprakash Narayan: *Socialist Unity and the Congress Socialist Party*, 1941, page 3.

11 *Ibid*, page 26.

12 *Open Forum*, no. 12, Bengal Party Headquarters, 1950, quoted by Madhu Limaye: *Communist Party, Fact and Fiction*, page 23.

13 *The Communist*, volume I, no. 12, September 1936, page 23.

14 Jayaprakash Narayan: *Socialist Unity and the Congress Socialist Party*, 1941, page 24.

CHAPTER FIVE

1 The *Daily Worker* (London) of 1st February 1940, wrote: 'Hitler repeated once again his claim that the war was thrust upon him by Britain. Against this historical fact there is no reply. Britain declared war, not Germany. Attempts were made to end the war but the Soviet-German peace overtures were rejected by Britain.'

2 P. Sundarayya, now leader of the CP in the Indian Parliament, had written in the *National Front* of 3rd April 1938: 'The immediate issue before us in India is not the fight against fascism but the fight for a true democracy in our own country. India's part in the coming international struggle for power is the struggle for her own freedom'. *National Front* of 2nd October 1938, wrote editorially: 'The Indian people can play a positive and decisive rôle only if they enter the war with complete control over their army and their foreign policy is determined by their own government. To agree to anything else would be a betrayal of our independence movement. But the National Congress must also declare that India will not participate even in such a war except as a free nation . . .

'Only as a people free to determine their course of action will the Indian people line up with Britain in the war against fascist aggressors.'

3 In a pamphlet entitled *The Congress Socialist Party and the War* dated March 1940, the communists wrote: 'With the outbreak of the war and with the consequent sharpening of all conflicts, conflict between the bourgeoisie and the proletariat, conflict between the landlords and the peasants, conflicts between the British Government and the Indian people – Gandhism has entered into its last and most reactionary phase. No longer is Gandhiji's leadership, in even a restricted sense, unifier of the people's movement, no longer has it any progressive rôle whatsoever. Compromise on the issue of war is the biggest danger that faces the national movement and Gandhism to-day means the line of that compromise . . .

'This does not mean organisational break from the Congress which is even to-day dominated by Gandhites, but it does mean relentless struggle against and exposure of Gandhism as a political line, as a technique, and as an organisational principle; it does mean sharpest opposition to Gandhian leadership; it does mean isolation of that leadership and determined effort to smash its influence . . .

'The CSP leadership has made its final break with Marxism and has completely gone over to Gandhism . . . The circle is completed. Masanism has triumphed.'

4 In April 1941, Jayaprakash Narayan issued a pamphlet entitled *Socialist Unity and the Congress Socialist Party* already referred to in Chapter 3. In this he detailed his unsuccessful efforts at socialist unity and the calculated disruption of which the communists had been guilty.

5 In July 1941, the Politbureau published a pamphlet entitled *Soviet-German War* on the following lines: 'The Communist Party declares that the only way in which the Indian people can help in the just war which the Soviet is waging is by fighting all the more vigorously for their own emancipation from the imperialist yoke. Our attitude towards the British Government and its imperialist war remains what it was. We must continue, nay, intensify our struggle against both. There can be no change in our policy until a people's government which unequivocally renounces imperialist aims in this war as well as in India and in the colonies comes to power. We can render really effective aid to the Soviet Union only as a free people. That is why our campaign for the demonstration of our support and solidarity with the Soviet Union must be coupled with the exposure of the imperialist hypocrisy of the Churchills and Roosevelts, with the demand for the intensification of our struggle for independence.' (Quoted by Acharya Narendra Dev in his *Socialism and the National Revolution*.)

6 In the years 1937–38, when World War 2 was already looming on the horizon and the attitude that the Indian people should adopt in case of such a war was being canvassed, a straight question had been addressed to the Indian communists in the columns of the *Congress Socialist*, the weekly organ of the Congress Socialist Party: What would be the attitude of the Indian Communist Party towards such a war in case Britain and Russia found themselves on the same side? To this question, which was repeated more than once, no clear answer was forthcoming from the communist ranks.

A decade later, Ranadive had this to say in the course of an article in the *Communist* of February 1949: 'The battle against proletarian internationalism started nearly eleven years back. Both the Sixth Congress and the Seventh Congress of the Communist International had correctly laid down that the defence of the Soviet Union was the acid test of internationalism. Basing himself on this, one of the Party leaders wrote an article in 1936, frankly stating that the communists would support the Soviet Union in her fight against Hitler's aggression, and if Britain were on the same side as the Soviets that fact would not alter the communists' attitude to war. This stand was officially repudiated by the then Politbureau and it was stated that in such an event the communists would not support the joint war but would fight Britain.'

7 On 12th July 1952, communist adherents observed a 'Release the

Détenus Day'. The sponsoring appeal for the occasion issued by Mr N.M. Joshi said: 'It is to be noted that the very large proportion of the *détenus* who are still in jail are detained on the ground of being communists, since the beginning of the year have expressed in unmistakable terms a change in their attitude towards the war, and that those of the communists who are free have been for some months giving an enthusiastic support to the war by their speeches and in other ways . . . (those in prison) are denied the freedom even to support the war.'

8 Commenting on the Working Committee's resolution, the CP weekly organ, *The People's War* on 19th July 1942, wrote: 'After nine days of labour the Working Committee has brought forth an abortion. The resolution it has produced has bankruptcy writ large upon it. From the rut of inactivity it now seeks to lead the nation into the politics of blind desperation and disaster.'

Writing on the same subject in *The People's War* of 16th August 1942, P. C. Joshi, the General Secretary of the Party, said: 'The Working Committee has tied the rope round the neck of the nation and handed over its ends to the imperialist bureaucracy. This was the lead that was being glorified as "national struggle".'

9 R. Palme Dutt of the British Communist Party in a letter to the CPI (published in *The People's War*) of 2nd August 1942, wrote: 'By the time this reaches you, events will have moved very much further and you may be in the midst of big issues. The general line is clear; maximum mass mobilisation against fascism; full co-operation in practical action with all who oppose fascism, irrespective of political differences; no action of the present rulers so long as they stand by the alliance to resist fascism, should deflect us from this line, which is in the interests, not merely of the world front of the peoples, but of the Indian people whose future cannot be separated from the world front of the peoples.'

10 Thus in the course of a Resolution adopted by the first Congress of the CPI held in Bombay on 23rd May 1943, it is laid down: 'The groups which make up the fifth column are the Forward Bloc, the Party of the traitor Bose; the CSP which betrayed socialism at the beginning of the war and pursued a policy of opportunism and disruption and ended in the camp of the Trotskyite traitors; and finally, the Trotskyite groups which are criminal gangs in the pay of fascists. *The Communist Party declares that all these three groups must be treated by every honest Indian as the worst enemy of the*

nation and driven out of political life and exterminated.' (Italics on the original) (Limaye's CP *Facts and Fiction* – pages 48 and 49)

The People's War of 12th September 1943 wrote: 'The CSP, Forward Bloc and Trotskyites are parties organised on the basis of . . . a fifth columnist policy . . . we communists call these parties Fifth Column Parties . . . The Fifth Column groups want the deadlock to continue because under cover of this they hope to organise their cadres so that when the time comes for Jap invasion they may blow up the rear to help the Japs and deliver our people to Jap enslavement.'

11 The resolution passed by the First Congress of the CPI held in Bombay on 23rd May 1943, said: 'It is the patriotic duty of the worker to strengthen defence by taking initiative for organising more production and better transport and against stoppage of work *irrespective of what the boss or the bureaucrat does* . . . Communists take *a bold and open stand against strikes* as they injure the defence of the country by holding up production.'

12 Commenting editorially, *The People's War* of 9th August 1942, wrote: 'Vivisection of India is a sin, says Gandhiji. And this sums up the opinion of the national leadership and emphasises the gulf that must be bridged before it is too late . . . Nationalist opinion has been loud in its proclamation that under a free India, there must be no oppression of the minority by the majority. But a minority which distrusts the majority cannot be satisfied with such assertions. Its fears must be completely allayed. Its equal status must be guaranteed in a form easily understood. It must be given the right to secession, the right to form an independent state . . . To look upon the right of secession as the special fad of Jinnah, as the conspiracy of a few communists to divide India in the interests of British imperialism, is to ignore the new Muslim awakening, as also of other nationalities, *eg*, Andhras, Karnatakis, Maharashtrians, etc, the awakening of a distinct nationality to new life, individual national consciousness.'

On 15th October 1944, by which time Mahatma Gandhi had been released, had tried to negotiate an agreement with Mr Jinnah and failed, *The People's War* commented editorially: 'We hope . . . more and more non-Muslims than before will see that Pakistan is a just demand for the Muslim homelands.'

CHAPTER SIX

1 In an interview with Mr M. Limaye, Joint Secretary of the Socialist Party, in November 1947 (quoted by Mr Limaye in his pamphlet, *Communist Party: Facts and Fiction*,) R. Palme Dutt said: 'Your talk about leaving the Congress is untimely and mistaken and you should not only remain in the Congress but agitate for the readmittance of the communists into the national organisation. The Congress is now divided into two camps, the progressive camp led by Pandit Nehru, Sheikh Abdulla and others and the reactionary bloc led by Sardar Patel. It is the supreme duty of all of us to support Nehru. If Nehru offers you seats in his cabinet, you should readily accept the offer.' The socialists did not accept the advice, and finally left the Congress in 1948. The communists had already been expelled from the Congress in 1945.

2 With the failure of the Moscow Conference in 1947, communist co-operation with the governments of the Western European countries was suddenly withdrawn. The Italian communists were in consequence thrown out of the De Gasperi Cabinet and Maurice Thorez ousted from the French Government. With the ending of coalition governments, a series of strikes followed in France and Italy.

3 In *The International Situation*, Zhdanov also said: 'The new policy of the United States is designed to consolidate its monopoly position and to reduce its capitalist partners to a state of subordination and dependence of America. But America's aspirations to world supremacy encountered an obstacle in the USSR, the stronghold of anti-imperialist and anti-fascist policy and in its growing international influence; in the new democracies, which have escaped from the control of British and American imperialism; and in the workers of all countries, including America itself, who do not want a new war for the supremacy of their oppressors. Accordingly, the new expansionist and reactionary policy of the United States envisages a struggle against the USSR, against the new democracies, against the labour movement in all countries, including the United States, and against the emancipationist anti-imperialist forces in all countries.'

In the same address, Zhdanov further said: 'The fundamental changes caused by the war in the international scene and in the position of individual countries has entirely changed the political landscape of the world. A new alignment of political forces has arisen. The more the war recedes into the past, the more distinct become two major trends in post-war international policy, corresponding to the division of the political forces operating in the international arena into two major camps: the imperialist and anti-democratic camp, on the one hand, and the anti-imperialist and democratic camp on the other. The principal driving force of the imperialist camp is the USA. Allied with it are Great Britain and France. The Ramadier Socialist Government in France does not hinder that country from playing the part of satellite of the United States and following the lead of its imperialist policy on all major questions. The imperialist camp is also supported by colony-owning countries, such as Belgium and Holland, by countries with reactionary anti-democratic régimes, such as Turkey and Greece, and by countries politically and economically dependent on the United States, such as Near-Eastern and South American countries and China . . .

'The anti-imperialist and anti-fascist forces comprise the second camp. This camp is based on the USSR and the new democracies. It also includes countries that have broken with imperialism and have firmly set foot on the path of democratic development, such as Rumania, Hungary and Finland. Indonesia and Viet Nam are associated with it; it has the sympathy of India, Egypt and Syria.'

4 Party Thesis, page 39. The Indian interpretation of the international crisis was, if anything, more optimistic than that of Zhdanov. It presumed that the downfall of the capitalist powers was inevitable and round the corner and that revolution was ripe. For example, the thesis said: 'The defeat of Hitler Germany and Fascist Japan in World War 2 has completely altered the international landscape and moved the balance decisively in favour of the working class and its revolutionary movement . . .' 'Not only the military, but also the economic, organisational and industrial prestige of the Soviet Union has increased tremendously and the people in capitalist countries contrast the planned, organised life in the Soviet Union with the anarchy in capitalist society . . .' 'Europe for the capitalists is on the brink of a disaster. In Britain it is the Labour Government that stands between the mounting discontent and capitalist rule. In America, which is getting more and more in the mire of the crisis, which is hungrily searching for markets all over the world and is

attacking the living standard of its own people and the freedom of other nations – the crisis opens new battles between the financial autocrats and the common people.'

The same facile optimism ran through the analysis of the political situation in the colonies and the newly-freed countries. It said: 'The post-war revolutionary epoch has brought the colonies to the path of armed struggle against the imperialists and their allies. So powerful are these struggles and so great their revolutionary sweep that the achievement at one stroke of People's Democracy (as in the countries of Eastern Europe) becomes an immediate attainable objective. The imperialists and their bourgeois collaborators are overthrown and power passes into the hands of the toiling people led by the working class, which assures not only complete national independence but also the liquidation of the capitalist social order and the building of socialism.'

Referring to India, the Thesis explained the departure of the British and the National Government that followed as below:

'In India, the British imperialists saw the menacing tide of revolution, irrepressible and advancing, and realised that the days of the old order were over . . .

'The way to bar the revolution, to save the old order, was to purchase the very leaders who were at the head of the national movement and thus broaden the social base of the Government, split the revolutionary forces and strike at them . . .

'. . . therefore agreeable to compromise, imperialism struck a deal with the bourgeoisie, whose leaders had placed themselves at the head of the national movement and who were immensely useful in beating down the revolutionary wave . . .

'. . . The object was to instal a reactionary Government of vested interests in power which, while protecting the imperialist order, would screen imperialist designs . . .'

'The establishment of the Central Government headed by Pandit Nehru has not solved a single problem of the democratic revolution. Its establishment does not mean that the Indian people have won either freedom or independence, nor does it ensure that they will be moving in the direction of democracy and freedom for the people . . .

'On the contrary . . . it is manoeuvring to find an advantageous position for itself in the Anglo-American bloc.'

In contrast to the adulation for Nehru expressed by the Party under the leadership of P. C. Joshi immediately following independence in 1947, it is interesting to read what the Thesis had to say on the subject in 1948. It said: '. . . on the question of democratic policies, there exist illusions about Nehru. Nehru is seen as a fighter against Patel's policies and almost made to appear as the leader of the democratic forces . . . an illusion is created that, if Nehru's hands are strengthened as against Patel, the Government will be transformed into an instrument as the people's will . . . This estimate of Nehru is anti-Marxist and serves to tie down the masses to the bourgeois leadership. It must be clearly understood that Nehru is as much a representative of the bourgeoisie as Patel is. They both defend the class policies and interests of the bourgeoisie which is now collaborating with imperialism . . . He (Nehru) often outdoes Patel on vital issues.'

5 Hinting at the pattern of struggle, the Thesis said: 'The building of the Democratic Front is a process of struggle. It advances through a series of joint campaigns and partial struggles, jointly conducted, and through local united fronts . . . The core of the new Front would be the Communist Party together with the mass organisations led by the Party, trade unions, kisan sabhas and students' and youth organisations.'

The Thesis asserts confidently that 'The economic crisis, which will smite the agrarian areas most ruthlessly, will set in motion colossal forces.'

It quoted the example of Telengana where 'the people . . . have liberated over 2,000 villages and are conducting a bitter struggle for land, for freedom and for democracy. Thereby they have demonstrated how the struggle can grow and develop when the basic issue of land for the tiller is made an integral party of the democratic struggle, when the issue of abolition of autocracy and power for the people is placed in the forefront, when the masses are led by fighting organisations and are free from the paralysing influence of the bourgeoisie'.

6 P. C. Joshi, who was bitter at that time for being expelled, wrote in a pamphlet, called *Views:* 'The majority of Provincial Committees have been "reorganised" from top . . . The technique of dissolving the reorganising Party committees is following. First, a whisper campaign is started against the "disloyal" Party comrades from top, then a large number of cadres who are critical are just "dropped", not called to Party meeting, comrades are individually met and taken into confidence and then with the help of a section of the leadership, it is placed not before a local Party conference as demanded by the

Party Constitution but before an arbitrarily fixed Conference of active elements (no principles are followed in determining who are to be called active). It is called upon to elect or suggest a new leadership.'

'*Meetings of units are called or banned by the organiser sent from above.* Comrades are encouraged to spy on each other and whoever is supposed to be critical or not enthusiastic enough about the new leadership are quietly "dropped" from Party meetings, secretly slandered and provoked to make irresponsible remarks or just forced into passivity.'

7 Published by the Pacific Institute, Academy of Sciences, USSR.

8 The *Communist*, January 1950, pages 108–109.

CHAPTER SEVEN

1 The issue of the *Communist* of July 1949 conceded: 'In many provinces the Party began to reel under it and unstable elements began getting demoralised and even running away from the Party ... Even in those provinces where repression was not so brutal and nothing compared with the worst in the Southern provinces, wavering and unstable elements, accustomed to legal conditions and never having faced repression began to waver and vacillate before it, raising doubts about the party line.'

There were resignations and serious differences of opinion everywhere. In early 1950 twelve members from Maharashtra resigned. The Home Member of Bombay Province said in a Press Conference that many communist *détenus* were coming forward to give an undertaking of good behaviour so as to obtain release from prison, which they did. According to one report several comrades faced expulsion from the Party for not creating trouble inside the jails. In fact there were rifts within the jails throughout the country and these were so serious that the prisoners asked to be kept in separate blocks.

2 *Parliamentary Debates*, volume 11, no. 2, 25th February 1950.

3 Joshi tried to prove his charges by quoting facts and incidents as follows: 'Contrast our understanding of the "ever mounting revolutionary upsurge" with the following:

'We gave the call for an All-India Railwaymen's strike on 9th March 1949, and it was a complete fiasco, it remained a call on paper, unanswered by any section of railwaymen, even our followers. Railways used to be our best organised unions and we claimed a majority of organised railwaymen.

'In June our comrades in Bengal jails (including our well-known TU leaders) went on hunger-strike and were fired upon. We gave a call for general strike. Another flop. Bengal together with Tamilnad used to be our best organised Trade Union Province.

'In November 1949 we gave a call for All-Bengal Jute strike. Not one factory responded.'

'On 2nd January 1950, we called for one day's protest strike of All-India Textile workers. Our press claims 75,000 struck in Bombay. Semi-official news agency gives the figure 1,500, some Bombay dailies 4,000. No strike in other textile centres. Textile together with Railways used to be our strongholds.'

He goes on to say: 'There is no escaping the reality for anyone with eyes to see that our Party has become detached from our own class, that the very masses that have been traditionally following us can no more be mobilised by us ... Our comrades in jail are being called upon to commit suicide, through repeated hunger strikes, mandatory instructions are being sent to them from outside the hunger-strike on pain of expulsion and they are supposed to offer resistance by erecting "barricades" of furniture and hit armed policemen with whatever they can and for as long as they can. Lathi charges are merciless and firings indiscriminate. Majority of our jail comrades will be of no use for active work when they get out.

'The hunger-strike is supposed to "rouse tempo" outside but the campaign outside is thinning out more and more. There is a hunger-strike on now in Calcutta and we have not been able to get more than 1,000 persons out on the streets. Mostly it is 100–200 petty bourgeois students, mostly brothers and sisters from Party familiies and of jailed comrades.

'It is the petty bourgeois youth section of the Party that alone can be mobilised for present day "actions" and raids. There are hardly any worker militants in the "bands" and of course the average worker is far more sensible ...

'Practical failure on the mass front, especially the fiasco of the Railway strike, speeds up the passage from sectarian deviation into pure and simple terrorism in the second half of 1949, with the masses holding aloof and Patel (Home Minister of the Government of India) happy with getting both documentary and factual evidence to "justify" belatedly his entire repressive policy against the Party.'

Referring to the peasant movement, he says: 'Our present tactical line is, start with the most pressing demand to launch mass action and then seize land etc, as soon as possible and go forward to establishing liberated areas backed by guerrillas ... This line has led to the virtual liquidation of the Kisan (Peasant) movement. The AITUC at least meets sometimes but the All-India Kisan Sabha (Peasant organisation) has not met even once in two years.

4 The *Communist*, volume II, no. 4.

5 The Government of Hyderabad State gave publicity on 13th January 1951 to a 400-word secret letter addressed to the Central Committee of the Party by a Telengana communist functionary in Telengana in the course of which he warned the Party leadership that 'if the Party and its large number of leaders and workers who are still in the front are to be saved from complete annihilation, it must abandon its present adventurist tactics immediately'. Demanding an immediate cessation of violent activities in view of the heavy losses which the communists have suffered at the hands of the people, the Congress workers, the police and the army during the past few months, this communist leader conceded that the 'peasants themselves are against the Party's activities in its present form'. According to this letter the chief factors responsible for the near extinction of the forces fighting to establish this Indian 'Yenan' were 'the might of the Indian army and its striking power, coupled with the deep-rooted illusions in the minds of the masses about the Congress régime and its nature'.

6 Two previous members of the politbureau, D. Venkateshwara Rao and Biresh Misra, were allowed to resign and the Politbureau was reconstituted with Chandra Rajeshwar Rao, who was to continue as the General Secretary, E. M. S. Nambudiripad, Dange, Yusuf and Ghate or A. K. Ghosh as members.

7 The Preventive Detention Act was passed in February 1950 for one year to enable the Government to arrest people on suspicion and detain them without trial for one year. Sardar Patel, the then Home Minister, stated plainly at the time of proposing the Bill in Parliament, that it was directed against the communists, as they 'constitute a danger to the existence and security of the State' ... 'obviously we cannot deal with these people in terms of ordinary law ... When the law is flouted and offences are committed, ordinarily there is the criminal law which is put into force. But where

the very basis of law is sought to be undermined . . . we feel justified in invoking emergency and extraordinary laws.'

8 Justifying this drastic measure, Mr C. Rajagopalachari had said in Parliament on the 15th February 1951: 'The measure that I am asking the House to continue with certain amendments is certainly an infringement of what may be called a normal principle of criminal justice . . . It is a confession of abnormalcy. But the Government cannot be contacted on an unreal basis.'

He said that if subversive elements were to be left loose and allowed to operate as they chose, and the ordinary procedure for trial of offences were alone available, 'we would undoubtedly be unable to cope with the situation . . . Where the security of the Union or of any of the States in the Union and the safety of the public or any other vital matter, such as essential supplies, is involved, we cannot afford danger to grow in secret preparation and organised plots. We must nip the thing in the bud'. (*Statesman*, 16th February 1951)

9 Writing editorially on this, the *Times of India*, Bombay, in its issue dated 28th February 1951, stated:

'From Assam in recent days has come disquieting news. Widespread terrorist activities are reported in the strategic north-eastern districts embracing Assam, Manipur and Tripura. Though the Burma Government have re-established their authority over a large part of their country, the Burma communists are by no means liquidated, and the Hammer and Sickle hold sway over wide areas of the frontier. Peking may not harbour expansionist desires, but communism is potentially expansive and explosive, and anxiety is heightened by the Union Home Minister's reference to encouragement for the Assam terrorist from across the border . . . The Communist Party Congress in Calcutta three years ago served as a useful cloak for transborder contact men. Official spokesmen have more recently suggested that the Naga Hills territory, where large quantities of arms were left behind after the last war, serves as a supply depot for the terrorists.

'India's eastern frontiers have intermittently been infected with violence and unrest since 1949. Failing in their efforts to incite the railway workers, terrorist leaders turned their attention to the tribal people who comprise nearly forty per cent of the total population and their tactics have yielded good dividends . . . The Assam picture repeats the pattern of Telengana and Andhra.'

10 This document came to light as recently as January 1954 when it formed one of several secret documents of the CPI to come into the hands of the Democratic Research Service, Bombay, and to be published by that body as part of a book *The Communist Conspiracy at Madurai* (an analysis of the proceedings of the closed sessions of the Third Congress of the CPI with full text of secret documents) published by the Popular Book Depot, Bombay 7, in March 1954, price Rs 1/12/–, 7s or $1.00.

11 Published in Bombay for the CPI by Jayant Bhat. See also *Communist Conspiracy at Madurai.*

12 The preamble to the Constitution of the CPI states:

'The Communist Party of India, is the political party of the Indian class, is its vanguard and most organised detachment, the highest form of its class organisation.

'The Communist Party of India fulfils the rôle of the leadership of the proletariat, the toiling peasants and the other sections of the toiling people, organising them in the struggle for the victorious anti-imperialist and agrarian revolution, for complete national independence, for the establishment of a people's democratic State led by the working class, for the realisation of the dictatorship of the proletariat to build up socialism and a classless society, according to the teachings of Marxism-Leninism ... The Communist Party of India demands of its members active participation in the work of the Party and selfless sacrifice for the fulfilment of the programme of the Communist Party of India and of the international communist movement. It demands also the adherence of the members to the Constitution of the Party, the implementation of all decisions of the Party and the strengthening of fraternal international relations. The Communist Party of India', the preamble concludes, 'shall work in all the organisations of the toiling people and among the masses, seeking to win them over from all reformist influence, for the immediate establishment of a People's Democratic State in India and for building Socialism, the first stage of communism'.

(*The Constitution of the Communist Party of India*, published by V.M.Kaul for the Communist Party of India, Raj Bhavan, Bombay 1, 1948, pages 3–4.)

CHAPTER EIGHT

1 This refers to the debates in the course of framing the Constitution.

2 Even the Communist Party was given full freedom to contest elec-

tions except where it was violating the peace and trying to overthrow the government by violence. The Party was banned during the elections in only three regions in India.

3 This refers to a clause in the constitution that no private property or business will be confiscated by the State without the payment of compensation.

4 This again is false. Rights and liberty of the individual are fully guaranteed on the model of the American constitution and in fact the Constitution had to be amended this year to enable the government to deal effectively with the communist menace. The amendment enabled the government to assume power of preventive detention in times of stress threatening the security of the State.

5 *Telepress Bulletin no. 8. US Bribes to Indian Socialist Leader Revealed.* Delhi, Telepress – Two leading members of the Indian Socialist Party who recently resigned their membership revealed many startling facts proving the gross interference of the United States in giving financial assistance to the Socialist Party and that this money is being used for American propaganda has caused a tremendous stir here.

It was revealed that when the socialist leader, Dr R.M.Lohia was in the United States in the summer of 1951 he received from the United States through the American Socialist leader, Norman Thomas, $45,000 to cover the special needs of the Indian Party. Actually the greater part of this money was kept by Lohia and India's two other leading socialists, J. Narayan and Asok Mehta. As this was known to the United States Government it put pressure on Narayan and Mehta to organise a broad campaign to overcome the dissatisfaction caused among the people by the outrageous terms attached to the United States' food aid granted last summer.

Narayan, Mehta and Lohia, frightened that the Socialist Party and the Indian public would hear of their retention of the United States' gift to their Party, agreed to help the Americans get control of the Victory Press and the Jaya Hind Bookstall Company in which the Socialists had a controlling interest. Through Mehta the United States bought a large number of shares in these companies which following the suggestion of the United States Information Service in Delhi began issuing propaganda literature condemning India's neutral foreign policy and leading the American way of life and United States policy in Asia.

T

The United States Agent, Clare Timberlake, acting for the United States Embassy recently gave Narayan 30,000 dollars for the Socialist Party Election campaign. In return, Narayan assured Timberlake that the socialists would support those candidates in the General Elections now taking place in India, who supported United States policy. He said they would support pro-American candidates whether they belonged to the governing Indian National Congress Party or the right wing Hindu Maha Sabha or Bharatiya Jan Sangh Parties.

6 In a circular letter dated 23rd November 1952, Ajoy Ghosh, General Secretary of the CPI, wrote to all Provincial Committees and District Committees:

'As regards our election policy it was made clear at the All-India Party Conference that we shall not in a place where Congress and some reactionary Party like Jan Sangh are the only contestants support either of the candidates. The argument that compared to Jan Sangh the Congress is progressive has no basis and reality and should not be allowed to deceive anybody ... We do not and cannot as a general rule support all candidates set up by the Socialist Party where we are not contesting. Many of those Socialist candidates have had nothing to do either with socialism or with any progressive ideology or movement ... Such candidates we shall not support even when we support right wing reactionaries set up by the Socialist Party even if they have done political work. They are rabid reactionaries who denounce Left Unity who have declared that they prefer Congress victory to victory of the communist and who are avowed enemies of the Soviet Union and People's China, and supporters of the Anglo-American war bloc. For example the *Janata*, organ of the Socialist Party in Bihar writes editorially in its issue of 28th September: 'China is the enemy not merely of India but of the whole of Asia, the whole of the world ...

'Capitalism is a dying force. Its end is near. To-day the world has to meet the danger represented by communism. New China is embodiment of this danger.'

'Such is the real face of right wing socialists. There are socialist candidates who do not fall in any of these categories ... Such socialist candidates should be supported where we are not setting up any candidate and where we have no electoral agreement ... In such a case the anti-Unity and reactionary policy of the right wing socialist leaders should be exposed and also it should be explained why we are supporting the particular socialist candidate ...

'Some comrades may give the analogy of the British Labour Party and point out the defeat of the Congress is our objective in the elections, we should support the candidates set up by the Socialist Party just as the CPGB supported candidates set up by the British Labour Party, despite the reactionary policy and record of the British Labour Party. The analogy is false. The British Labour Party represents the organised working class ... Socialist Party of India despite its claim does not represent the organised working class of India, nor the unity of the democratic forces ...

'Moreover, it should be borne in mind that to-day when the issue of war or peace dominates the whole political scene in every country of the world we cannot support a Party whose leadership on the all-important issue of Peace takes a stand which in many respects is even more reactionary than that taken by the Congress.'

7 *Social Action*, the journal of the Indian Institute of Social Order, Poona, wrote in its issue of April 1952:

'Instead of attributing the communist success to a host of secondary causes and circumstances such as the failure of the monsoon, the food shortage, prohibition, etc, and thereby confusing the whole issue, let us try to analyse the fundamental reasons which are deeper and more lasting than the transitory causes and circumstances which are so often unthinkingly proposed. The fundamental reasons for communist gains would seem to be: first, a vague, all-defined, illogical and often emotional admiration for things communist, an admiration that has been on the increase since China turned communist. This admiration is greatest among the educated middle class, especially those with a "modern" education. Such people are immensely impressed by reports of the material progress made in the Soviet and by the news of recent reforms in China, while their critical faculties seem to be dead to reports from other sources of the atrocities and loss of freedom in communist dominated countries. Even those who are opposed to communism because of its violent methods, find it difficult to shake off a sneaking regard for its doctrine. Even the Prime Minister himself has on more than one occasion, as recently at the Delhi Press Conference, expressed his admiration for certain fine sentiments and idealism possessed by communism, while condemning it for being "utterly reactionary in outlook".'

CHAPTER NINE

1 *Hindu*, Madras, 7th April 1952.

2 *Hindu*, Madras, 7th April 1952.

3 *Hindustan Times*, Delhi, 25th April 1952.

4 *Hindustan Times*, Delhi, 12th May 1952.

5 *Times of India*, Bombay, 5th September 1953.

6 *Times of India*, Bombay, 25th May 1952.

7 Among the more recent of such statements on record is one made by Mr Nehru at Trivandrum in the heavily infiltrated state of Travan-core-Cochin. 'Referring to the communists the Prime Minister said their ideology was good. That was his aim too. But they functioned in a destructive way.' (*Times of India*, 30th December 1952)

Again at Hyderabad less than a month later, he said: 'The communists talked a lot of progress and equality of people and abolition of the gulf between the rich and the poor. As far as those ideals were concerned, they were good ones, but the method of violence which the communists sometimes adopted was utterly wrong.' (*Times of India*, 20th January 1953)

8 'Darem' in *Times of India*, Bombay, 9th September 1952.

9 *Free Press Journal*, Bombay, 3rd January 1952.

10 *Cross Roads*, 30th May 1952.

11 Peking Radio – Chinese Home Service Broadcast, 18th June 1952.

12 *Hindustan Times*, Delhi, 30th March 1953 and *Cross Roads*, Bombay 5th April, 1953.

13 *National Standard*, Bombay, 31st March 1953.

14 *Cross Roads*, 5th April 1953.

15 *Hindustan Times*, Delhi, 13th April 1953.

16 *Thought*, Delhi, 7th March 1953.

17 *Hindustan Times*, Delhi, 11th May 1953. *Blitz*, Bombay and *Cross Roads*, 16th May 1953.

18 The alarming extent to which good and well-meaning people may be misinformed and misled is perhaps best evidenced by the words of welcome in New Delhi to a Chinese communist 'cultural' mission in November 1951 by an eminent and respected academic figure like Dr Zakir Hussain, Vice-Chancellor of Aligarh University, de-

livered in the presence of a distinguished gathering including cabinet ministers.

'Already your effort has borne fruit. The People's Government has united nearly 500 million people as they were never before united. It has given the "land to the tiller"; it has generated a tremendous enthusiasm for production; it has brought together the peasant, the worker, the petty *bourgeoisie* and the national *bourgeoisie* in one great urge to build up a poltical and economic system in which each can make the fullest contribution and from which all can derive the greatest benefit. You have evolved the "common programme" through full and free discussion and you have created a loyalty and devotion to the purposes of this programme which assure its success. You have the best wishes of the Indian people for the attainment of the ends to which you aspire'.

19 *Evening News of India,* Bombay, 17th June 1953.

20 A correspondent in the *Harijan* of 30th May 1953, was provoked to refer to the process 'in which the Government including the Prime Minister have been fully participating: a constant, parrot-like uninformed reiteration and admiration of Russian and Chinese "achievements", thus creating an atmosphere of enthusiastic reception of communism. Communists and persons like Dr Kumarappa, some professors and editors of the "bourgeois" press have been indulging in both. The combined result of these efforts and processes has been that among a vast section of influential people, there is a rejection of India and their minds have been prepared for accepting Russo-Chinese "liberation". That is the worst that could happen to a country, its past traditions, present labours and future hopes'.

21 *Cross Roads,* 22nd March 1953.

22 Prime Minister Nehru in his speech at the All-India Congress Committee on 17th January 1953, in which he reported on the Indian Plan presented to the UN General Assembly, said:

'It did not recognise voluntary repatriation of prisoners, nor was there any question of prisoners being asked whether they wished to return or decline to do so. It did not recognise the right of asylum for prisoners of war, which applied to political refugees. There was to be no screening of prisoners. It ensured that all prisoners would be released from the custody of the detaining side and in neutral territory. The presumption was that they would go back to their country of origin. In fact, repatriation would have begun as soon as these prisoners were released from detention.'

In his closing speech in the UN Assembly just prior to the vote, Mr V.K. Krishna Menon, the Indian spokesman, observed:

'In the procedure effecting return, there are no further processes of separating the wheat from the chaff, or what is usually called "screening". There are no interrogations; there are no questions to be asked. And there will be no restrictions from guards whom in the past the Chinese have called the guards of Syngman Rhee and Chiang-Kai-shek ... There will be no offering of temptations to prevent returning ... There will equally be no question of groups of people who want to go and groups who do not want to go – I mean this in quotation marks – who will be kept separate so that they will be marked men ... The first act of release by the detaining side is the first act of repatriation.'

23 *National Standard*, Bombay, 18th May 1953.

24 *Free Press Journal*, Bombay, 22nd May 1953.

25 *Blitz*, Bombay, 23rd May 1953.

26 *Times of India*, Bombay, 14th June 1953.

27 *Sunday Standard*, Bombay, 14th June 1953.

28 *Cross Roads*, 12th July 1953.

29 *Hindustan Times*, Delhi, 1st August 1953.

30 *Cross Roads*, 9th August 1953.

31 *Times of India*, Bombay, 13th August 1953.

32 *Blitz*, Bombay, 3rd January 1953.

33 *Hindustan Times*, Delhi, and *Times of India*, Bombay, 17th January 1953.

34 *Hindustan Times*, Delhi, 7th March 1953.

35 *National Standard*, Bombay, 21st April 1953.

36 *Cross Roads*, 26th April 1953.

37 For a detailed analysis of the activities and publications of this organisation, *vide* Philip Spratt's article in *Freedom First*, Bombay, June 1953.

38 *Hindustan Times*, Delhi, 12th January 1953.

39 *Cross Roads*, 30th August 1953.

40 *Blitz*, Bombay, 28th March 1953.

41 *Times of India,* Bombay, 20th April 1953.

42 *Times of India,* Bombay, 4th May 1953 and *Cross Roads,* Bombay, 10th May 1953.

43 *Cross Roads,* Bombay, 13th January 1953.

44 *Times of India,* Bombay, 10th March 1953.

45 *Cross Roads,* Bombay, 29th March 1953.

46 *Times of India,* Bombay, 30th March 1953.

47 *Times of India,* and *Free Press Journal,* Bombay, 28th May 1953.

48 *Times of India,* Bombay, 20th April 1953.

49 *Current,* Bombay, 25 February 1953.

50 *Times of India,* Bombay, 28th April 1953.

51 Vide *Kashmir and the Communists,* by Tilak Raj Chadha, a prominent member of the Praja Socialist Party, in *Thought,* Delhi, 17th January 1953.

52 *Thought,* Delhi, 17th January 1953.

53 *Thought,* 17th January 1953.

On 30th May 1953, *Thought* again wrote: 'In Kashmir, they (the communists) have a distinct advantage over their potential opponents in that they operate through the National Conference, which is the ruling party there. It was a sight for the gods to see some time back when some of the known communists were having free ride and hospitality in Jammu and Kashmir at the expense of Sheikh Abdullah's Government. The Speaker of the Kashmir Constituent Assembly, is, of course, a notorious instance of com-communist success in infiltration into key positions in organisations which they ultimately seek to destroy. Even in a State like Delhi, where the Congress leaders ought to know better, a thoughtless fraternisation between the leaders of the Congress and known communist workers is going on. The so-called Friends of New Kashmir Society reeks with communist influence and parrots the phrases and slogans which the communists have popularised in India.'

54 The communist leader, Dhanwantri, in his inauguration speech, though himself known to be the architect of some of the vital policies of the Kashmir Government since 1947, quoted instances to the public, 'based on personal knowledge', to establish his charges of inefficiency against the present governmental machine. His speech was also marked by great emphasis on points of 'fundamental

disagreement'. On the other hand, the communist spokesman arrogated all credit to his own Party for 'a few good turns' done by the State Government in respect of agrarian reforms and the end of hereditary princely rule. (*Bombay Sentinel*, 3rd September 1952)

55 *Cross Roads*, 17th May 1953: *Hindustan Times Weekly*, 17th May 1953, and *Janata*, 7th June 1953.

CHAPTER TEN

1 Published by the Popular Book Depot, Bombay 7, pp 160. Rs 1/12/–; 7s; or $1.00.

Commenting on these disclosures, the Delhi correspondent of the *Times of India*, Bombay, wrote:

'Weight is lent to the conclusion of the DRS that the adoption by the Communist Party of legal and constitutional methods is only a facade to conceal its preparation for an armed insurrection by the fact that knowledgeable circles here are prone to agree with it. Their own sources of information have left it beyond doubt that the communists are playing a double game . . . The authorities are also believed to be in possession of some of the secret documents that were circulated to a few members of the CP. What has attracted special attention is a document entitled: "Not Peaceful But Revolutionary Path'."

The *Statesman*, Delhi, of 7th January 1954 said in its survey of the Political scene:

'Large extracts from these documents have already been reproduced in the Press and the Central Home Ministry has also been provided with a printed copy by the Democratic Research Group of Bombay. Official quarters in Delhi have no reason to believe that the papers are not authentic, which is a good enough testimonial for those responsible for their publication.'

Capital, Calcutta, of 11th February 1954, commented:

'. . . More embarrassing must be the present situation in which the country has an opportunity of hearing what the party has been told in secret. What may be called the "inner contradictions" of the party have now made available to the Democratic Research Service of Bombay a mass of very significant documents, which conclusively expose not only the deception the party plans to work on the country and on some guileless political groups, but also the dishonesty obtaining inside the party itself.

'. . . When the war came in 1939, politicians were blamed for not reading *Mein Kampf*. Omission to read the documents mentioned above carries the possibility of heavier penalties'.

2 *New Age*, weekly journal of the CPI, 3rd January 1954.

3 *Communist Conspiracy at Madurai*, p 159.

4 For full text, see *Communist Conspiracy at Madurai*, p 87.

5 For full text of letter from the CC of the CPI to these PDF leaders, see *Communist Conspiracy at Madurai*, p 142.

6 For full text, see *Communist Conspiracy at Madurai*, page 55.

7 For full text, see *New Age*, 10th January 1954.

8 See *Communist Conspiracy at Madurai*, page 142.

9 See *Communist Conspiracy at Madurai*, page 142.

CHAPTER ELEVEN

1 The *Hindu*, Madras, 24th October 1952.

2 *Vide* Thesis and Statutes of the Communist International adopted by the Second World Congress, Moscow, 17th July to 7th August 1920. Article 3 states: 'All parties and organisations comprising the Communist International bear the name of the Communist Party of the given country (section of the international).'

Article 6 reads: 'The executive committee appeals on behalf of the Communist International and issues instructions obligatory to all the parties and organisations which form part of the Communist International'.

Among the 21 conditions laid down by Lenin for admission to the Communist International is this: 'Each party desirous of affiliating to the Communist International should be obliged to render every possible assistance to the Soviet Republics in their struggle against all counter-revolutionary forces.'

The Programme of the Communist International (Chapter v, Section 3) adopted by the Sixth World Congress, Moscow, September 1928, lays down: 'In view of the fact that the USSR is the only fatherland of the International Proletariat, the principal bulwark of its achievements and the most important factor for its international emancipation, the international proletariat must on its part facilitate the success of the work of socialist construction in the USSR and defend her against the attacks of the capitalists by all means in its power.'

3 *Problems of Communism*, January 1953 (volume 1, no. 2); see also *Times of India*, Bombay, 7th October 1952, for Reuter-Press Trust of India report.

4 *Times of India*, Bombay, 20th December 1952.

5 *Times of India*, Bombay, 20th December 1952.

6 *Cross Roads*, Bombay, 28th December 1952.

7 *Illustrated Weekly of India*, Bombay, 17th August 1952.

8 *Statesman*, 5th January 1953.

9 *Bombay Sentinel*, 13th January 1953.

10 *Times of India*, 15th January 1953.

11 *Times of India*, 6th March 1953.

12 *Evening News of India*, 22nd April 1953.

13 *New York Times*, 6th March 1953

14 *Times of India*, 13th March 1953.

15 *Times of India*, 28th March 1953.

16 *Times of India*, 7th April 1953.

17 In December 1950, the Indian Government placed on exhibition in New Delhi a collection of firearms and literature captured from communist agents in Telengana. The display included modern rifles as well as ancient flintlocks; swords, daggers and crude bombs; wireless sets and large quantities of printed material, some of it on paper not of Indian origin nor printed in India. The exhibition drew attention pointedly to the fact that, for the first time in history, the communists in India had arms, though not in adequate quantities.

18 On 17th March 1953, was arrested on the Assam border a Soviet citizen of Indian origin with an Indian name. He was found without a permit at Minjong within the 'Inner Line' of the North East Frontier Agency. The man claimed he was a Soviet citizen and stated he was not aware that the place where he was arrested was within the 'Inner Line'. He failed to explain, however, how he managed to lose his way there just about the time that Red Chinese troops were reported to be trespassing on the Indian side of the country's N.E. Frontiers. (*Current*, 17th June 1953.)

19 *Thought*, 21st June 1952.

20 *Andhra Patrika*, 23rd November 1952.

21 *Bharat Jyoti*, 10th May 1953.

22 *Hindu*, 24th May 1952.

23 *Times of India*, 23rd January 1953.

24 *Hindustan Times*, 6th February 1952.

25 See *The Communist*, volume III no. 3, July–August 1950.

26 *Cross Roads*, 22nd March 1953; see also *Cross Roads*, 7th June 1953

27 *Times of India*, 20th May 1953.

28 *Free Press Journal*, 22nd May 1953.

29 The analysis attempted nearly three years back by *Janata*, the organ of the Socialist Party of India, on 14th January 1951, still holds good: 'While giving its decision, Moscow will be influenced by its reading of the international situation as well as its estimation of the Government of India. If they think that the war is imminent, then they would like the Indian communists to undermine the foundations of the Indian State. If they feel that war is not likely to come soon, and that Nehru's policy is indirectly helping them, then they may direct the Communist Party of India to return to the path of democratic agitation, and at the same time secretly and silently to build up the illegal organisation of the Party. The first course is the old adventurist policy and will spell their utter ruin. The second course is a more subtle way of undermining the democratic form and spirit and the danger has to be noted and combated at every stage.'

30 See Proceedings of the Indian Congress for Cultural Freedom, March 1951, and Proceedings of the Second Annual General Meeting of the Indian Committee for Cultural Freedom, Madras, September 1953 (Indian Committee for Cultural Freedom, 127 Mahatma Gandhi Road, Bombay 1)

31 An exception is the resolution passed by the session of the All-India Mahasabha at Bhopal in December 1952 opining that 'in foreign affairs India must take note of the grave menace of communism which is a danger to the principles which India holds dear and sacred. India firmly believes in the principles of democracy and is opposed to totalitarianism or regimentation of life'. (*Hindustan Times*, 1st January 1953)

32 *Sunday Statesman*, 18th January 1953.
On the other hand, it must be recorded that Mr M.N.Roy's

organ has expressed the view that 'even for the negative purpose of stemming the tide of communism, socialism in Asia is bound to be a broken reed'. (*Radical Humanist*, 15th March 1953)

33 *Hindustan Times*, 12th January 1953.

34 *Cross Roads*, 17th May 1953.
   See also subsequent denunciations of the Plan by A. K. Gopalan and S. A. Dange reported in the *Times of India*, 25th May, and the *Free Press Journal*, 26th May 1953, respectively.

35 *Cross Roads*, 3rd May 1953.

36 *Hindustan Times*, 18th May 1953.

37 *Current*, 27th May 1953.

38 *Thought*, Delhi, 15th August 1953.

39 This point of view found cogent expression in an editorial article appearing in the *Radical Humanist* (the organ of Mr M. N. Roy, the well-known ex-Comintern functionary) of 14th January 1951:
   'The dangers of communism lay, let it be made clear, not so much in men being poor but in men being alienated from their nature, only partly as a consequence of their poverty. It should therefore be clear that attempts intended or calculated to improve the living conditions of the people, in themselves of great importance, are not and cannot be a sufficient antidote to communism. Such improvements, even if they are actualised, may be largely deprived of their significance in the absence of a proper outlook. It is indeed regrettable that those who advocate the necessity for these improvements in the living conditions of the people against the communist promise of a paradise on earth try to win over the people on the basis of an economic appeal . . . If democracy appears to be weak and undefended to-day, let it be noted that it is so because of its lack of any genuine and sound foundations. And the only way of laying such foundations is to promote in increasing numbers the rise of intelligent, rational and discriminating human beings.' Reverting to this theme, Roy wrote again in *Thought* on 15th August 1953:
   'The siren call of communism reaches the Indian masses through the educated middle class. As a matter of fact, in the underdeveloped countries of Asia, communism is a middle-class movement . . . Economic aid . . . by itself will not go very far. It must be supplemented by what may be called spiritual aid.'

40 *Blitz*, 20th January 1951.

41 *Current*, 15th April 1953.

42 On her return to India from Moscow in June 1953, Rajkumari Amrit Kaur, Health Minister in the Union Government, paid gushing tributes to the miraculous achievements of Soviet medicine. (*Times of India*, 20th June 1953)

43 *Bombay Sentinel*, 6th March 1953.

44 See *Cross Roads*, 22nd March 1953, for a round up of the Indian Press not unfairly entitled 'Indian Press salutes Stalin'.

45 *Cross Roads*, 22nd and 29th March, and 19th April 1953.

46 Writing from Delhi on 6th March, the correspondent of the *Free Press of India* stated: 'The only section in Parliament and outside which is happy about these developments is the Communist Party which, with characteristic naïvete, foretells disintegration of the "Third Force" once it agrees to coalesce with the Congress. In such an eventuality, the field, it seems, would be clear for them to go ahead as "it won't take much time for the people to be disillusioned". ' (*Free Press Journal*, 7th March 1953)

47 *Times of India*, 3rd January 1953.

48 *Times of India*, 29th May 1953.

49 *Hindustan Times*, 6th April 1953.

50 *Hindu*, 24th May 1953.

51 *Bombay Sentinel*, 28th May 1953.

52 *Illustrated Weekly of India*, 17th August 1952.

53 *Thought* of 30th May 1953, observed: 'When Mr C. Rajagopalachari says that communism has passed its peak in India, he is probably unaware of these happenings in the North. There are two things which must always be borne in mind by those who want to devise a suitable strategy to fight the menace of communism. There are: (1) That communism can never trade on its own and (2) that it must have outside military assistance to succeed in its final aim. In the North both these things may come into operation before long.'

The *Statesman* of 27th May 1953, commented: 'Mr Rajagopalachari's "precipitous decline" is something of which few apparent symptoms seem yet to be discernible.'

54 *Cross Roads*, 26th April 1953.

55 The *Statesman*, Calcutta, 13th November 1953.

56 Two American writers who have shown rare insight in the workings of the Asian mind are Mr Arthur Goodfriend and Prof M.A. Lineberger. In his book *The Only War We Seek*, Goodfriend writes: 'They (the Chinese communists) reached the people by means of education and political indoctrination. We tried too often to win them with charity . . . We can, as we did in China, keep mum about the shameful record of Russian communism. Or we can attack the soft underbelly of communism by reciting its record on the values most precious to Asians and others—religion, the family, national independence and the ownership of the land . . . Unless we are prepared to face up to the problem, the United States and the free world may be betrayed into a grievous error. The governments of under-developed peoples may rally to our side—but behind this facade, the people may remain aloof and even antagonistic'.

Prof Lineberger, in his article in the Annals of the American Academy of Political and Social Science, November 1951 writes: 'The Americans believe in spiritual things, but they try to buy them by material means—by dollars, by gifts, by aid. The communists believe in material things, but they offer people something to join, something to do, something to fight. We Americans offer property; the communists offer a reason for being alive. People who join the communist side feel that they are needed, that the communists want them. You could not join the American side, if you were an Asian. There isn't anything to join.'

In this context, US policy in regard to India has been found deplorably wanting. See editorial note entitled *Failure of a Mission* in *Freedom First* (organ of the ICCF), April 1953, page 3.

57 *Cross Roads*, 25th January 1953.

58 *Current*, 14th January 1953.

59 For an interesting effort at drawing a parallel, see *Nehru and Benes* by Rev T. Mascarenhas in *The Examiner* of 14th and 21st June 1952.

60 *Hindu*, Madras, 9th February 1954.

61 *Hindu*, Madras, 10th February 1954.

62 *Hindu*, Madras, 9th February 1954.

63 *Hindu*, Madras, 10th February 1954.

64 *Hindu*, Madras, 11th February 1954.

65 *Times of India*, Bombay, 10th February 1954.